iOS Forensic Analysis for iPhone, iPad and iPod touch

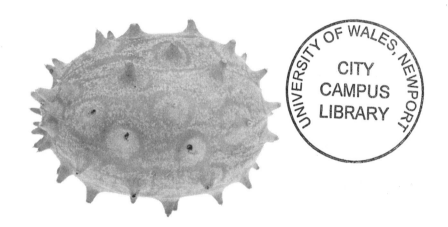

Sean Morrissey

Apress®

iOS Forensic Analysis for iPhone, iPad and iPod touch

ISBN-13 (pbk): 978-1-4302-3342-8

ISBN-13 (electronic): 978-1-4302-3343-5

Printed and bound in the United States of America (POD)

President and Publisher: Paul Manning
Lead Editor: Michelle Lowman
Technical Reviewer: Tony Campbell
Editorial Board: Steve Anglin, Mark Beckner, Ewan Buckingham, Gary Cornell, Jonathan Gennick, Jonathan Hassell, Michelle Lowman, Matthew Moodie, Duncan Parkes, Jeffrey Pepper, Frank Pohlmann, Douglas Pundick, Ben Renow-Clarke, Dominic Shakeshaft, Matt Wade, Tom Welsh
Coordinating Editor: Kelly Moritz
Copy Editor: Kim Wimpsett
Compositor: MacPS, LLC
Indexer: BIM Indexing & Proofreading Services
Artist: April Milne
Cover Designer: Anna Ishchenko

Distributed to the book trade worldwide by Springer Science+Business Media, LLC., 233 Spring Street, 6th Floor, New York, NY 10013. Phone 1-800-SPRINGER, fax (201) 348-4505, e-mail orders-ny@springer-sbm.com, or visit www.springeronline.com.

For information on translations, please e-mail rights@apress.com, or visit www.apress.com.

Apress and friends of ED books may be purchased in bulk for academic, corporate, or promotional use. eBook versions and licenses are also available for most titles. For more information, reference our Special Bulk Sales–eBook Licensing web page at www.apress.com/info/bulksales.

This book is dedicated to all those in uniform who serve our country and communities.

They work tirelessly to keep us safe and go mostly unappreciated.

I thank all who serve and keep us safe

Contents at a Glance

Contents v

Foreword x

About the Author xi

About the Technical Reviewer xii

Acknowledgments xiii

Introduction xiv

Chapter 1: History of Apple Mobile Devices 1

Chapter 2: iOS Operating and File System Analysis 25

Chapter 3: Search, Seizure, and Incident Response................................. 67

Chapter 4: iPhone Logical Acquisition... 87

Chapter 5: Logical Data Analysis.. 135

Chapter 6: Mac and Windows Artifacts 209

Chapter 7: GPS Analysis 227

Chapter 8: Media Exploitation 267

Chapter 9: Media Exploitation Analysis... 291

Chapter 10: Network Analysis 323

Index.. 343

Contents

▓ **Contents at a Glance**... iv

▓ **Foreword** x

▓ **About the Author** xi

▓ **About the Technical Reviewer**... xii

▓ **Acknowledgments**.. xiii

▓ **Introduction**..xiv

▓ **Chapter 1: Start Guide History of Apple Mobile Devices** 1

    The iPod 2

    The Evolution of Apple iPhones..2

        The ROCKR...2

        The Apple iPhone 2G 3

        The 3G iPhone..5

        The 3G[S] iPhone 6

        The iPhone 4 7

    The Apple iPad 8

    Under the Surface: iPhone and iPad Hardware..8

        2G iPhone Internals...9

        3G iPhone Internals...12

        iPhone 3G[S] Internals 14

        iPhone 4 Internals..15

        iPad Internals...16

    The Apple App Store 19

    Rise of the iPhone Hackers..22

    Summary 23

▓ **Chapter 2: iOS Operating and File System Analysis** 25

    Changing iOS Features 25

        iOS 1 25

        iOS 2 27

iOS 3 28

iOS 4 29

Application Development 31

The iOS File System 33

HFS+ File System 33

HFSX 35

iPhone Partition and Volume Information 36

OS Partition 41

iOS System Partition 41

iOS Data Partition 46

SQLite Databases 49

Address Book Database 49

SMS Database 50

Call History Database 50

Working with the Databases 51

Retrieving Data from SQLite Databases 53

Property Lists 61

Viewing Property Lists 62

Summary 66

Chapter 3: Search, Seizure, and Incident Response.................. 67

The Fourth Amendment of the U.S. Constitution...68

Tracking an Individual by Cell Phone 69

Cell Phone Searches Incident to Arrest..69

Changing Technology and the Apple iPhone...71

Responding to the Apple Device 72

Isolating the Device 75

Passcode Lock 77

Identifying Jailbroken iPhones..79

Information Collection of the iPhone 80

Responding to Mac/Windows in Connection to iPhones..84

Summary 85

References...85

Chapter 4: iPhone Logical Acquisition.. 87

Acquiring Data from iPhone, iPod touch, and iPad 87

Acquiring Data Using mdhelper 88

Available Tools and Software 92

Lantern..92

Susteen Secure View 2 107

Paraben Device Seizure 115

Oxygen Forensic Suite 2010 118

Cellebrite...125

Comparing the Tools and Results 130

Buyer Beware 130

Paraben Device Seizure Results 131

Oxygen Forensic Suite 2010 Results 131

Cellebrite Results 132

Susteen Secure View 2 Results 132

Katana Forensics Lantern Results 132
The Issue of Support 133
Summary 133

■Chapter 5: Logical Data Analysis 135

Setting Up a Forensic Workstation 135
Library Domain..140
AddressBook...142
Caches 144
Call History 147
Configuration Profiles 149
Cookies 149
Keyboard 150
Logs 152
Maps 154
Map History...155
Notes...156
Preferences..156
Safari 157
Suspended State...159
SMS and MMS 160
Voicemails...162
WebClips 163
WebKits 164
System Configuration Data 168
Media Domain...170
Media Directory...170
Photos.sqlite Database 175
PhotosAux.sqlite Database 175
Recordings 176
iPhoto Photos 176
Multimedia 177
Third-Party Applications 178
Social Networking Analysis 179
Skype 180
Facebook 182
AOL AIM 184
LinkedIn 184
Twitter..185
MySpace 185
Google Voice 186
Craigslist..189
Analytics 191
iDisk 192
Google Mobile 192
Opera 193
Bing..194
Documents and Document Recovery 194

Antiforensic Applications and Processes..197
    Image Vaults..198
    Picture Safe...198
    Picture Vault..199
    Incognito Web Browser...200
    Invisible Browser 201
    tigertext 202
Jailbreaking 207
Summary 207

Chapter 6: Mac and Windows Artifacts 209

Artifacts from a Mac 209
    Property List..209
    The MobileSync Database 210
    Apple Changes to Backup Files Over Time 211
    Lockdown Certificates...212
Artifacts from Windows 212
    iPodDevices.xml..212
    MobileSync Backups...213
    Lockdown Certificates...214
Analysis of the iDevice Backups 214
    iPhone Backup Extractor...214
    JuicePhone 216
    mdhelper...218
    Oxygen Forensics Suite 2010 219
Windows Forensic Tools and Backup Files...220
    FTK Imager..221
    FTK 1.8 222
    Tips and Tricks..223
Summary 225

Chapter 7: GPS Analysis 227

Maps Application 227
Geotagging of Images and Video 237
Cell Tower Data...248
    GeoHunter...255
Navigation Applications 260
    Navigon...260
    Tom Tom 265
Summary 265

Chapter 8: Media Exploitation 267

What Is Digital Rights Management (DRM)?...267
    Legal Elements of Digital Rights Management 268
    Case in Point: Jailbreaking the iPhone 271
    Case in Point: *Apple v. Psystar*..273
    Case in Point: Online Music Downloading..274
    Case in Point: The Sony BMG Case 275
    The Future of DRM 275
Media Exploitation 276

Media Exploitation Tools 277

Image Validation 284

Summary 287

References 288

Chapter 9: Media Exploitation Analysis 291

Reviewing Exploited Media Using a Mac 291

Mail 295

IMAP 296

POP Mail 296

Exchange 298

Carving 299

MacForensicsLab 299

Access Data Forensic Toolkit 303

FTK and Images 306

EnCase 314

Spyware 317

Mobile Spy 318

FlexiSpy 321

Summary 322

Chapter 10: Network Analysis 323

Custody Considerations 323

Networking 101: The Basics 324

Networking 201: Advanced Topics 331

DHCP 331

Wireless Encryption and Authentication 333

Forensic Analysis 334

Network Traffic Analysis 337

Summary 342

Index 343

Foreword

Sometimes when you fly, you have a chance to see what consumers are using for personal devices. You could tell e-books were taking off when you started seeing them regularly on planes. On the last trip I took, I was amazed to see the number of people using Apple iPads on the plane. In every row, at least one person was using an Apple iPad. Unseen, of course, was the Apple iPhone, but I knew that probably just as many individuals were using that device daily as well. Out of all my friends, I would say at least 50 percent of them have an Apple iPhone. In my family, we all own one, including my extended family. The dominance of Apple mobile devices is clear.

Every individual who uses an Apple device has detailed information about their daily habits stored on their personal mobile devices—more than we have ever seen on computer workstations or laptops. Since the devices are portable and usually never leave the side of the individual using it, they are considered trusted. As a result, the amount of data one might be able to recover from these devices during an investigation is crucial to case work today and in the future.

As businesses begin to adopt Apple devices into their infrastructure and assign them to their employees, knowing how to properly examine and recover detailed evidence from these mobile devices is something that is going to grow significantly beyond just a law enforcement requirement.

Running on each one of these devices is a proprietary operating system based on Mac OS X called iOS, and this book will aid any investigator in understanding and learning the latest iOS analysis techniques. Law enforcement and IT security will need to have the knowledge to properly acquire and analyze data from these devices, which are being adopted quicker than any other technology for personal use. Forensic analysis of iOS is no longer an option on your resume; it is a critical skill. This book helps bridge a crucial gap in knowledge that currently exists with many forensics professionals. Thanks go to Sean for taking the time to write this wonderful book and continuing to share his knowledge with the community.

Rob Lee
SANS Institute

About the Author

 **Sean Morrissey** is currently a computer and mobile forensics analyst for a federal agency and is a contributing editor for *Digital Forensics Magazine*. Sean is married to his wife of 23 years, Dawn, and also has one son, Robert, who is currently serving in the U.S. Army. Sean is a graduate of Creighton University and following college was an officer in the U.S. Army. After military service, Sean's career moved to law enforcement where he was a police officer and sheriff's deputy in Maryland. Following service as a law enforcement officer, training became an important part of Sean's development. Sean was a military trainer in Africa and an instructor of forensics at the Defense Cyber Crime Center. During this time, Sean gained certifications as a Certified Digital Media Collector (CDMC) and Certified Digital Forensic Examiner (CDFE) and was a lead author on the book *Mac OS X, iPod, and iPhone Forensic Analysis* (Syngress, 2008).

Sean also founded Katana Forensics from his roots as a law enforcement officer for departments that didn't have the luxury of gaining access to high-priced tools. Katana was founded to create quality forensic tools that all levels of law enforcement can use.

About the Technical Reviewer

 **Tony Campbell** is an independent security consultant, writer, speaker, and publisher who specializes in developing secure architectures, writing security policy, and implementing low-level security engineering for government and private sector clients. He is also responsible for TR Media's *Digital Forensics Magazine* (www.digitalforensicsmagazine.com), an independent publication targeting the computer forensics community that now ships to more than 30 countries worldwide. Previously in his long and varied IT career, Tony worked in publishing as part of the Apress editorial team (after working on three Windows-related books for Apress), and he has written or contributed to a further six independent technology books and has written more than 200 articles for various computer magazines, such as *Windows XP Answers, Windows XP: The Official Magazine*, and *Windows Vista: The Official Magazine*. In the far and distant past, Tony worked in the British Meteorological Office where he trained as a weatherman; however, after failing the compulsory screen test with too many ummms, uhhhhs, and odd expressions, he decided a job in IT better suited his demeanor.

Tony now lives in Reading, Berkshire, in the United Kingdom and can be contacted via the *Digital Forensics Magazine* web site.

Acknowledgments

First I would like to thank my two contributors, Chris Cook for his legal analysis and Alex Levinson for his expertise in network forensics.

Chris Cook is both an attorney and computer forensic analyst. He has extensive education and experience in the areas of computer forensics, cyber crime, and e-discovery. Chris is an active member of the bar in Texas and the District of Columbia. He holds a juris doctorate degree from the Catholic University of America, Columbus School of Law; a master's of forensic science in computer forensics from George Washington University; and a bachelor's degree with special honors in government from the University of Texas at Austin. Chris currently provides direct legal and computer forensics support to a federal government agency. Chris recently worked as a discovery manager for an international computer forensics and e-discovery consulting firm. Chris has also worked as a staff attorney for a global securities practice law firm in the Washington, DC, area where he assisted with the representation of corporate clients involving sensitive enforcement matters brought by the Securities and Exchange Commission (SEC) and other federal regulators.

Alex Levinson is an undergraduate student at the Rochester Institute of Technology, with a major in information security and forensics. Following high school in Indiana, Alex moved to San Francisco and attended Heald College of San Francisco for Information Technology with an emphasis in network security. He transferred to Rochester Institute of Technology in the spring of 2009. Alex has a diverse background spanning offensive and defensive cyber security, forensics, and software development. Alex was a top placing competitor in the 2010 US Cyber Challenge and has been published in IEEE for his work in mobile forensics. Alex joined Sean as the senior engineer of Katana Forensics in the spring of 2010.

Second, I would like to thank the following companies that donated demonstration software: Access Data, Guidance Software, Paraben, Oxygen, Susteen, and Alwin Troost. Without them this book would not have been possible. Thank you also goes to TechInsights and Semiconductor Insights for providing iDevice hardware images.

I would like to also thank Apress and Tony Campbell, who were instrumental in this book getting published.

Lastly, I would like to thank my wife, Dawn, who put up with me during the past year while I wrote this book.

Introduction

This book was a journey that began with the introduction of the iPhone 2G back in January 2007. This fascinating piece of engineering took the cell phone market by storm. Since then, manufacturers have done everything they can to knock Apple off the smartphone hill. Android has crept up but just hasn't measured up to the total experience that Steve Jobs and Apple has given its users of mobile devices. With the iPod, Apple changed the way we consume multimedia; with the iPhone, Apple changed the way we communicate and use cell phones. The iPad was yet another revelation. The iPad has seemed to squash the sales of netbooks. With the rise in popularity of these devices, they've also become more and more prevalent in criminal cases.

This book will take you down the road of examining these devices, from the hardware that powers them to the software that runs these amazing marvels of technology. We will examine all facets of forensics, from the incident response of these devices to tools that assist in examining an iDevice (any iPhone, iPad, or iPod) and from GPS to property lists. We will examine some legal implications that involve the iPhone and jailbreaking. As you will see in this book, the canons of forensics should be maintained, and procedures that are derived from underground sources, however they are measured, should be used as tools of last resort. You'll learn that the process of least invasive to most invasive should be paramount to mobile forensics. Examiners are constantly looking to examine phones quicker but not necessarily sticking to the traditions of forensics. This book will show that there can be a huge number of artifacts that can be located in the logical space. Immediately diving into breaking the phone is not a preferred method. You will see that these methods can be destructive and therefore detrimental to a case. Along with the devices, there are now approximately 300,000+ applications in circulation, not counting those from the third-party Cydia store. Some of these applications can look very innocent but at the same time can be very dangerous. Examiners tend to overlook the world of third-party apps. This book will teach you which applications are best for finding artifacts that can help in solving crimes.

This book will also help you form strategies for artifact retrieval and analysis. Imagine that an iPhone has been given to you for analysis. What do you do? This book will help you in formulating a game plan and maximize the data that can be retrieved from these devices. Do you use a logical forensic tool? Do you go in for the kill and jailbreak the phone and access the RAW device? These are questions that need to be answered by the examiner and stay within his skill set in order to keep from destroying the evidence at hand.

Although we can only guess what Apple has in store for us in the future, it is very clear that any future iDevice will not look too much different internally in reference to the structure of the data. So, a good foundation in iOS forensics will aid in analyzing any devices potentially released in the future by Apple. This book will give that foundation so that you can analyze any iDevice and report the artifacts.

Chapter 1

History of Apple Mobile Devices

Before we delve into artifacts and analysis, let's take a look at the history of Apple's mobile devices. Apple had a history of trials and failures until the release of the iPhone, which is the phone that actually changed the mobile phone game. For instance, in 1988, Apple started the development of the Newton (see Figure 1–1), an early version of a PDA tablet. The first Newton project was the Message Pad 100, released in August 1993, and the last was MessagePad 2100, released in November 1997. The Newton line of products was subsequently killed upon the return of Steve Jobs to Apple in 1997.

Figure 1–1. *The Apple Message Pad vs. the Apple products of today (courtesy of Apple)*

There were six models of the Newton, and all had an ARM processor, with a clock speed of 20MHz to 162MHz. The Message Pad also had its own operating system called NewtonOS. The platform had a touchscreen, handwriting recognition, and applications that were able to share information in "soups." Soups were not unlike what we see in the iPhone's databases, where one application can refer to data in another application. For example, the SMS database can cross-reference data in the AddressBook database, and you can see names in place of phone numbers in the GUI.

The Newton had a calendar, contacts, and notes—everything a normal PDA used at that time. Despite this, the device just didn't seem to grasp the attention of the general public. Instead, devices such as the Palm were leading in the personal digital assistant (PDA) market.

The failure of the Newton didn't seem to deter Steve Jobs, who just returned to Apple as CEO, in developing newer technologies. In fact, it soon became evident that Steve Jobs' focus was to bring Apple back from the brink of death and develop new technologies. Before the birth of the iPhone, Steve Jobs turned his focus to a device that would forever change Apple—the iPod. The iPod (and iTunes) was the springboard for the eventual inception of the iPhone and iPad.

The iPod

The Apple iPod didn't ignore Apple's PDA roots. Each iPod had the ability to store calendar and contact information, and subsequent generations of iPods gave the consumer the ability to view photos and then video. The original iPod was capable only of syncing with a Mac because of its FireWire interface. Windows users saw the utility of the iPod and were clamoring for it, so Apple switched to USB and has never looked back.

The sales of iPods soared into the stratosphere and, with more than 300 million iPods sold worldwide, forever changed the landscape of how consumers listen, view, and purchase multimedia. As opposed to the failure of the Newton, the iPod was a success story that numerous competitors attempted to match but failed. The iPod and eventual success of its Mac lines of computers changed the way that consumers saw Apple; they began to look to Apple for future innovations and devices that again would change our world.

The Evolution of Apple iPhones

The iPod kicked off the revitalization of Apple, but it's the iPhone that has made it last. Apple took what it learned from the success of the iPod and applied it to the world of mobile communications.

The ROCKR

Before Apple decided to eventually come out with its own cell phone, in 2005 it had a joint venture with Motorola with the ROCKR, as shown in Figure 1–2.

Figure 1–2. *The ROCKR (courtesy of Motorola)*

The ROCKR was the first cell phone that had a version of iTunes, but in 2006 Apple discontinued its support of iTunes on the ROCKR. So, it was surprising that Steve Jobs and Apple would release a cell phone that would revolutionize the cellular industry. Even though the ROCKR was another failure of Apple, it was seen as a testing ground for the iPhone.

Hence, in January 2007, Steve Jobs introduced the iPhone to the world. It was a Multi-Touch device that had its own operating system, iPhone OS. Bringing back the PDA roots of the Newton and the iTunes from the ROCKR, it was a game changer in the cell phone market.

The Apple iPhone 2G

The first iPhone was referred to as the 2G, shown in Figure 1–3.

Figure 1–3. *The Apple iPhone 2G (courtesy of Apple)*

The iPhone was capable of using the second-generation cellular network Edge. The iPhone 2G also had the ability to communicate with 802.11 technology and used

Bluetooth for accessories such as hands-free headsets. The Apple 2G iPhone was first released with 4GB of internal storage and then released in September 2007 with 8GB and 16GB versions. New technologies such as a MultiTouch input method from the user interface were a huge breakthrough for Apple (and cell phones in general). The main functions of the iPhone were not just cellular communication, but web access, e-mail, and PDA functions. The Apple iPhone also connected to iTunes and YouTube.

The iPhone was clearly designed to be used as a multiple application device, not just a cell phone. Since the App Store didn't exist yet, the iPhone was able to place web apps on its device. These web apps were the precursor to the apps that are now seen on today's iPhones. (Web apps were just links to web site pages that run a given function.)

Web Apps

Prior to the App Store and during iPhone OS version 1.0, Apple created web applications that were similar to widgets on the Mac platform. These apps were small applications in the following categories: Calculate, Entertainment, Games, Productivity, Search Tools, Sports, Travel, Utilities, and Weather. The applications were accessible from Safari and on the iPhone home screen, as shown in Figure 1–4. These applications didn't generate any data on the iPhone except for the icon on the screen and its hyperlink.

These web apps still exist, and some are still being developed. The numbers are not anywhere the size of the App Store, but they were the precursor to the tremendous success of the App Store.

Figure 1–4. *Apple web applications, the precursor to the iTunes App Store*

Competitive Advantages

The iPhone connected people, and the integration of the iPhone camera was a first step in a quest to remove the need for digital cameras and use your iDevice to capture your life.

Apple also showed that keeping with one carrier increased the sales of the device, and competitors mimicked that model—some with more success than others. Research in Motion (RIM) developed the Blackberry Storm and was connected to Verizon, Palm's Pre was developed by Palm and was connected to Sprint, and Google's Nexus was connected to T-Mobile. Most of these eventually split from their exclusive carriers and branched out to other carriers; however, Apple did not. Apple has stuck with AT&T, even with the complaints about service, and the iPhone has been a cash cow for both Apple and AT&T.

Since the iPhone's release, other manufacturers have been scrambling to match Apple and produce other smartphones to compete. Research in Motion developed the Storm and Storm 2 in hopes of keeping its edge over Apple. Palm developed the Palm Pre, which was seen as a failure that brought the eventual demise of Palm. HTC developed numerous Android-powered devices, and Motorola developed the Droid. Every competing device was always asked, "Is this the iPhone killer?" Every device just didn't seem to match the capabilities of the iPhone. Apple also never stood still, and again the mystique of the "new iPhone" continued to propel the iPhone's sales and reach.

The Motorola Droid also hasn't generated the same buzz as even one release of any of the iPhones. The Google Nexus 1, even with its impressive hardware, has been beset with problems, and any problems that arise from the phone gets directed to the manufacturer of the phone, in this case HTC. The Nexus was quietly removed from the market, and other generations of HTC and Motorola phones have attempted to compete directly with the iPhone. Still, Apple has still stayed above the rest with the ability to support not only the hardware but also the operating system.

The 3G iPhone

The second generation of iPhones commonly referred to as the 3G was the iPhone that switch from the Edge network to the faster 3G network. Figure 1–5 shows the updated iPhone 3G.

Figure 1–5. *The Apple iPhone 3G (courtesy of Apple)*

Apple released the iPhone 3G in June 2008 and by June 2009 had two variants, 8GB and 16GB models. The 16GB iPhones were the first iPhones available in black and white. The biggest feature of the 3G iPhone was that is contained Assisted GPS. This gave more functionality to the Google Maps applications, allowing the user to use this application as a simple GPS turn-by-turn road map. The GPS was not that accurate, but with future firmware updates, the device got better. The GPS function of the 3GS also allowed geotagging of images that were taken from the internal camera, which was previously seen only in high-end digital cameras. This allowed investigators to place a subject at a certain place at a point in time.

Version 2.0 of the firmware also saw the debut of the App Store. This was a marketplace that would offer applications to users of the iPhone. Nobody thought that the App Store would be the premiere model for other manufacturers to follow. For example, Android released the Android Market to showcase and sell apps, Palm Pre's has an App Catalog, and RIM has its own version of an app store. To date, Apple has 300,000+ applications in its store. Its competitors haven't even come close to the effectiveness of Apple's App Store. The applications, which are developed by an army of developers who utilize the software development kit (SDK), can take advantage of the phone's accelerometer, GPS, video, audio, and PDA functions.

The 3G[S] iPhone

In June 2009, Apple released its newest iPhone, the iPhone 3G[S], shown in Figure 1–6.

Figure 1–6. *The Apple iPhone 3G[S] (courtesy of Apple)*

The 3G[S] was also the released with the new 3.0 software. The 3G[S] arrived with a compass and a new 3.0-megapixel camera that was able to shoot and edit video. The 3.0 software was also a boom for developers because it was given access to third-party hardware via the USB port and Bluetooth. The 3GS was another game changer with the addition of the two new technologies on the phone. The video capability was a good boost for Apple and for investigators, because even when a video is taken and possibly edited, the original stays on the phone, until it is eventually deleted. The 3.0 software also added voice recordings, which added one more possible artifact to investigators. The GPS on the phone was more capable and with better accuracy. The compass added a compass heading to the geotagging feature, so now you can gather images with latitude, longitude, altitude, and compass headings. The phone still maintained its relationship with AT&T.

The iPhone 4

The iPhone 4 (shown in Figure 1–7) was a center of controversy and drama. Leaks of the new device were becoming more and more intense until Gawker Media/Gizmodo purchased a device that later was revealed as the fourth-generation iPhone.

Figure 1–7. *The Apple iPhone 4G (courtesy of Apple)*

On June 21, 2010, Steve Jobs announced at the Worldwide Developers Conference the introduction of the new iPhone 4. The iPhone 4 was a completely redesign from Jonathan Ive, who heads the Industrial Design team at Apple. The stainless steel case was incorporated as part of the new antennae system on the phone. The iPhone 4 was centered on a new processor and a larger battery. A front-facing camera that used Apple's Face Time technology was a mode for video conferencing with iPhones and other devices and carriers. The iPhone 4 sported a new 5-megapixel camera and LED flash.

The launch of the iPhone 4 was also the launch of iOS 4, a newer and more powerful operating system. iOS4 gave the development community five APIs in order to multitask operations on the iPhone. The user was also allowed to change the environment by replacing the wallpaper and lockdown screens. With applications such as iMovie, video editing was also possible, not just clipping in iOS3. Face Time, a new application that allowed for video chat via Wi-Fi, was not available at first on the 3G network.

The Apple iPad

The Apple iPad was announced on January 26, 2010 (shown in Figure 1–8).

Figure 1–8. *The Apple iPad (courtesy of Apple)*

When Steve Jobs announced this device, there was a sense that Apple was shifting the way we do things again. Like the iPod changed the way we consume media and like the iPhone forever changed the way cell phones are produced and used, the iPad can change the way we read. It's not meant to replace the iPod or iPhone but to complement them.

So, what does this mean for forensics? There will be a huge migration in doing productivity work, and we will be begin to find artifacts that we've never seen before on an iDevice, such as numerous documents, spreadsheets, and PDFs. As more developers take advantage of syncing items from a computer to the iPad, these type of artifacts will grow exponentially. The first iPad uses iPhone OS 3.2, which means all the things we have been doing with the iPhone and iPod touch will still apply. In 2010, there will be an upgrade available to iOS4, which has some differences. It has a mini-SIM card, but it's unable to use the 3G network to place calls. It's larger than an iPod touch, so it's not as portable. It has the same processor as the iPhone 4 and comes in 16GB, 32GB, and 64GB variations.

Under the Surface: iPhone and iPad Hardware

How the interface functions in the iPhone 2G, 3G, and 3GS hasn't changed too much over the years. The major exterior change from the iPhone 2G to the iPhone 3G was the switch from a stainless steel housing to a hard plastic one, and then the iPhone 4 made a radical change to the design of the iPhone line. The 2G, 3G, 3GS iPhone devices have a slot on top for a SIM card, volume control, a ringer on/off button, and two speakers and one microphone. The iPhone started with a 2-megapixel camera, and in the iPhone 3G/3GS it was changed to a 3-megapixel camera. In the following sections of this chapter, you will see the operation, use, and guts of iDevices.

2G iPhone Internals

Figures 1–9 and 1–10 show the internals of the iPhone 2G. You will see in the development of the iPhone how things get small and in the iPhone 4 how things get even smaller in order to make room for a larger battery.

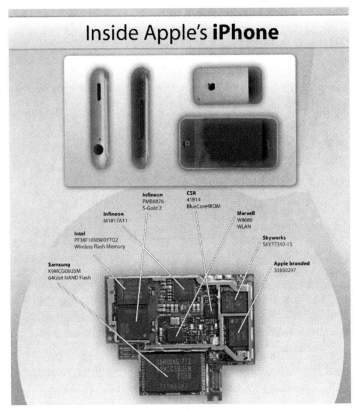

Figure 1–9. *The internals of the Apple iPhone 2G (courtesy of Semiconductor Insights)*

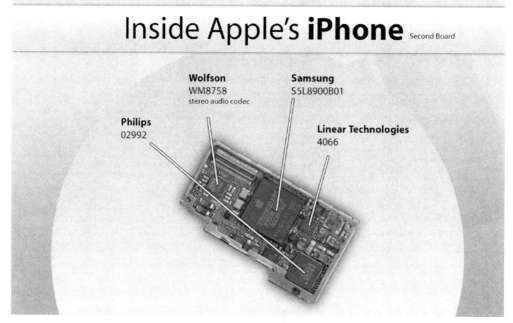

Figure 1–10. *Another view inside the Apple iPhone 2G (courtesy of Semiconductor Insights)*

The 2G exterior is unique compared to all the versions of the iPhone. The front of the phone is the iconic black with a silver rim. The rear is aluminum, and a portion at the bottom is black. The iPhone 2G does not have a removable battery, which has been a matter of soreness for users who never received long life from its internal power supply.

The iPhone 2G was released in June 2007 and was discontinued in July 2008. The OS that was released with the 2G was OS 1.0, and owners of the 2G iPhone are still able to upgrade to the latest version of the operating system, which currently is 3.x. The hardware of this phone gave unprecedented access to the Internet via the 2G Edge network with a wireless connection, and the screen made cruising the Internet easier than any other phone that had been developed at that time. With full rendering of web pages, pinching and zooming made navigating around a web page better than any other phone at that time. Also, 2G provided the ability to listen to music and watch video and send and receive e-mail. Table 1–2 breaks down the 2G hardware.

Table 1–1. *2G Hardware*

2G Hardware	Manufacturer	Description
Application processor	Samsung	SSI8900B01. A chip that has an ARM11766JZF-S CPU core, 16KB L1 cache. This chip has an eight-stage integer pipeline, ARM Trust Zone, MBX Lite 3D graphics co-processor at 60MHz, a vector floating-point coprocessor, and 128MB DDR integrated SDRAM. The Samsung SS18900B01 has a maximum clock speed of 667MHz.
Baseband processor	Infineon	PMB8876 S-Gold Quad Band GSM/GPRS/Edge 850/900/1800/1900MHz.
Connectivity	Marvell	W8686 802.11 b/g.
	CSR	41B14 Blucore4ROM (Bluetooth).
Graphics	PowerVR	MBX Lite 3D graphics co-processor at 60MHz.
Memory		128MB DRAM.
Display	Phillips	LPCC2221/02992 Touchscreen controller.
	National Semiconductor	24-bit RGB display interface. Glass capacitive Multi-Touchtouchscreen, with a resolution of 320×480 and was scratch resistant was made on the device. The Multi-Touch sensor could distinguish between a finger rather than a stylus. A stylus did not conduct enough electrical connectivity to activate the Multi-Touch sensor.
Audio	Wolfson	WM8758 Stereo audio codec.
Storage	Samsung	K9MCG08USM 64Gb NAND flash memory chip in 4GB, 8GB, and 16GB.
USB	Apple	30 pin USB proprietary connection.
Camera		2.0 Megapixel.
Sensors		Ambient Light, Proximity, Moisture.

3G iPhone Internals

As it be came to be, Apple released a major change to the iPhone in its appearance and added some performance upgrades. The most pronounced was the addition of GPS, which gave developers another arena to add functionality to their applications. The iPhone 3G also switched from the Edge network to the 3G network that improved network performance.

This model was release with a lot of fanfare in July 2008. The hardware was faster, the storage was bigger, and it came in black and white cases. The upgrade in power and speed became important with the introduction of the App Store. The iPhone 3G became a complete package that now could do just about anything with apps. Figure 1–11 gives insight to the internals of the iPhone 3G. The daughterboard is lost, and all is placed on one circuit board. Table 1–11 breaks down the hardware.

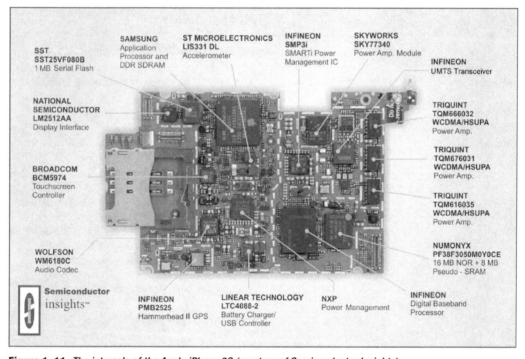

Figure 1–11. *The internals of the Apple iPhone 3G (courtesy of Semiconductor Insights)*

Table 1–2. *3G Hardware*

3G Hardware	Manufacturer	Description
Application processor	Samsung	SSI8900B01. A chip that has an ARM11766JZF-S CPU core, 16KB L1 cache. This chip has an 8-stage integer pipeline, ARM Trust Zone, a vector floating-point coprocessor, and 128MB DDR integrated SDRAM. The Samsung SS18900B01 has a maximum clock speed of 667MHz.
Baseband processor	Infineon	PMB8878 X-Gold Tri-Band UMTS/HSDPA 850/1900/2100MHz.
Connectivity	Marvell	W8686 802.11 b/g.
	CSR	41B14 Blucore4ROM (Bluetooth).
Graphics	PowerVR	MBX Lite 3D graphics co-processor at 60MHz.
GPS	Infineon	Hammerhead II AGPS Assisted GPS chip that gives the iPhone location services.
Memory		128MB DRAM.
Display	Broadcom	BCM5974 Touchscreen Controller.
	National Semiconductor	LM2512AA 24-bit RGB display.
		Glass capacitive Multi-Touchtouchscreen, with a resolution of 320×480 and was scratch resistant. The Multi-Touch sensor could distinguish between a finger rather than a stylus. A stylus did not conduct enough electrical connectivity to activate the Multi-Touch sensor.
Audio	Wolfson	WM8758 Stereo audio codec.
Storage	Samsung	K9MCG08USM 64Gbit NAND flash memory chip in 8GB and 16GB.
USB	Apple	30-pin USB proprietary connection.
Camera		2.0 megapixel.
Sensors		Ambient Light, Proximity, Moisture.

iPhone 3G[S] Internals

The iPhone 3GS was a dramatic change from the 3G with improvements in the operating system, such as an upgraded processor, voice control, and an improved camera that allowed the capture of video.

The 3G[S] was released on June 3, 2009. iOS 3 was released with this iPhone. The 3GS gave the ability to create video from the iPhone camera, it had a faster processor, and it was hailed as a faster platform than its predecessor, the iPhone 3G. The iPhone 3GS did out-perform the 3G, but it still was plagued with problems with its reception. Some hoped for tethering, which never produced itself in the United States. However, survey after survey showed that owners of the iPhone 3GS were generally pleased even though the service provider, AT&T, consistently took flak for inferior performance. Figure 1–12 shows the insides of the iPhone 3G. Table 1–3 breaks down the hardware.

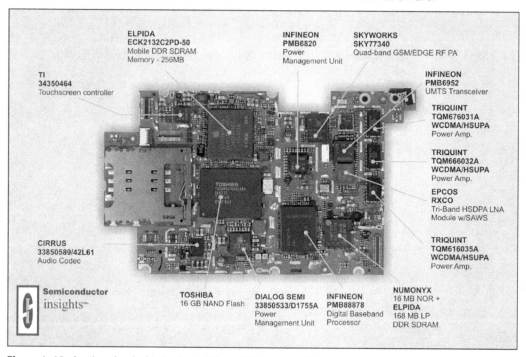

Figure 1–12. *Another view inside the Apple iPhone 3G (courtesy of Semiconductor Insights)*

Table 1–3. *3GS Hardware*

3GS Hardware	Manufacturer	Description
Application processor	Samsung	Samsung S5PC100 is 32-bit ARM Cortex A8 RISC microprocessor and a 64/32-bit internal bus architecture; could operate up to 833MHz. The iPhone 3G[S] was under-clocked at 600MHz to conserve battery life.
Baseband processor	Infineon	PMB8878 X-Gold Tri-Band UMTS/HSDPA 850,1900, 2100MHz.
Connectivity	Broadcom	BCM4325 802.11a/b/g . Bluetooth2.1+EDR.
Graphics	PowerVR	200MHz SGX.
GPS	Infineon	Hammerhead II AGPS. Gave the iPhone geotagging capabilities.
Memory		256MB DRAM.
Display	TI	34350464 touchscreen controller. Glass oelophobic technology Multi-Touch touchscreen, with a resolution of 320×480, and was scratch resistant and fingerprint resistive.
Audio	Cirrus	33850589/42L61 Audio Codec.
Storage	Toshiba	TH58NVG702 NAND flash memory chip 16GB and 32GB.
USB	Apple	30-pin USB proprietary connection.
Camera		3.0-megapixel with video with a rate of 30fps.
Sensors		Ambient Light, Proximity, Moisture.

iPhone 4 Internals

The iPhone 4 was a radical new design from its predecessors. Made of Helicopter (Gorilla) glass and stainless steel, this iPhone compared to the iPhone 3GS seemed more of a phone and less of a toy. The ruggedness brings back memories of the iPhone 2G but with a classic and more substantive mobile phone experience. The iPhone 4 came with two cameras, one front facing and one rear facing. A new feature called Face Time brought communicating to a higher level. Now we are able to see those we talk to, like in iChat AV. Unfortunately, this is available only through the wireless network. The iPhone 4 also has a brilliant high-def (Retina) screen, greater speed with the new A4 processor, more RAM than ever placed onto an iDevice, and longer life battery. Table 1–4 breaks down the hardware.

Table 1–4. *iPhone 4 Hardware*

iPhone 4 Hardware	Manufacturer	Description
Baseband	Skyworks	SKY77541GSM/GPRS front-end module
Power amp	Triqunt	TQM666092 & TQM666901 power amp
Radio/amplifier	Skyworks	SKY77452 W-CDMA FEM
Radio/transmit and receiver	Apple/Infineon	338S0626GSM/CDMA transceiver
Radio/amplifier	Skyworks	SKY777469 Tx-Rx FEM for Quad-Band GSM/GPRS/Edge
Gyroscope	Apple	AGD1 STMicro three-axis gyroscope
Processor	Apple	ARM Cortex A4 processor
Connectivity/80211 and GPS	Broadcom	BCM4329KUGB 802.11n and Bluetooth 2.1 + EDR antennae
Connectivity	Broadcom	BCM4750IUB8 single-chip receiver
Memory	Samsung	K9DG08USM-LCB0
DRAM memory	Samsung	K4XKG6432GB
Display	Wintek	Capacitive glass
Camera		5MP autofocus

iPad Internals

The Apple iPad was the device that was to precede the iPhone. However, as it turned out, the iPhone was released first, and the iPad was released after the iPhone 3GS and before the iPhone 4. The iPad is a tablet device that runs iOS 3.2 and created a new niche in portable devices that complemented the iDevice line.

Since the iPad runs iOS, it is really a giant iPod touch but with a few differences. This device has a gigantic battery that allows 7+ hours of numerous functions. The gaming and video possibilities are enormous, and commercial television networks as well a publishing houses are looking to the iPad as a solution to their floundering businesses.

The iPad has a huge screen to view numerous periodicals and view TV shows and news. The iPad has its own version of Pages, which gives users the ability to modify documents and presentations. The iPad was such a big hit that it had 3 million sales in three weeks. Figure 1–13 shows the internals of the iPad and how Apple was able to place a huge battery in the device, which gives it outstanding life without having to recharge. Table 1–5 breaks down the hardware.

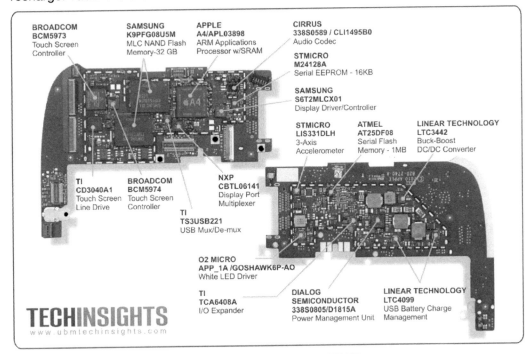

Figure 1–13. *The internal view of the Apple iPad (courtesy of TECHINSIGHTS)*

We have reviewed the mobile devices that Apple has released. But to the untrained eye, how can you look at a device and determine whether it is 2G, 3G, 3GS, iPhone, or the various generations of iPod touch devices? Some generations of iDevices can be visually identifiable by their complete design change, such as the aluminum backing of the 2G or the plastic backing of the 3G or the radical change of the iPhone 4 and glass housings.

Some are not so easy, though. For example, it is sometimes hard to distinguish between the iPhone 3G and 3GS. Generations of iPod touch devices are equally hard to know the generation. On the back of all iDevice, Apple has stamped model numbers, and Table 1–6 shows the generation of iDevices and their associated model number. This can assist an examiner in readily identifying the correct generation of iDevice.

Table 1–5. *Apple iPad Hardware*

iPad Hardware	Manufacturer	Description
Processor	Apple	A4
Touchscreen	Broadcom	BCM5973, BCM5974
Memory	Samsung	K-PFG8U5M Nand Flash
Audio	Cirrus	338S0589/CLI1495B0
LED Driver	02 Micro	APP_1A/GOSHAWK6P-AO
Accelerometer	STMicro	LIS331DLH 3 Axis
RAM	Samsung	K4X1G323PE DDR SRAM
DC Regulator	Linear Technologies	3442N7667LT9L
Audio Processor	Cirrus	338S0589 BO YFSAB0BY1001 SGP
Bluetooth	Broadcom	802.11n BCM4329XKUBG
Display	LG	SW0627B

Table 1–6. *Generation of iDevice*

iOS Device	Model Number
iPhone 2G	A1203
iPhone 3G	A1241
iPhone 3GS	A1303
iPhone 4	A1332
iPod touch 1G	A1213
iPod touch 2G	A1288
iPod touch 3G	A1318
IPod Touch 4G	A1367
iPad WiFi	A1219
iPad 3G+ WiFi	A1337
AppleTV 2G	A1378

The Apple App Store

One of the greatest successes of the Apple iPhone was actually the Apple App Store. The store has become the digital iTunes of the iPhone. When the iPhone was first introduced, the App Store was a creation waiting to unfold with the development of the new iPhone iOS and the iPhone 3G. Prior to the iPhone 3G, there were limited applications that were available to the iPhone: Calendar, Camera, Weather, Maps, Notes, Clock, Settings, and, in the Dock, Phone, Mail, Safari, iPod. In March 2008, Apple released the iPhone SDK. This release was to give developers the tools necessary to create applications for the upcoming new iPhone OS 2.0. Upon the release of the iPhone 3G and iPhone OS 2.0 came the App Store to iTunes, as well as 500 new applications that were free or paid-for applications.

The Apple App Store opened on July 10, 2008. The medium that distributed these applications was iTunes. When a developer sells an app in the App Store, the developer receives 70 percent of the sales, and Apple receives 30 percent. The Apple 3G came preloaded with iPhone OS 2.0, which had App Store support. The Apple iPhone 2G was also capable of the same iOS but was a download from iTunes. With iPhone iOS 3.0, this was carried forward with the ability of developers to add updates that could be fee based. This was seen as a boost for game developers who could charge for additions to games. Today there are more than 300,000 applications available from the Apple App Store.

An account needs to applied for through iTunes in order to purchase applications. Applications can be brought into the iPhone via two methods—iTunes and from the iPhone App Store application directly on the iPhone, iPod touch, or iPad. Within iTunes, the iPhone, iPod touch, or iPad have to be connected to a Mac or Windows computer. A user can go online to the App Store and grab free or for purchase Apps. Figure 1–14 is a view of the App Store from iTunes.

Figure 1–14. *The iTunes App Store*

Once the apps have been downloaded to iTunes, the user can connect the device to the computer and add the app. One major improvement for the application section of iTunes is that it now mimics how each home page is laid out so the user can add, remove, and move applications to and from iTunes easily. When the iPhone is connected, all the changes can be updated on its next sync. The interface of the application section of iTunes is shown in Figure 1–15.

Figure 1–15. *The interface of the iTunes application section*

The second way to add applications to the phone is right from the phone itself, as depicted in Figure 1–16. There is an App Store application on the phone that goes directly to the App Store on the Web. Here, free and paid for apps can be purchased. There is one limitation, which is that some apps are larger than 20MB to be downloaded via the 3G network, and a Wi-Fi connection is requested by the app. The App Store application is similar to the App Store on the Web. Apps can be searched by name, by category, or by popularity.

Figure 1–16. *Accessing the App Store through and iPhone*

If the iPhone is returned to a Mac or Windows computer for a sync, the applications will be transferred to iTunes in the event that a restore is needed in the future.

Rise of the iPhone Hackers

Ever since the release of the iPhone, a legion of misguided hackers have descended on the iPhone to give users the ability to use the iPhone on multiple carriers and to use applications that didn't go through the Apple's application review process. The hacking community's ideology was that the iPhone shouldn't be tied one carrier.

First the hacks to the iPhone were crude and often "bricked" phones, in other words, made them useless. This started a cat-and-mouse game with Apple and the hackers. After the release of OS version 1.1.1, it was announced that the iPhone could not be hacked—that was until the iPhone dev team released a hack that cracked 1.1.1. The hackers never thought that their endeavors would amount to anything malicious until two attacks on the iPhone targeted jailbroken iPhones and were able to track these phones within the provider's network.

In June 2010, a hacker was able to penetrate the AT&T network and was able to collect information from prominent personalities in the United States including the chief of staff to President Barack Obama. Hackers have also revealed how malicious code that can be placed onto the phone from within Apple's own App Store–reviewing process. Spyware has been developed for the iPhone that works only on jailbroken phones. The remedy for all this is? Simple—placing the original operating system on the IPhone.

On July 26, 2010, the U.S. Copyright Office ruled that jailbreaking mobile devices doesn't violate copyright law. This ruling allowed for owners of iPhones and other cell phones to circumvent the protections on the phone to allow for the lawful addition of legally purchased applications and allow the phone to be used on other networks. In a sense, this allows for jailbreaking and breaks exclusivity for cell phones. However, this ruling did not take into account the rampant network security problems that Apple and AT&T and others may have with these jailbroken devices.

Summary

Apple has created marvelous devices that were devised to assist all types of people. Apple mobile devices are powerful and beautiful. But with all great and wonderful things, there are those who take these inventions and turn them into objects of evil and wrongdoing.

A good foundation in iOS forensics is to have a grasp of the Apple ecosystem and its effect on forensics. These devices are a social phenomenon and are a growing part of the cell phone landscape, and examiners will see these devices in our labs more and more. Now that you have seen the overall functions of iDevices and their capabilities, you can begin to poke and prod the artifacts that it leaves behind. This book will go into those artifacts and how to extract and examine them.

iOS Operating and File System Analysis

In Chapter 1, we discussed the evolution of devices; in this chapter, we'll look at changes in the operating system (OS) and the addition of the App Store to the iOS environment, and then we'll delve into the details of the iDevice file system in order to provide context for investigations.

Changing iOS Features

iOS, the operating system for the iPhone, iPod, and iPad, was first released with the first-generation iPhone in June 2008. This revolutionized the way cell phones would be created in the future. HTC, Motorola, and Google have since jumped into the smartphone market with their Android phones, as has Research in Motion with its Blackberry phones.

The following subsections describe the history of iOS development.

iOS 1

The first iPhone, using iOS version 1.0, gave users a new experience. This phone came with the following applications:

- SMS
- Calendar
- Photos
- Camera
- YouTube
- Stocks

- Maps

- Weather

- Notes

- Clock

- Calculator

- Settings

- iTunes

- Phone

- Mail

- Safari

- iPod

This iPhone user interface (UI) has a top portion that displays network strength, network type of network, time, Bluetooth icons, and battery strength. Below the top portion of the UI are the home screens. Each screen can hold 16 applications, which at first were web apps that could be downloaded from Apple or bookmarks from Safari that could be added to a home screen. You can swipe left or right to access each screen. The dock has four icons. At first this could not be changed, but revisions of the OS allowed for any application to be placed in the dock, as shown in Figure 2–1.

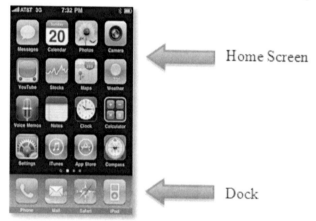

Home Screen

Dock

Figure 2–1. *The iPhone home screen, with four fixed icons on the dock*

Since the iPhone 2G was released with iOS version 1.0, there have been many revisions and improvements to the OS. Major revisions followed a release of a new device. Smaller revisions came out to either fix a problem or to thwart hackers. For example, iOS 1.1.3, which was released in January 2009, addressed a large number of items. Some of the most notable are as follows:

- Addition of apps to the iPod touch

- The ability for icons on the home screen to be rearranged and placed on a maximum of nine separate screens

- Updates for Google Maps

- iTunes gift cards that can be redeemed through the iPhone itself

- SMS messages that can be sent to multiple contacts

- An increase SMS storage

iOS 2

The first big revision to the iPhone was iOS 2.0, which was offered in the iPhone 3G. The first big addition to the OS was the App Store, a marketplace for applications that could run on the iPhone. Apple also released its SDK (Software Development Kit) to assist developers that wanted to create applications on the App Store for free or for purchase. This again was a boon for Apple—the sale of applications and downloads has to this day exceeded 2 million apps. The SDK was released in March 2009 and iOS 2.0 was available for download as of July, 2008. As with previous revisions, it was backward compatible with all previous models of iPhones. All applications that were developed had to be screened by Apple prior to release. This has at times given US government agencies reason to investigate why some applications did not win approval. The most noticeable of them all was Google Voice.

The second biggest addition to the iPhone was GPS (Global Positioning System). This allowed numerous applications to use the GPS API for a multitude of purposes. When GPS first became available to the iPhone, it's was not very accurate, and images didn't get tagged. With subsequent firmware updates and the advent of the iPhone 3GS, the accuracy improved. The two major iOS2/3G applications that used GPS were Google Maps and the Camera application, which geotagged images that were taken with the iPhone camera. However, one should be aware, when the iPhone is inside a structure, the geographic accuracy of the images degrades. This will be apparent when someone examines the images that have been geotagged by the iPhone.

As with iOS 1, iOS 2 had numerous updates. From 2.0 to 2.2.1, there were many enhancements made to the OS. The following were some of the most notable:

- The ability to turn on Wi-Fi even when Airplane mode is turned on

- Support for SVG (Scalable Vector Graphics)

- The ability to save photos from the Mail application

- The addition of the App Store

- Parental controls

- Applications that prompt the user three times to allow location services

- Microsoft Exchange support

- Support for Apple's MobileMe service

- Push e-mail

- Multiple e-mail deletion

- The ability to view Microsoft word documents

- The ability to watch videos in landscape or portrait orientation

- The inclusion of parental controls in the Camera app

- EXIF data, which remains when images are e-mailed from the phone

iOS 3

In June 2009, Apple released iOS 3. This version had many features that were missing in the previous versions:

- Cut, copy, and paste

- Turn-by-turn navigation

- The ability for YouTube account holders to sign in from the phone

- Call history that allowed more granular information, such as call length

- The ability to change the My Number field in the phone settings

- The addition of video capture (3GS only), which included the ability to trim video on the phone itself

- Images that include thumbnails of the original photos. This granted the user to view and possibly delete photos from the Camera application without exiting and going to the Photos application.

- The addition of an autofocus function to the camera (3GS only)

- The renaming of the SMS application to Messages, which signaled the possibility of MMS. (However, in the United States this came months after the release of iOS 3.0.)

- The ability to use MobileMe to turn on the Find My iPhone feature from a setting on the phone and within the Mobile Me account. This allowed you to use remote wiping, add a pass code, or place a message on the screen of the phone remotely.

- CalDAV and LDAP support

- Spotlight searching

- Tethering (available for certain carriers, but not in the United States)

- Voice memos

- Encrypted backups

- Hardware encryption (3GS only)

- Voice control

- The ability for developers to add devices from the USB port

Further revisions of iOS 3 added the following:

- Fraud protection in Safari

- Customizable home screens within Safari

- Improved Exchange support

- Push notifications

iOS 4

On April 7, 2010, Apple announced the release of iOS 4. This was a major step forward for Apple. The most notable feature of the new OS was that it allowed for selective multitasking. Prior to this, the only application that was able to run in the background was the iPod app. Apple announced that it added 1,500 new APIs for developers to utilize for the Apple device family. Of those 1,500, Apple announced that 7 APIs would allow developers to run their applications in the background. The APIs that allowed this were for the following:

- Background audio

- Voice over IP

- Background location (GPS)

- Push notification

- Local notification

- Task completion

- Fast app switching

Some of the most notable features of iOS 4 are as follows:

- Multitasking

- Folders

- Wallpaper and home screen personalization

- Enhanced mail, including the following:

  - A unified mailbox

  - Multiple Exchange mailboxes

  - Fast inbox switching

- Threading
- Open attachments with multiple applications
- iBooks
- Enterprise features, including the following:
  - Mail encryption with a PIN code
  - Mobile device management
  - Wireless app distribution
  - Multiple Exchange accounts
  - SSL VPN support
- Game Center features, including the following:
  - Social gaming network
  - Matchmaking
  - Leader boards
  - Achievements
- iAd
- 5× digital zoom for both pictures and video
- Faces and places in photos (with iPhone-created media)
- Spell checking
- Wireless Bluetooth keyboard support

iOS is a scaled-down version of OS X. iOS devices use a variant of the Mac OS X kernel, and development is based on Xcode and Cocoa.

There are four major components that compose iOS, as follows (these same components have been made available to developers for app development):

- Cocoa, which includes the following:
  - Multitouch for both events and controls
  - Accelerometer
  - Camera support
- Media, which includes the following:
  - OpenAL
  - Video playback
  - Image file formats
  - Quartz

- Core animation

- OpenGL

- Core Services, which includes the following:

  - Networking

  - SQLite databases

  - Core location

  - Threads

- OS X kernel, which includes the following:

  - TCP/IP

  - Sockets

  - Power management

  - File system

  - Security

Application Development

Beginning with iOS 2, Apple allowed the development of application for its App Store. The iPhone SDK gave application developers the access they needed to write applications for all devices. For a developer to release software to the App Store, the developer had to enroll into the iPhone Developer Program, the initial interface of which is shown in Figure 2–2. A standard program had a cost of $99 and an enterprise program had a cost of $299. The developer also had to sign an extensive agreement with Apple in order to develop and add applications to the App Store. Apple also had a strict and sometimes time-consuming approval process. Over time, Apple has loosened some of its rules, and has even accommodated apps such as Google Voice and applications developed with Adobe Flash.

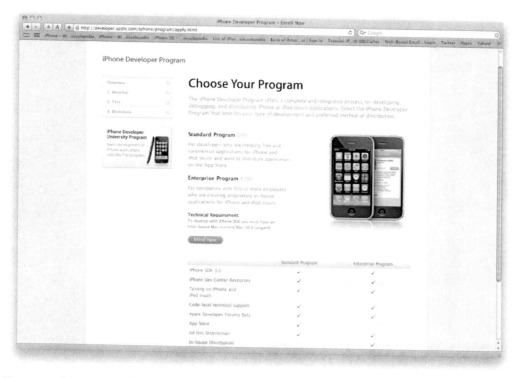

Figure 2–2. *The iPhone Developer Program*

HACKING

One of the biggest challenges that Apple has faced is the army of hackers that descended onto the iPhone. The original hackers of the iPhone justified their actions by virtue of the fact that the iPhone and iOS didn't allow certain functions (e.g., MMS, tethering, customization) or third-party applications other than those available from the App Store. Some hackers also took the stance that the iPhone was insecure, and they wanted to show Apple the flaws that it had. Some of the more notorious groups were the iPhone Dev Team and the Chronic Dev Team. Some of their more maverick members have splintered to develop jailbreaks to further their own ambitions and fame. The modus operandi of all these hackers was notoriety—becoming known to the masses—which became an intoxicating motivation. By late 2009, other hackers had developed viruses and exploits to jailbroken iPhones. These exploits invaded the provider's network to seek out and find jailbroken iPhones. This was a concern that Apple addressed in its counter to the Electronic Freedom Foundation's claim to allow jailbreaking as an exception to the DMCA (Digital Media Copyright Act). The Library of Congress decided that jailbreaking your phone was an exception. However, the deciders of this policy didn't take into account the increase of threats that would invade AT&T and Apple. So Apple and AT&T would have to protect their networks and OS. Since the release of the first Apple mobile device, Apple and the hackers have played a cat-and-mouse game. The first jailbreaks were crude and were prone to crashing the phone and making the iPhone nonfunctional, otherwise known as "bricking" the phone. Some of the jailbreaks and unlocks had the following monikers:

■ Pwnage

■ Qwkpwn

■ RedSn0w

■ Yellowsn0w

■ iLiberty

■ Purplera1n

■ Blackra1n

■ Greenpois0n

All circumvented the security measures of the iPhone by either replacing the OS with one engineered on user-created firmware, or just patching the kernel and/or bootrom, which allowed the device to run unsigned code.

The iOS File System

HFS+ File System

In 1996, Apple developed a new file system that would accommodate storing large data sets. As physical disk size was increasing at breakneck speed, a file system had to be developed to support the growing need for storage. Hence, Apple developed the Hierarchical File System (HFS). The structure of HFS can be complicated to understand. At the physical level, the disks formatted with HFS are in 512–byte blocks. These are similar to Windows-based sectors. There are two types of blocks on an HFS system: logical blocks and allocation blocks. The logical blocks are numbered from the first to the last on a given volume. They are static and are the same size as the physical blocks, 512 bytes. Allocation blocks are groups of logical blocks used by the HFS system to track data in a more efficient way. To reduce fragmentation on an HFS volume, groups of allocation blocks are tied together as clumps. This organization is shown in Figure 2–3.

In terms of date and time, Apple has used absolute time, otherwise known as local time. UNIX time is used as well. The iOS system utilizes both of these time schemes. Since absolute time does not take into account the differences in time zones, one must be cognizant to identify the location of the system to understand actual the data and time of artifacts.

Data within the HFS file system utilizes a catalog file system or B*tree (balanced tree) to organize files. This balanced tree uses a catalog file and extents overflows in its organization scheme. B*trees are comprised of nodes. These nodes are grouped together in linear fashion, which makes data access faster. When data is added or deleted, the extents are constantly balanced to keep its efficiency. Each file that is created on an HFS file system is given a unique number—a catalog ID number. The HFS volume header tracks the numbering of the catalog ID and will increment by one each file added. These numbers can be reused, but this is tracked by the HFS volume header.

Typically, the reuse of catalog ID numbers is mainly seen in server environments, where large numbers of files are created. This number is consistently used to bind each node together in a file.

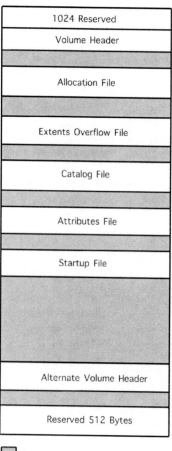

Figure 2–3. *The structure of an HFS+ file system*

- The first 1024 bytes are reserved for boot blocks.

- *Volume header*: The next 1024 bytes are for the volume header, which contains information in regards to the structure of the HFS volume. There is a backup volume header at the last 1024 bytes of the HFS volume. There are also volume header signatures. HFS plus the volume header signature is seen as "H+." For HFSX it is "HX."

- *Allocation file*: The allocation file simply tracks which allocation blocks are is use by the file system.

- *Extents overflow file*: This tracks all the allocation blocks that belong to a file's data forks. The contains a list of all extents used by a file and the associated blocks in the appropriate order.

- *Catalog file*: The HFS+ file system uses a catalog file system to maintain all the information in regards to files and folders within a volume. These are in a hierarchical system of nodes:

  - Header node

  - Index node

  - Leaf nodes

  - Map nodes

The location of the Header node is tracked in the volume header. Within that, the catalog ID number is stored as well. This number is assigned by the catalog file, which gets the next number from the volume header that tracks the last number assigned. The catalog file will increment that number by one and assign it to that file, and is in turn store in the Header node.

- *Attributes file*: This file is reserved for future use of data forks.

- *Startup file*: This file was designed to assist in booting a system that did not have built-in ROM support.

- After the startup file is where all the data in a volume is stored and tracked by the file system.

- *Alternate volume header*: A backup of the volume header and is primarily used for disk repair.

- The last 512 bytes are reserved.

HFSX

All Apple mobile devices use HFSX as the file system. HFSX is a variation of HFS+ with one major difference. HFSX is case sensitive. This means that two files on the file system can have the exact same name—but the case sensitivity is what allows the file system to differentiate between the two. For example:

```
Case sensitive.doc
```

```
Case Sensitive.doc
```

Both of these files can exist on a HFSX file system. On OS X on a desktop or laptop, the following error occurs when the two file names with different cases are attempted to be saved. If the same were attempted on an HFS+ system, the following error will be seen, as shown in Figure 2–4.

Figure 2–4. *Error message from saving on an HFS+ system*

iPhone Partition and Volume Information

The partition and volumes of the iPhone also have some history to them. Apple TV, another product of Apple, also came out with a scaled-down version of OS X. It had only one user and two partitions—an OS and data partition. Like the iPhone, Apple TV was designed to hold multimedia and access the Internet and iTunes. AppleTV appears to be a project test bed for HFSX for Apple and the use of a jailed system. Today the new AppleTV now utilizes the HFSX and jailed system of iOS 4. Figure 2–5 demonstrates the similarities between the iPhone and Apple TV.

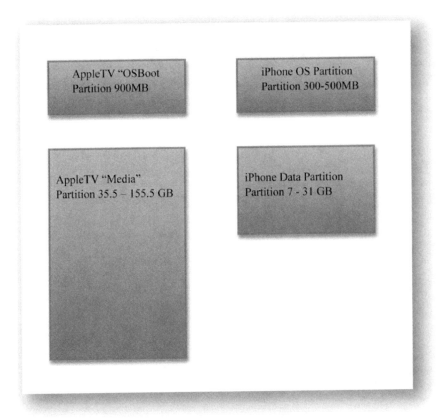

Figure 2–5. *The similarities between the iPhone and Apple TV*

Using two tools on the Mac from the command line, we can see the partition structure of the iPhone. Hdiutil is a command-line binary that is already on the Mac, and there are h the following switches, pmap and imageinfo, which can give the picture of the iPhone. Hdiutil is a great program for looking at the structure of an iOS system. HDiutil with the option pmap gives an overall view of the partitioning scheme on a device. Hdiutil with the option imageinfo gives a granular look at each partition and information in regards to each.

To acquire partition information of the iPhone

1. Open the Terminal application.

2. Navigate to /Applications/Utilities/Terminal. From the command line, type **hdiutil pmap**, and then drag and drop an image of the iPhone from the finder to the terminal and press Enter, as depicted in Figure 2–6. You'll see the output shown in Figure 2–7.

Figure 2–6. *Steps to acquire partition information on the iPhone*

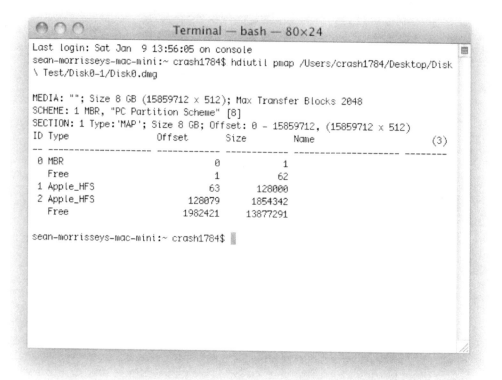

Figure 2–7. *Output of the partition acquisition*

3. Next, from the terminal, type the command **hdiutil imageinfo**, and then drag and drop a raw disk image or .dmg and press Enter, as shown in Figure 2–8.

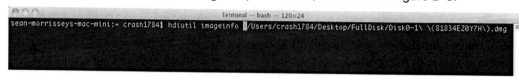

Figure 2–8. *Type the command hdiutil imageinfo, and then drag and drop a raw disk image or .dmg*

You'll see the output shown in Figure 2–9.

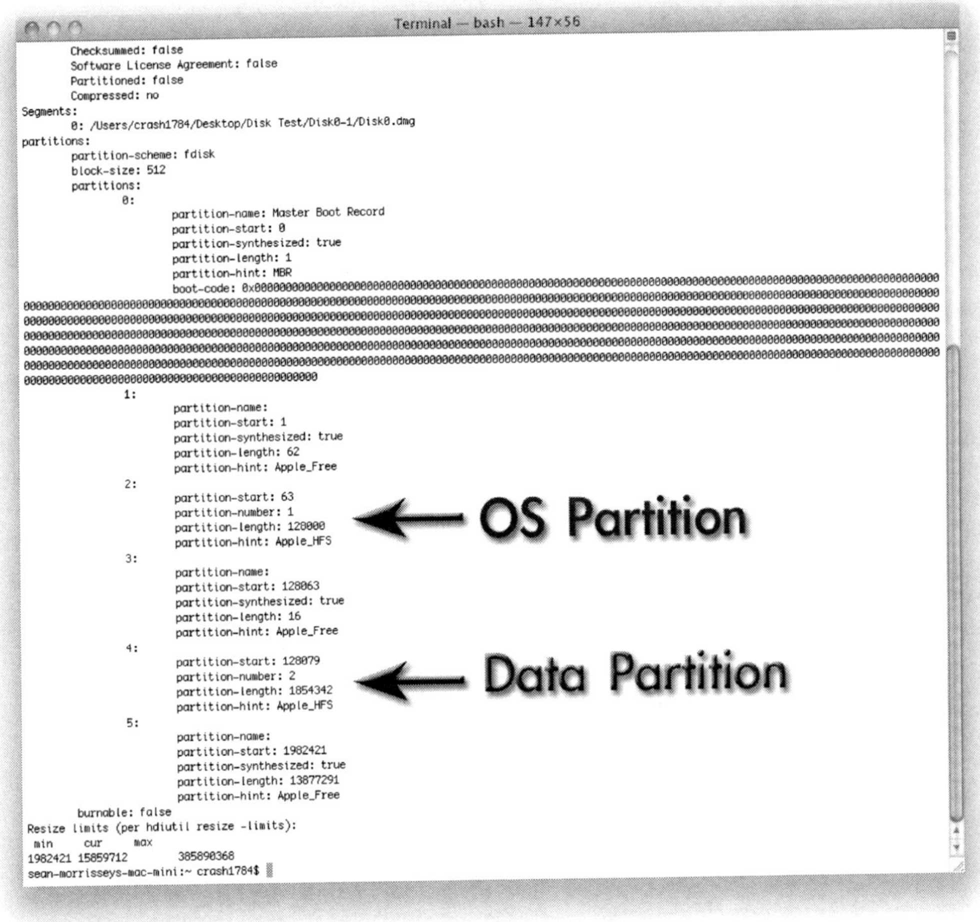

Figure 2–9. *The OS partition and the data partition*

The previous two images show the partition scheme of the Apple iPhone OS. However, the information from hdiutil is incorrect. If the image were correct, Mac OS would be able to mount the iPhone image. If we look at what hduitil reports as the start of each partition, as shown in Figure 2–10, the answer becomes clear.

```
ID  Type                          Offset        Size        Name                                (3)
--  ---------------------------   -----------   ---------   -------------------------------   --------
 0  MBR                                     0           1
    Free                                    1          62
 1  Apple_HFS                              63      128000
 2  Apple_HFS                          128079     1854342
    Free                              1982421    13877291
```

Figure 2–10. *Hduitil reports as the start of each partition*

When OS X attempts to mount this volume it sees the first HFS volume at sector 63 and the second HFS volume at 128079. The actual starting sector is as follows: the OS volume header is at sector 504 and the data volume header is at sector 1024632. It is because of the offsets of these volumes that even a Mac cannot mount a Disk0 (the complete raw image of the physical disk) image properly. The disk utitlity can mount images of either the OS partition (DiskOs1) or data partition (DiskOs2) themselves, with out any errors. When a raw image of Disk0 is in the process of mounting, the following error shown in Figure 2–11 occurs. Further details on mounting RAW images can be seen in the Media Exploitation chapter.

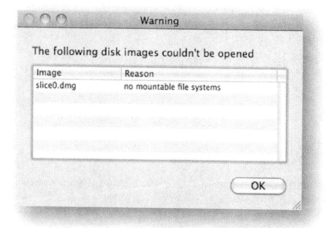

Figure 2–11. *Error produced when a RAW image of Disk0 is in the process of mounting*

However, if the gathered .dmg of the whole raw disk was copied, the offsets can be corrected and the image can be mounted properly. Creating a plug-in for MacFUSE can assist in allowing the Mac OS to properly mount the complete Disk0. Information in regards to creating a plug-in can be found at http://code.google.com/p/macfuse.

OS Partition

The OS partition is a read-only volume. This can be seen by following the path located at private/etc/fstab. Open the fstab file with TextEdit, and the following information is then shown in Figure 2–12.

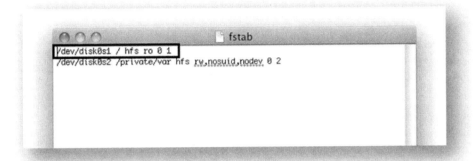

Figure 2–12. *Opening the fstab file in TextEdit*

As on all Macs, the partitions are divided in into disks and slices. The RAW disk is "Disk0." There is only one disk on the iPhone, hence you see Disk0. The OS partition is "Disk0s1" and the Data partition is "Disk0s2." Next you see both partitions from Figure 2–12, and the /dev/disk0s1 and then / hfs denoting an HFS volume after that. Next to hfs is ro. This means that the volume is read-only. The data partition /dev/Disk0s2 is a read/write HFS volume. Due to the fact that the system partition is read-only, all the data that is on this volume is usually non-evidentiary unless the phone has been jailbroken. The relevance of this file is that if you see /dev/disk0s1 / hfs rw, the system has been jailbroken. This is a good artifact to use to validate if an imaging process has tampered with the UNIX jail of the iDevice system.

iOS System Partition

The system partition (shown in Figure 2–13) of the iOS device is described in Table 2–1. The contents of this partition are usually non-evidentiary; however, sometimes an examination could be necessary.

Figure 2–13. *The iOS system partition*

Table 2–1. *The System Partition of the iOS Device*

Directory	Description
Application	Has symbolic links that point to the /var/stacsh directory
Etc	Has a symbolic link to /private/etc
Tmp	Has a symbolic link to
User	Has a symbolic link
Var	Has a symbolic link to /private/var
Damaged files	Can contain artifacts of a previous jailbreak
Bin	Contains one command-line binary, launchctl
Cores	Empty
Dev	Empty
Developer	Empty

Directory	Description
Library	As with any OS X system, contains system plug-ins and settings:
	Application support: Bluetooth models and PIN codes
	Audio: Contains the audio plug-in
	Caches: Empty
	File systems: Empty
	Internet Plug-Ins: Empty
	LaunchAgents: Empty
	LaunchDaemons: Empty
	Managed Preferences: Contains a symbolic link to Mobile
	Printers: Empty
	Ringtones: Contains system-installed ringtones
	Updates: Empty
	Wallpaper: Contains numerous PNG files and thumbnails (non-evidentiary)
private	Contains the Etc and Var folders:
	Etc: Contains fstab, master.passwd, passwd files (both master and passwd: same)
	Var: Empty
sbin	Contains command-line binaries
System	Library folder that contains system preferences and settings; includes /System/Library/CoreServices/SystemVersion.plist: Firmware Version
Usr	Contains more command-line binaries and time zone data

private/etc/passwd is the password file of the OS. Tools like John the Ripper, which can be downloaded at www.openwall.com/john/, allow for cracking the root and mobile passwords. The root and mobile passwords are encrypted using a DES algorithm that requires a 2–character salt key and an 8-character text password, which yields an 11-character value. With jailbroken iPhones, a more advanced user can change these passwords. A password for root that has never changed since the first iPhone is "Alpine," as shown in Figure 2–14.

Figure 2–14. *The password Alpine has not changed since the first-generation iPhone.*

Due to the design of the iPhone, there are procedures that can break the phone or use copyrighted software to bypass the security measures in order to image an iPhone. As will be discussed in this book, there are numerous areas of investigation that will maintain the integrity of the evidence and still locate valuable artifacts and secure convictions. For each firmware version, the OS partition has volume names that correspond to the iOS version. Table 2–2 shows the iOS version and the corresponding volume name of the OS system partitions.

Table 2–2. *The iOS Version and the Corresponding Volume Name*

iOS Version	Volume Name
1.00	Alpine 1A420
1.0.0	Heavenly 1A543a
1.0.1	Heavenly 1C25
1.0.2	Heavenly 1C28
1.1.1	Snowbird 3A109a
1.1.2	Oktoberfest 3B48b
1.1.3	Little Bear 4A93
1.1.4	Little Bear 4A102
2	Big Bear 5A347
2.0.1	Big Bear 5B108
2.0.2	Big Bear 5C1

iOS Version	Volume Name
2.1	Sugar Bowl 5F136
2.2	Timberline 5G77
2.2.1	SUTimberline 5H11
3	Kirkwood 7A341
3.0.1	Kirkwood 7A400
3.1	Northstar 7C144
3.1.2	Northstar 7D11
3.1.3	SUNorthstarTwo 7E18
2.00	Big Bear 5A345
2.00	Big Bear 5A347
2.0.1	Big Bear 5B108
2.0.2	Big Bear 5C1
2.1	Sugar Bowl 5F136
2.2	Timberline 5G77
2.2.1	SUTimberline 5H11
3.00	Kirkwood 7A341
3.0.1	Kirkwood 7A400
3.1	Northstar 7C144
3.1.2	Northstar 7D11
3.1.3	SUNorthstarTwo 7E18
3.2	Wildcat7B367
4.0	Apex8A306
4.1	Baker8B117

iOS Data Partition

Over the years, there has been little change in the makeup of this data partition. You can see some of the changes in the file system from logical acquisitions. The bulk of the evidence that can be acquired from this device comes from the read/write partition, also known the data partition, as shown in Figure 2–15.

Figure 2–15. *Data partition directory structure*

Table 2–3 shows the directories and accompanying items of interest.

Table 2–3. *The Directories and Corresponding Items of Interest*

Directory	Items of Interest
CommCenter	No artifacts
Dhcpclient	One plist that contains the last IP address and router information for that device
db	No artifacts
Ea	Empty
Folders	Empty
Keychains	Keychain.db, which contains user passwords from various applications
Log	Empty
Logs	General.log: The OS version and serial number Lockdownd.log: Lockdown deamon log
Managed Preferences	Empty
Mobile	Bulk of the user data (described in detail in other chapters)
MobileDevice	Empty
Preferences	System configuration: Network artifacts backed up
Root	Caches: GPS location information Lockdown: Pairing certificates Preferences: No artifacts
Run	System log
tmp	Manifest.plist: plist backup
Vm	Empty

The data partition is riddled with a lot of information that will assist in any investigation. When an Apple device gets backed up from iTunes, it gathers information from the Mobile directory. Table 2–4 shows all the artifacts that are acquired logically by the means described in Chapter 5, and items that are also stored as backups on a Mac or PC.

Table 2–4. *Artifacts Organized by Directory and Whether They Are in Backup*

Directory	In Backup	Artifact
Mobile/Application	√	Plists, SQLite databases
Library/AddressBook	√	Contacts and images
Library/Caches		SQLite database: MapTiles
Library/Calendar	√	SQLite database: Events
Library/CallHistory	√	SQLite database: Call logs
Library/Carrier Bundles		Carrier information
Library/Caches/Com.apple.itunesstored		iTunes purchase information
Library/ConfigurationProfiles	√	Plist password history
Library/Cookies	√	Plist: Internet cookies
Library/DataAccess	√	E-mail account information
Library/Keyboard	√	.dat file: Dynamic text
Library/Logs	√	Log files
Library/Mail	√	In Logical Data, no artifacts
Library/Maps	√	Plist: Bookmarks, directions, history
Library/Mobileinstallation	√	Applications that use Locations
Library/Notes	√	SQLite database: Notes
Library/Preferences	√	Plist: System and user settings
Library/RemoteNotification	√	Plist: Apps that have push notification
Library/Safari	√	Plist: Bookmarks, history
Library/SafeHarbor		Location of where app data is stored
Library/SMS	√	SMS and MMS data
Library/Voicemail	√	.amr files: Voice messages
Library/Webclips		
Library/WebKit	√	SQLite databases: Gmail account info, cached e-mail messages
Media/DCIM	√	iPhone camera photos
Media/PhotoData	√	Additional photo information and thumbnails
Media /iTunes_Control		Music and video from iTunes
Media/Books		Books from the iBookstore and synced PDFs

Chapter 5 will discuss the artifacts of the iOS data partition in greater detail.

SQLite Databases

The iDevice OS uses the SQLite database format to store information on the phone. An examination of the logical extraction shows numerous SQLite databases for the operation of the phone and by developers of applications. The iPhone also uses these databases to cross-reference information from one database to the other, which gets displayed on the UI. These databases interact with each other to give the user an informative experience. The big three databases are the Address Book, SMS, and Call History databases.

Address Book Database

This database has 18 tables. Table 2–5 provides the information that would be relevant in an investigation.

Table 2–5. *The Address Book Database*

Table	Relevant Data
AB Group	Group information
ABGroupChanges	Non-evidentiary
ABGroupMembers	Contacts associated each group
ABMultiValue	When a contact has multiple values, phone numbers, e-mail address books, company URLs, etc.
ABMultiValueEntry	Street addresses for contacts
ABMultiValueEntryKey	Non-evidentiary
ABMultiValueLabel	Non-evidentiary
ABPerson	Name, organization, department, notes, etc.
ABPersonChanges	Non-evidentiary
ABPersonMultiValueDeletes	Non-evidentiary
ABPersonSearchKey	Non-evidentiary
ABPhoneLastFour	Non-evidentiary
ABRecent	Recently used e-mail addresses
ABStore	Non-evidentiary
FirstSortSectionCount	Non-evidentiary
FirstSortSectionCount	Non-evidentiary
_SqliteDatabaseProperties	Non-evidentiary
Sqlite_sequence	Non-evidentiary (but contains good information on the structure of the database)

SMS Database

The SMS database is the container that keeps records of text messages sent and received by the Messages application. Table 2–6 shows the tables that make up this database.

Table 2–6. *The Tables and Relevant Data of the SMS Database*

Table	Relevant Data
_SqliteDataBaseProperties	Contains database properties (non-evidentiary)
Group_member	Assigns an incoming text a group ID that then will pull all the text messages from the iPhone owner and the party having the conversation
Message	Contains the content of the message, date and time, and whether the message was sent or received; also lists the associated group ID
Msg_group	Gives the group ID and ID of the last message in that group
Msg_Pieces	Tracks all MMS messages
Sqlite_sequence	Provides a sequential list of all tables in the database

In Figure 2–16, you can see the ROWID (row identification),which is a number for the message, the address (the phone number that the text came from), and the date and time of the text. The date and time values are in Unix time and can be converted using several free tools. The flags are for sent and received text messages.

Figure 2–16. *The ROWID, address, date, text, and flags*

Call History Database

The Call History database is a simpler database, and the only one that has restrictions. The Call History database will only hold 100 calls. The Address Book database is the hub of a lot of other applications on the iDevice. A lot of data correlation occurs between this database and others. For example, the Call History database correlates the numbers from the sent and/or received call with the names associated with those numbers in the Address Book database. Table 2–7 describes the tables and artifacts of relevance.

Table 2–7. *Tables and Relevant Data Artifacts*

Table	Relevant Data
SqliteDatabaseProperties	
Call	Contains phone numbers, date and time info, and the duration of the call; also flags incoming, outgoing, and missed calls, and calls that have voicemails
Data	Tracks the number of bytes the iPhone has sent and received
Sqlite_sequence	Contains a sequential list of tables in the database

Working with the Databases

Now that we've looked at the databases and how they relate to each other, Figure 2–17 gives a visual representation of how the databases work with each other. The relationship of these databases was devised to allow you to better visualize data in the iPhone interface. For instance, in the call logs, the GUI shows a person's name. The Call Log database then queries the Address Book database for the actual number and the name associated with that number, and then displays the name instead of a number. When a phone call is sent or received that isn't located in the Address Book database, the number is shown in the interface. The SMS database also correlates data from its tables that contain calls with numbers stored in the Address Book database and names associated with the stored numbers There are a multitude of other applications on the iDevice that use the Address Book database. Figure 2–17 shows the relationships between the Address Book, Call History, and SMS databases.

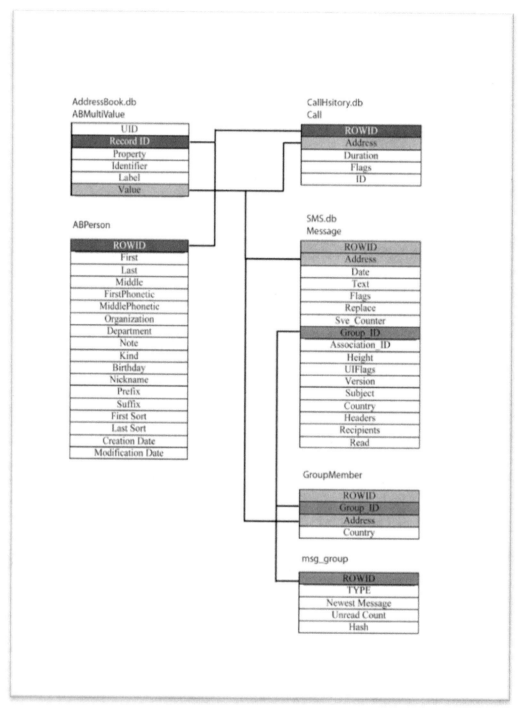

Figure 2–17. *The relationships between the Address Book, Call History, and SMS databases*

Retrieving Data from SQLite Databases

There are applications that can assist in extracting data from SQLite databases that can be used in other applications or tools. One of these SQLite database applications is SQLite Database Browser. The interface of this application is shown in Figure 2–18.

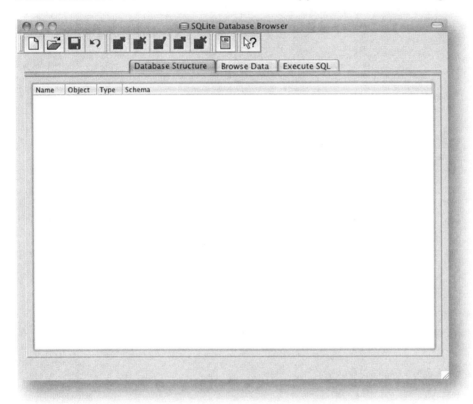

Figure 2–18. *The interface of the SQLite Database Browser application*

To add SQLite Database Browser, click the Open icon and navigate to the relevant database, as shown in Figure 2–19.

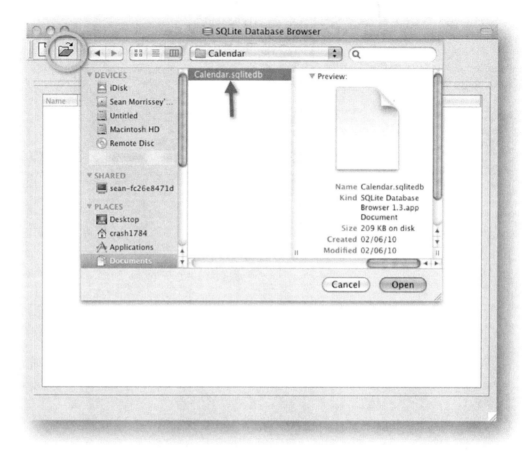

Figure 2–19. *Adding SQLite Database Browser*

After the relevant database is brought into SQLite Database Browser, one can browse through the tables in the database. First move to the Browse Data tab and then pick the table to review from the Table drop-down list. This is shown in Figure 2–20.

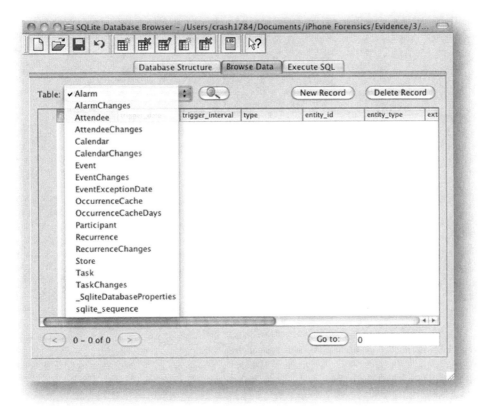

Figure 2–20. *Move to the Browse Data tab, and then pick the table to review*

The data can be exported from SQLite Database Browser to a CSV (comma-separated value) format, which in turn can be opened with applications such as Microsoft Excel, as shown in Figure 2–21.

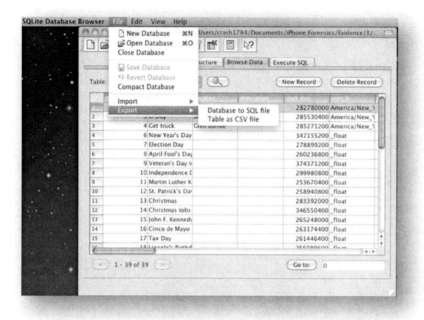

Figure 2–21. *The CSV format can be opened in other applications*

Another application worth mentioning is Froq, developed by Alwin Troost. This application is proprietary and can be purchased at www.alwintroost.nl/?id=82. This application has a lot of functionality and is an excellent tool for viewing the tables of a database and exporting the portions of the database needed for a given investigation. The interface of Froq is shown in Figure 2–22.

Figure 2–22. *The interface of the Froq application*

To view a database of interest, perform the following steps :

1. Go to the Froq menu bar and select connect | connect.

2. The next box will ask you to select an existing connection or create a new one. Select a new connection by clicking the +, as shown in Figure 2–23.

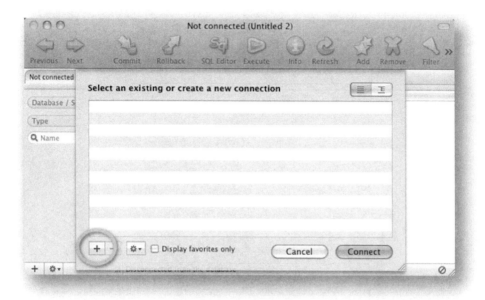

Figure 2–23. *Creating a new connection*

3. In the expanded window, give the connection a name—for example, Calendar.

4. For the database type, select SQLite.

5. From the Browse tab, navigate to the relevant database. (Steps 4 and 5 are shown in Figure 2–24.)

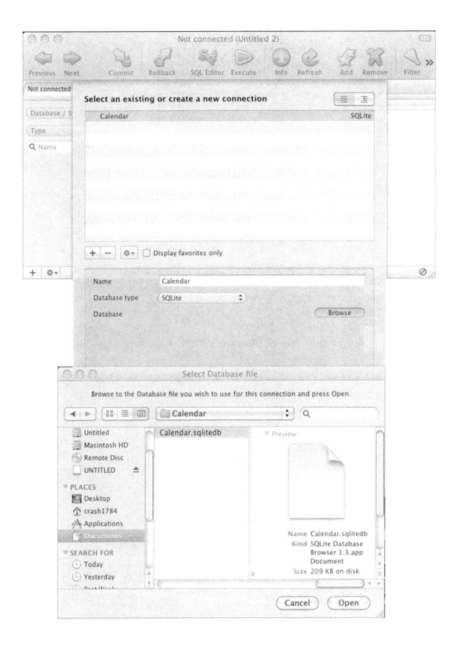

Figure 2–24. *Selecting SQLite as the database type, and browsing to the relevant database*

6.   Then the database will be brought into Froq for analysis. The tables can be selected from the left pane, and the data can be seen in the right pane, as shown in Figure 2–25.

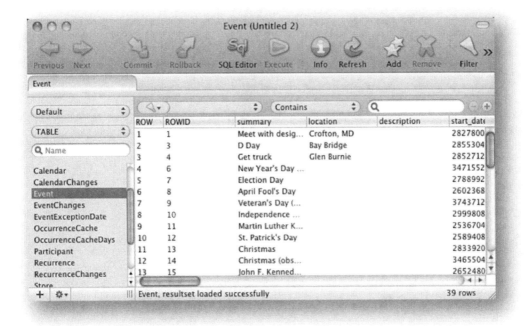

Figure 2–25. *Database brought into Froq for analysis*

To export data from this application, return to the top toolbar.

7. Select Resultset | Export.

8. There are three types of settings: Custom, export as an excel spreadsheet, or as SQL statements.

9. Under the columns, you can be as granular as necessary for the data that is required. For example, select "Export as Microsoft Excel document." Then select the "Export all rows" radio button from the "Source rows" section, and select the columns needed.

10. Then select "Export." The resulting screen is shown in Figure 2–26.

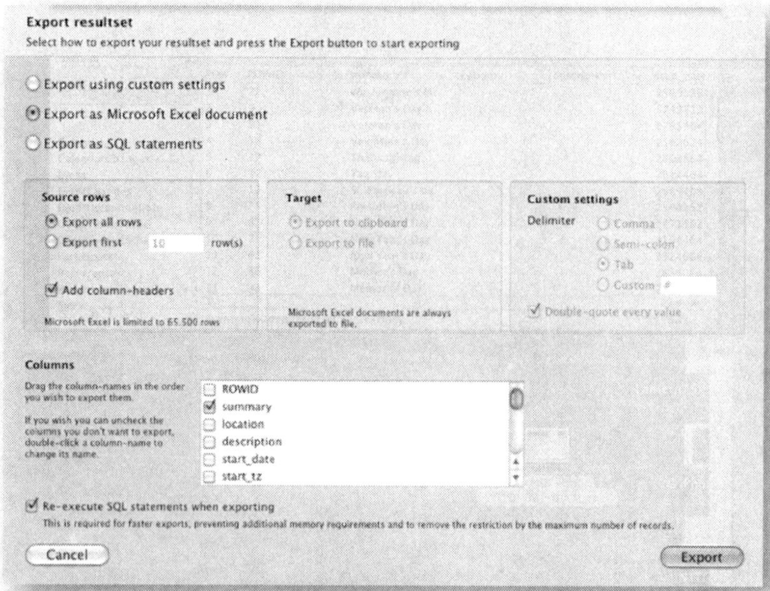

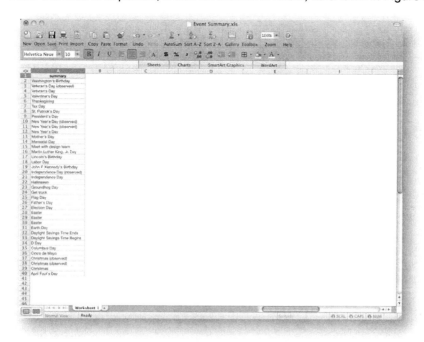

Figure 2–26. *The "Export resultset" screen*

After the data is exported, it can be viewed in Excel, as shown in Figure 2–27.

Figure 2–27. *The exported data viewed in Excel*

Property Lists

Property lists are XML files that are commonly seen in standard OS X systems. Since iOs is a modified OS X system, it stands to reason that we will also see property lists within the directory structure. The iOS data partition is riddled with property lists that can contain valuable information. Table 2–8 shows the property lists that contain data of relevance.

Table 2–8. *Property Lists and Relevant Data*

Directory	Property Lists and Artifacts
Db	
Keychain	
Managed preferences	Com.apple.springboard.plist: Add artifact
Mobile/library/Cookies	Cookies.plist: Web-related artifacts
Mobile/Library/Mail	Accounts.plist: E-mail accounts
	Metadata.plist: Dates and times of e-mail pulls
Mobile/Library.Maps	Bookmarks.plist: Map bookmarks created by the user
	History.plist: All routes and searches
Mobile/Library/Preferences	Com,apple.BTserver,airplane.plist: Shows that airplane mode was initiated on the device for Bluetooth
	Com.apple.commcenter,plist: Stores ICCID and IMSI numbers
	Com.apple.maps.plist: Recent map searches and last latitude and longitude of last map tile seen
	Com.apple.mobilehpone.settings.plist: Call-forwarding numbers
	Com.apple.mobilephone.speeddial.plist: All favorite contacts for speed dial
	Com.apple.mobilesafari.plist: Recent Safari searches
	Com.apple.MobileSMS.plist: Any unsent SMS messages
	Com.apple.mobiletimer.plist: List of world clocks used
	Com.apple.preference.plist: Keyboard language last used
	Com.apple.springboard.plist: Lists of apps that are shown in the interface, password protection flag, wipe enable settings, last system version
	Com.apple.weather.plist: Cities for weather reports, date and time of last update
	Com.apple.youtube.plist: URLs of all videos bookmarked, history of all video watched, videos searched by user
Library/Safari	Bookmarks.plist: All Internet bookmarks—created and standard
	History.plist: Web browsing history
	Suspendedstate.plist: Web page title and URL of all suspended web pages that are held in the background so that users can jump from one page to anther easily (a maximum of eight pages can be

saved at one time)

Viewing Property Lists

Apple has given examiners a free tool to view property lists, the Property List Editor (also known as the plist) The Property List Editor is part of the developer tools, and is an optional install on the OS X installation disk. The newest versions can be downloaded from the Apple Developers web site, at http://developer.apple.com/technologies/tools. The Property List Editor can display these XML-formatted files in a readable manner, similar to how they are viewed on a Windows system (i.e., not in their raw form). Once the Property List Editor has either been installed from the OS X disk or downloaded from the Internet, the following steps can be followed to view a given property list:

1. Navigate to /Developer/Applications/Utilities/Property List Editor.

2. Double-click the application.

3. From the Property list file menu, select Open.

4. Next, navigate to the location of the plist you wish to view.

5. Select the plist.

6. Press the Open button.

7. View the artifacts from the plist editor interface.

The one thing that detracts from this free tool is the way it reports the artifacts. One can grab screenshots of the relevant data and add those images to a report. There is another application, OmniOutliner 3, an app bundled with OS X 1.4 (Tiger). It is a for-pay app, and it's available at www.omnigroup.com/products/omnioutliner. You can use this tool to view plists easily bring them into an existing report. The following describes how to view and report plists with OmniOutliner 3.

First you have to set up your Mac so that you can automatically open all plists with OmniOutliner.

1. From Finder, find any plist on your volume (Library/Preferences is a good choice).

2. Right-click the plist.

3. Select Get Info, as shown in Figure 2–28.

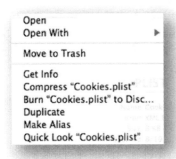

Figure 2–28. *Select Get Info from this drop-down menu*

4. From the Get Info dialog box, expand the "Open with" portion of the window (shown in Figure 2–29).

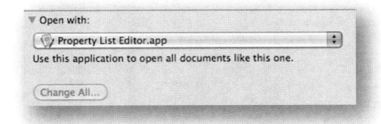

Figure 2–29. *Expand the "Open with" portion of the window*

5. Now click the drop-down list and select Other, as shown in Figure 2–30.

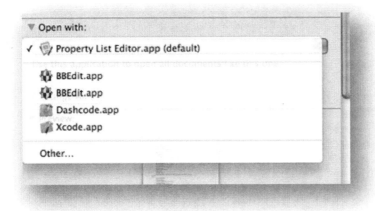

Figure 2–30. *Select Other.*

6. The next window will be another finder window in the application directory. You will have to change Recommended Applications to All Applications, as shown in Figure 2–31.

✓ Recommended Applications
   All Applications

Figure 2–31. *Change Recommended Applications to All Applications.*

7. Then locate OmniOutliner and highlight the application.

8. Then select the Always Open With box, and click the Add button, as shown in Figure 2–32.

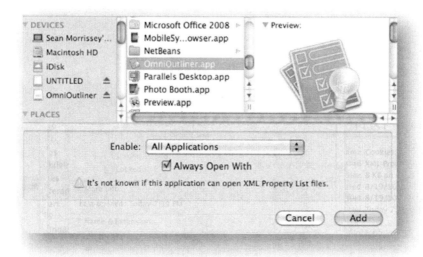

Figure 2–32. *Select Always Open With.*

All property lists will automatically open with OmniOutliner instead of the Property List Editor. If you wish to switch back to the Property List Editor, repeat the same steps, but select Property List Editor instead. Now that you have switched to OmniOutliner, the next steps will go through using OmniOutliner.

9. Select a property list to examine and double-click the file. OmniOutliner will automatically open the plist.

10. The values are separated into Key and Value columns, as shown in Figure 2–33.

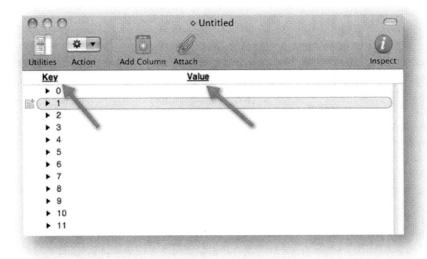

Figure 2–33. *Separate Key and Value columns*

11. To expand all the keys, go to the menu bar and select View | Expand All. Now you'll be able to view all the keys and values.

12. To report data from Omni Outliner

    a. Either expand all or just the items of relevance.

    b. Then go to the menu bar and select File | Export.

    c. Enter a file name, where you want the file saved, and what format to export it in, as shown in Figure 2–34.

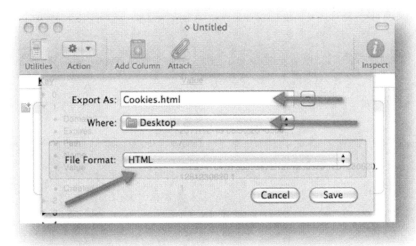

Figure 2–34. *Choose a file name, where to save the file, and the file format.*

Summary

The iOS operating and file systems have changed since its introduction in 2007. Since then the Apple device family has expanded and changed the way we communicate and now how we compute, it is important to understand the inner workings of the devices to intelligently articulate some of the processes that are accomplished to facilitate artifact extraction. As shown in this chapter, there can be a mountain of data that can be captured from the devices. In this chapter, we reviewed the history of the iOS operating and file system, and artifacts that reside in the system and data partitions. We also looked at tools that can examine many of the artifacts that are on any iDevice. As we saw, most of the evidence on the iDevice is stored in SQLite databases and property lists. The following chapters will go into more detail on the artifacts of iDevices and their relevance.

Chapter 3

Search, Seizure, and Incident Response

Imagine for a moment that an officer has stopped your vehicle and detained you for speeding. The officer approaches your car, walks around your vehicle, and, after speaking with you, requests to search your iPhone. What do you do? Do you have the right to say no? The Constitution—specifically the Fourth Amendment—offers protection from unreasonable search and seizure. Does the Constitution protect you from unlawful search and seizure of your iPhone? This question may seem easy to answer, but it actually depends on the circumstances and events that are occurring.

On its face, the Fourth Amendment to the United States Constitution protects an individual from unreasonable searches and seizures, except for certain exceptions, such as searches incident to a lawful arrest. However, technology is advancing faster than case law can interpret and protect an individual from unreasonable search and seizure of electronic devices. Wireless devices sold today are capable of storing large amounts of data, including not only call information but also contact lists, e-mails, and even Internet browser history.

The idea of a cell phone originated in 1947 when Donald Ring formulated the idea of clustering geographic areas into cells (Farley, 2007). In each of these cells, there would be an antenna and transceiver unit that would reduce power consumption and make it easier to expand into widespread areas. By 2000, there were more than 109 million cell phone subscribers, and cell phones had become smaller and more practical to use. The technology built into cell phones is constantly changing, so users are able to incorporate and utilize more features than just making a phone call.

As technology advances, cell phone features include the ability to use multimedia applications and store personal information including addresses, phone numbers, call lists, and text messages. Today, cell phones are more like handheld computers, allowing the user to not only make phone calls but communicate via the Internet and e-mail, store mass amounts of data, and perform functions as if at a normal desktop computer.

Currently, an officer may search an individual's cell phone for easily accessible information (Stillwagon, 2008). However, the standard, bright-line rule that officers apply after making an arrest may not be sufficient to guarantee an individual's rights under the Fourth Amendment. For instance, should officers have the option to search the entire contents of a cell phone, even if it's not an ordinary cell phone but a smartphone such as an Apple iPhone with 16GB of stored data? After all, the advances in technology have made the information management that's readily available in a handheld device possibly equal reams of paper.

The framers of the U.S. Constitution could not have envisioned the advances in technology that are available today, and lawmakers are constantly struggling to keep up with technology. Imagine being arrested for a crime and having your cell phone seized and searched, and while searching the cell phone, officers find information that is personal and has nothing to do with the crime for which you were arrested. In this scenario, officers have open access to your personal information with no recourse available to you if they misuse or misappropriate that information.

Courts currently allow police officers to seize cell phones and conduct searches after placing an individual under arrest (Stillwagon, 2008). However, an individual's rights surrounding the private information stored on a cell phone is not settled, because courts have been struggling to interpret and apply the correct law to the highly technologically advanced cell phone. We'll explore the Fourth Amendment more in the following section.

The Fourth Amendment of the U.S. Constitution

The underlying right that is codified by the Fourth Amendment of the U.S. Constitution is to prohibit "unreasonable searches and seizures" (Henderson, 2006). However, as highlighted by court cases and Henderson, the U.S. Supreme Court has interpreted that there is no protection from police looking at your financial records or your telephone, e-mail, and web site transactional records.

Searches conducted by police that do not meet limited circumstances should be preceded with a warrant to ensure an individual's Fourth Amendment rights are upheld. However, there are exceptions to the warrant requirement where an individual's reasonable expectation of privacy can be violated but still be considered constitutional (Stillwagon, 2008). Exceptions to the warrant requirement include consent, public view, exigent circumstances, and searches incident to arrest.

Generally, to have a reasonable expectation of privacy, the individual must have "an actual expectation of privacy," and that expectation must be "one that society is prepared to recognize as reasonable" (Stillwagon, 2008). In regard to cell phones, federal courts and the U.S. Department of Justice treat wireless electronic devices as "closed containers" for legal analysis purposes and have deemed them "searchable" when the search is conducted incident to a lawful arrest, as any other closed container might be.

Officers may also perform searches without a warrant under certain circumstances. If officers perform a search without a warrant and that search violates an individual's expectation of privacy, then courts must exclude any evidence obtained as a result of a tainted search (Stillwagon, 2008). Courts differ in whether they allow evidence obtained from wireless devices, because some courts view cell phones as technologically similar to pagers, and therefore reasonable, while other courts believe these types of searches are unreasonable.

However, the search incident to arrest is the primary exception in which courts allow cell phone searches (Stillwagon, 2008). This type of search must occur during a lawful arrest, and the search can only be in the area under the control of the person being arrested. During a search after a lawful arrest, officers are allowed to open any containers, which include cell phones that may be within the person's area of control.

Two landmark cases—Olmstead v. United States (277 U.S. 438, 1928) and Katz v. United States (389 U.S. 347, 1967)—have narrowed the interpretation of the Fourth Amendment (Henderson, 2006). In the Olmstead case, the Court concluded that the government could access telephone conversations without violating the Fourth Amendment. Further, in Katz, the Court clarified that the Fourth Amendment did not protect places but people. These two cases, taken together, conclude that the Fourth Amendment affords no reasonable expectation of privacy to an individual who uses a cell phone to dial a number and communicate information to a third party.

Tracking an Individual by Cell Phone

For law enforcement officers, an inherent advantage of cell phones is the ability to track the location of a particular cell phone at any given time (Henderson, 2006), and if police have the ability to track a cell phone, they have the ability to track an individual. Police officers have been able to link individuals to crimes using tracking information from cell phone records (Walsh, D., & Finz, S., 2004). For example, in the Scott Peterson murder case, officers reviewed Scott Peterson's cell phone location information, which assisted prosecutors in linking him to the crime scene and convicting him for the murder of his wife.

The Federal Communications Commission (FCC) initiated a proceeding in 2001 that forced cell carriers to roll out technology that used multiple overlapping cell sites to "triangulate" the location of cell phone calls (Fletcher, F., & Mow, L., 2002). Cell phone tracking technology was pushed by emergency personnel to aid in the prompt response to emergency locations. Police and government officials later discovered another inherent use for this technology: to track suspects, conduct investigations, and solve and prosecute crimes (Henderson, 2006). Thus, if you do not consent to being tracked, your only choice is to not carry a cell phone.

Cell Phone Searches Incident to Arrest

The root of the "search incident to arrest" exception to the warrant requirement of the Fourth Amendment of the U.S. Constitution comes from the 1914 Exclusionary Rule (Gershowitz, 2008). In 1914, the U.S. Supreme Court suggested that the government had the right to search a person "to seize the fruits or evidences of crime." Gershowitz explains that the case of Chimel v. California (395 U.S. 752, 1969) coined the precedent for this exception. In Chimel, police arrested the suspect while he was in his home and searched the entire house, including the garage and attic, to find items the suspect may have taken during a burglary. The Court in Chimel limited the search area during a search incident to a lawful arrest to weapons that could be used against the officer and preserve evidence.

As established through United States v. Robinson (414 U.S. 218, 235, 1973), the search incident to arrest doctrine follows a bright-line rule, allowing police to search the individual under arrest without first showing probable cause (Gershowitz, 2008). Technology has progressed much faster than the law underwriting rights an individual has against being searched. The law is vague in determining how to consider technological devices such as cell phones and the ability to search them. If you consider a device, a cell phone, or an iPhone as a "closed container," it would allow law enforcement to "open" it and search without probable cause. This justification falls under the "search incident to arrest" doctrine that has been followed for the past four decades.

The U.S. Supreme Court clarified the bright-line test eight years later after United States v. Robinson in the case of New York v. Belton (Gershowitz, 2008). In the New York v. Belton case, an officer had stopped a car for speeding, smelled marijuana, and arrested everyone in the car. This case clarified that officers may search the entire passenger area of a vehicle subject to a lawful arrest. The Court in this case specifically allowed officers to search any containers found in the passenger area, whether opened or closed, which has been later interpreted to include cell phones.

The most recent and potentially significant search incident to arrest opinion by the U.S. Supreme Court was in Thornton v. United States (Gershowitz, 2008). In this case, the driver had already exited and walked away from the vehicle before police arrived. The Court expanded the Belton case to allow officers to search vehicles after arresting the occupant who was "recently" in the vehicle.

These cases address and clarify the bright-line rules for searching an occupant's vehicle when the search is incident to a lawful arrest. Following these cases, there have been recent cases where courts have been forced to decide whether digital evidence found on electronic devices, including cell phones, is admissible under this same doctrine (Gershowitz, 2008). As evident in these case examples, the U.S. Supreme Court has interpreted the search incident to a lawful arrest exception extensively to offer guidance to officers.

In 2007, the Fifth Circuit examined United States v. Finley, which dealt with a recent case focusing on searching a cell phone (Gershowitz, 2008). In this case, police arrested Finley after staging a drug sale and, incident to his arrest, seized a cell phone. One of the officers searched Finley's cell phone and found incriminating text messages stored on it, which later were used to help convict him. The Fifth Circuit in Finley extended the right to officers to search cell phones because they could already open containers found on an individual when the search is incident to a lawful arrest. Prior to contrary authority, officers are able to search the contents of a cell phone when making arrests. The justification is also supported by the fact that an individual can delete incriminating evidence from a cell phone, similar to tearing up a piece of paper.

Changing Technology and the Apple iPhone

Cell phones are continuing to embrace technology and become more advanced each year. A cell phone in 2002 is nothing like a cell phone in 2010. In 2007, Apple released the first-generation iPhone. The iPhone is a wireless smartphone that combines the functions of a cell phone, camera, personal digital assistant (PDA), iPod, and Internet access via a mobile browser (Hafner, 2007). In the first three days of its release, more than a quarter million first-generation iPhones were sold.

Since that time, Apple has released updated versions of the iPhone and continues to lead the smartphone market. Customer satisfaction has been extraordinary. This will continue to fuel more sales of iPhones as new versions hit the market in the future (Roberts, 2007).

The storage capacity of the iPhone is currently between 8GB to 32GB. Thus, with this high storage capacity, law enforcement officers have the ability to access information ranging from text messages, e-mail, contacts, and call history, along with photos, music, and video. Further, the iPhone accesses the Internet using a web browser similar to that of an ordinary computer. Officers are able to retrace steps a suspect may have taken on web sites by reviewing Internet bookmarks and browser history and through forensic examination of deleted data.

Currently, the Fourth Amendment and the search incident to arrest doctrine make no distinction between the data found on a cell phone and iPhone (Gershowitz, 2008). Further, Gershowitz explains that it would be very difficult to alter the bright-line test to make a distinction between the types of cell phones on the market, because the rule is set up to make it easy for officers to stay within the confines of the Fourth Amendment. Even if courts were to make changes to keep up with different types of wireless technology, scholars argue it would not be efficient to have multiple rules for different cell phones because judges cannot predict how technology will evolve (Kerr, 2004).

Given the advanced technology and mass storage capabilities of the iPhone, technology has reached a point where the bright-line test may not be a "one-size-fits-all" type of test to apply to searching wireless devices. Gershowitz (2008) argues that changes to the bright-line test for the iPhone could be made without complicating the Fourth Amendment doctrine. For instance, officers are not constrained by limited resources when investigating the iPhone, because it's the individual with the technology, not the officer.

Another way to counteract the technology of the iPhone while protecting an individual's rights is to adopt a new test that allows an officer to limit the search content, such as searching only applications that are open (Gershowitz, 2008). The temptation to use a treasure trove of evidence against a suspect, however, would easily overcome a "new" bright-line test such as this. The iPhone or a BlackBerry device offers law enforcement a window into their suspect, not only via hard evidence but also in the sense that they can tell what kind of applications the suspect is interested in and what types of web sites they tend to visit. This could be very valuable character and habit information not directly related to the crime, which may unduly prejudice a jury or judge against the suspect.

As evident with the iPhone, technology is constantly changing with wireless devices. Both the courts and police officers are unable to keep up with the changes in technology. The bright-line test should be examined to guarantee that officers are not afforded too much freedom in conducting searches of cell phones, such as iPhones. To date, there have not been any major iPhone Fourth Amendment challenges in court (Gershowitz, 2008). Even after case law has been written that addresses advanced technological devices such as the iPhone, technology advancement will be opening new avenues in which to question the standard bright-line rule that involves conducting searches incident to a lawful arrest. The only clear-cut way to avoid being tracked or subjected to having your cell phone searched is to not carry a cell phone, iPhone, or the "next" phone of tomorrow.

Responding to the Apple Device

Now that we have the legal authority to search and seize an iPhone, there are some things that we have to consider and document while in the process of seizing. When an investigator, examiner, or other incident response personnel encounters an iPhone, iPod touch, or iPad, the following procedures should be used to mitigate loss of data and access to the device. The iPhone and iPad are just like a BlackBerry, which has the ability to *remote wipe*, which allows the owner to remove all data from the device and restore the settings to factory defaults, even when they are not physically in possession of the phone. This can be accomplished by the owner or a compatriot of the owner who has access to the MobileMe account associated with that device.

> **NOTE:** Apple controls these accounts, and the proper court orders will allow an investigator to gather MobileMe data.

The Find My iPhone service within a MobileMe account needs to have contact from the Web or the 3G network to the MobileMe account. First let's look at what a user has to do to accomplish wiping an iDevice. From the MobileMe account, the Find My iPhone service needs to be activated. Second, from the device, a MobileMe account has to be added. The Find My iPhone service needs to be turned on, as shown in Figures 3–1 and 3–2.

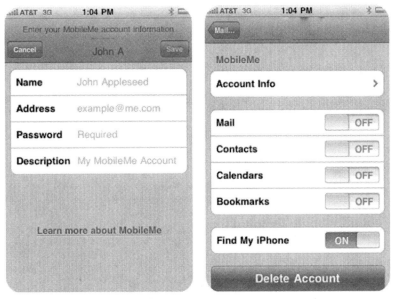

Figure 3–1. *Turning on the Find My iPhone feature*

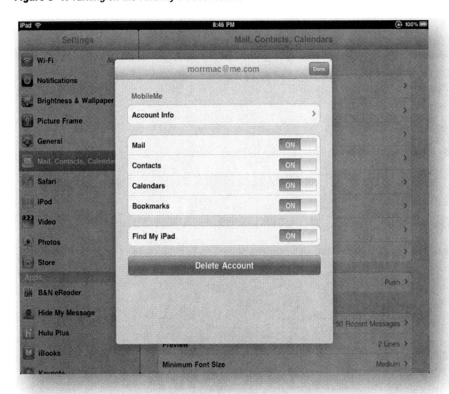

Figure 3–2. *Turning on the Find My iPad feature*

Once these steps have been completed, anyone who has access to the web-based MobileMe account can remotely wipe or lock the device. Figure 3–3 illustrates this.

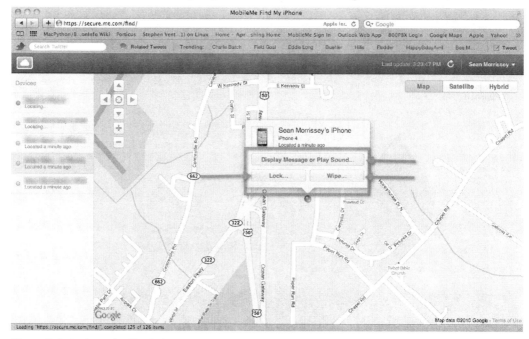

Figure 3–3. *Lock or wipe the device.*

The remote user can do two things:

- Place a passcode on the device (see Figure 3–4)
- Remote wipe the device

The process to place a passcode remotely is as follows:

1. Enter MobileMe.

2. Go to Find My iPhone.

3. Click the device.

4. Select Lock.

5. Insert a new passcode twice, and select Lock.

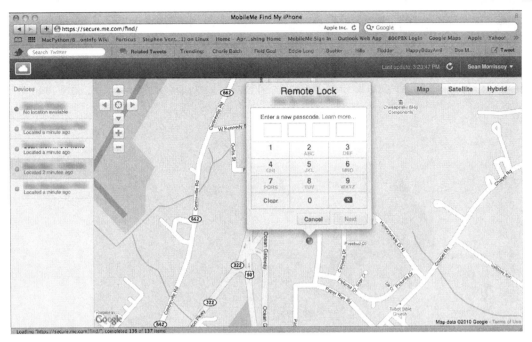

Figure 3–4. *Entering a remote lock passcode*

To remote wipe the device, the following steps have to be completed by the individual or co-conspirator:

1. As with locking, the user has to go to a MobileMe account.

2. Select Find My iPhone.

3. Select the appropriate device.

4. Select Wipe.

5. A warning is presented, and if accepted, the device will then be wiped.

Isolating the Device

To mitigate the possible data loss, when an iPhone is encountered and there isn't a passcode active, use the following steps to isolate the phone from cellular and wireless networks:

1. Tap the Settings icon.

2. Tap the top setting, Airplane Mode.

3. Switch from off to on.

4. Sometimes Airplane Mode can be activated and Wi-Fi will still be on. You can turn this off by tapping the Wi-Fi settings and turning the Wi-Fi off.

5. On the iPod touch and Wi-Fi iPad, it is only necessary to turn off the Wi-Fi.

If an Apple device has a passcode initiated and is locked upon response, isolate the device with a Faraday Bag, or in the case of the iPad, a large paint can be of some assistance.

These steps are demonstrated in Figures 3–5 and 3–6.

Figure 3–5. *Enabling Airplane Mode*

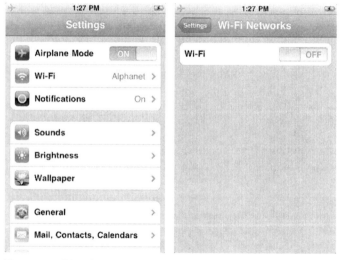

Figure 3–6. *Disabling Wi-Fi*

An additional step is removing the SIM card or mini-SIM cards from the iPhone or the iPad. Using a paper clip or a SIM card removal tool that comes with the device, you can eject the SIM card from the top or side of the Apple device, as demonstrated in Figure 3–7. The process is similar for an iPhone 4 or iPad. The SIM is on the right side on the iPhone 4 and the left side on the iPad.

Figure 3–7. *Removing the SIM from iPhone 2G, 3G, and 3GS phones*

This will isolate the phone only from the cellular network, not from any wireless access points.

Passcode Lock

Next you need to ascertain whether a passcode lock has been activated. To determine this, follow these steps:

1. If the Enter Passcode screen (see Figure 3–8) does not display upon responding to the device, then a passcode has been enabled. It then requires the person on the scene to locate and recover lockdown certificates. This is explained later in this chapter.

Figure 3–8. *Enter Passcode screen on iPhone*

2. You might also encounter a phone that has a passcode and the Auto-Lock has not been disabled.

3. Tap the Settings icon.

4. Tap General.

5. If you encounter the screen in Figure 3–9, the phone has a passcode.

Figure 3–9. *Passcode lock on iPhone*

6. From this screen, there is one additional setting that has to be changed to allow for a logical acquisition to be accomplished. It is important for the responder to have an iPhone charger as part of the tool kit.

7. Tap the Auto-Lock setting.

8. Change the 3 Minutes setting to Never, as shown in Figure 3–10.

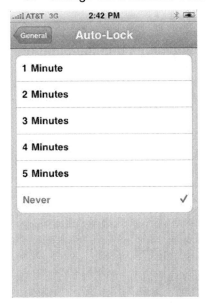

Figure 3–10. *Setting Auto-Lock to Never*

9. Attach the device to a forensic workstation, and retrieve a logical extraction using either a manual method from iTunes or the tools mentioned in Chapter 5.

10. If the device is encountered with a passcode, the responder should remove the SIM card or mini-SIM card from the phone as described previously and place the phone into a Faraday Bag. Bag and tag the SIM card and the device as required by your organization.

11. If in the passcode-enabled screen it says this is off, then a passcode is not enabled on the device. Bag and tag the device.

Identifying Jailbroken iPhones

The actual number of users who jailbreak their phones is minimal compared to the total sales of Apple devices. The reason most people jailbreak iPhones is to use the phone on other carriers, to customize the home screen, or to run applications that are not found in the App Store. Most users who have jailbroken their phones have reported performance reduction in their devices, and news reports state that hackers have attacked devices that have been jailbroken. That's because these devices circumvent the security features of the device, which allows rouge hackers to possibly gather personal information from their devices. Users jailbreak their phones using blackrai1n, Qwkpwn, Pwnage, or some other process.

There are visual ways of recognizing a jailbroken phone. With the release of iOS4, this has become harder to visualize, though. The home screen could have more icons that are not normally seen on any nonjailbroken phone. Figure 3–11 shows some of the suspected icons and the customization of the home screen, which can indicate that the device has been jailbroken.

Figure 3–11. *Indications of a jailbroken iPhone*

Responding to these devices is no different from nonjailbroken phones. Follow the previous procedures to collect the evidence on the iPhone.

Information Collection of the iPhone

Use the following steps to effectively gather system information from the iPhone upon the response:

1. From the home screen or lock screen, annotate the system date and time.

2. From the Mail, Contacts, and Calendars menu, record the e-mail accounts.

3. From the phone menu, annotate the telephone number.

4. From the General ➤ About menu, record the following information (see Figure 3–12):

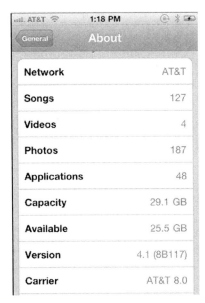

Figure 3–12. *General information about a particular iPhone*

- Size of the iPhone
- OS version
- The cellular carrier
- Serial number of the iPhone
- Model
- Wi-Fi and Bluetooth MAC addresses
- IEMI
- ICCID
- Modem firmware

The previous items should be written down in the responder's notes and/or photographed, as demonstrated in Figures 3–13, 3–14, 3–15, and 3–16.

Figure 3–13. *Photo evidence of date and time*

Figure 3–14. *Photo evidence of e-mail associated with the phone*

Figure 3–15. *Photo evidence of system information*

Figure 3–16. *Photo evidence of general information*

Responding to Mac/Windows in Connection to iPhones

It is important to know that there are items of evidentiary value on Mac and Windows computers. Therefore, your search warrants or consent search allows for the responder to grab the lockdown certificates from a possible syncing Mac/Windows computer. This will facilitate the process if a seized phone has a screen lock and requires the input of a four-number passcode or strong password. The new iOS4 now has the ability to add strong passwords.

If the connecting Mac/Windows machine is also seized, you can retrieve the lockdown certificates later. If the circumstances warrant that the certificates be acquired from the Mac/Windows computer, the following are the paths for various operating systems:

- **OS X:** /Private/var/db/Lockdown
- **XP:** C:\Documents and Settings\username\Local Settings\Application Data\Apple Computer\Lockdown
- **Vista:** C:\Users\username\AppData\Roaming\Apple Computer\Lockdown
- **Windows 7:** C:\ProgramData\Apple\Lockdown

In all the operating systems, copy the Lockdown folder. Save this to an external device for further use in acquisition. The property lists (*plists*) contain the authentication keys so that if the seized device has a passcode, these plists can assist the examiner in gaining access to the phone without invasive procedures. It is important to know the locations of these files so they are not forgotten during a response to any crime scene. It is also wise to incorporate language in search warrants that will allow you to locate these files on not just a Mac or Windows computer but on external devices as well, as depicted in Figure 3–17.

Figure 3–17. *Copying a lockdown certificate from a Mac*

Summary

As you have learned in this chapter, responding to an iDevice means isolating the device from the network and then acquiring information from that device while on scene—from getting device and account information to making sure that all artifacts are gathered at the time of seizure. By the time the search warrant is completed and you leave, all measures should be taken to get data and isolate the device so that an analysis of the iDevice can be accomplished. You also must not forget to write search warrants that allow for not only the seizure of the device but also artifacts from other types of media.

References

Elmer-Dewitt, P. (2008, May, 16). iPhone Rollout: 42 Countries, 575 million potential customers. Fortune. Retrieved March 30, 2009 from `http://apple20.blogs.fortune` `.cnn.com/2008/05/16/iphone-rollout-42-countries-575-million-potential-customers/`

Farley, T. (2007). The Cell-Phone Revolution. American Heritage of Invention and Technology. Retrieved March 24, 2009, from `www.americanheritage.com/events/articles` `/web/20070110-cell-phone-att-mobile-phone-motorola-federal-communications-commission-cdma-tdma-gsm.shtml`.

Fletcher, F. E., & Mow, L. C. (2002). What's happening with E-911? The Voice of Technology. Retrieved April 2, 2009, from www.drinkerbiddle.com/files/Publication /d6e48706-e421-411c-ab6f-b4fa132be026/Presentation/Publication Attachment/fdb0980a-7abf-40bf-a9cd-1b7f9c64f3c7 /WhatHappeningWithE911.pdf

Gershowitz, A. (2008). The iPhone meets the Fourth Amendment. UCLA Law Review, 56, 28.

Hafner, K. (2007, July 6). iPhone futures turn out to be a risky investment. The New York Times, p. C3.

Henderson, S. (2006). Learning from all fifty states: how to apply the fourth amendment and its state analogs to protect third party information from unreasonable search. The Catholic University Law Review, 55, 373.

Kerr, O. (2004). The fourth amendment and new technologies: constitutional myths and the case for caution. Michigan Law Review, 102, 801.

Krazit, T. (2009). Apple ready for third generation iPhone. Retrieved March 30, 2009, from http://news.cent.com/apple-ready-for-third-generation-of-iphone/

Roberts, M. (2007, July 25). AT&T profit soars: iPhone gives cell provider a boost. Augusta Chronicle, p. B11.

Stillwagon, B. (2008). Bringing an end to warrantless cell phone searches. Georgia Law Review, 42, 1165.

Walsh, D., & Finz, S. (2004, August 26). The Peterson trial: defendant lied often, recorded calls show, supporters mislead about whereabouts. San Francisco Chronicle, p. B1.

iPhone Logical Acquisition

One of the functions of the iPhone and iTunes is the ability to back up information in case of a catastrophic failure or to bring the phone to factory settings without losing any previous information. This is done using iDevice Backup in iTunes. There are GUI and command-line tools that can assist in analyzing the data retrieved from the device, and there are even free tools to acquire and analyze the logical data. You can use a combination of tools to assist you in many investigations.

Acquiring Data from iPhone, iPod touch, and iPad

In previous chapters, we analyzed some data from an iDevice. This chapter will focus on the acquisition from an iPhone, iPod touch, or iPad. This procedure can work on locked and unlocked phones. There are two ways to acquire this data from locked phones. In the first way, you locate the Mac or Windows computer that was synced to the device. The operating system of the computer will dictate where the pairing certificates are that allow the device to sync, regardless if it's locked or unlocked. The second way is to send the locked device to Apple to unlock the phone and allow the investigator to acquire the logical data. Apple will do this only for law enforcement, and a search warrant will be necessary to have Apple remove the passcode. All that is required for Apple to remove the passcode is the device and a court order.

To unlock phones where the examiner has the syncing computer, as in the first example, you need to retrieve the syncing property list. Table 4–1 shows the operating system type and the paths of the certificate files. These file are property lists (*plists*).

Table 4–1. *Operating System Type and Certificate File Paths*

Operating System	Path to the Certificate `.plist` File
OS X	`/private/var/db/lockdown`
Windows XP	`C:\Documents an Settings\[username]\Application Data\Apple Computer\Lockdown`
Windows Vista	`C:\Users\[username]\AppData\roaming\Apple Computer\Lockdown`
Windows 7	`C:\ProgramData\Apple\Lockdown`

After the plist (which is also the pairing certificate) has been found, place the file into the same folder on the Mac, /private/var/db/Lockdown, or the corresponding folder on for the Windows OS. Then start iTunes. Go to File ➤ Preferences ➤ Devices. Make sure that "Prevent iPods and iPhones from syncing automatically" is selected.

Then, using an iPod USB connector, attach the phone to the Mac. Once you've accomplished that, an icon that represents the phone will appear in the left sidebar under Devices, as depicted in Figure 4–1.

Figure 4–1. *Connecting the phone to the Mac*

Acquiring Data Using mdhelper

The following are the steps for acquiring data from the iPhone using mdhelper as a tool to parse the data. mdhelper is a free command-line utility that will work on iDevices below iOS4 to acquire, parse, and display archived data. The binary was created by Erica Sadun and can be downloaded at http://ericasadun.com/ftp/Macintosh.

This procedure is totally free, but it does not keep the MAC times intact of the backups acquired. This utility can also be used on existing backups found on Mac or Windows computer evidence.

1. Open the iTunes application.

2. Go to the Preferences menu from the top toolbar, as shown in Figure 4–2.

Figure 4–2. *Selecting the Preferences menu*

3. In the Preferences menu, go to Devices, and make sure that "Prevent iPods and iPhones from syncing automatically" is selected, as shown in Figure 4–3.

Figure 4–3. *Selecting the "Prevent iPods and iPhones from syncing automatically" option*

4. Prior to connecting the iPhone, the command-line binary mdhleper needs to be installed.

5. After the mdhelper binary is downloaded, copy the binary to any point in your $PATH, such as usr/usr/sbin/bin, and so on.

6. Return to iTunes, and plug in your iPhone or iPod touch.

7. When the icon for devices that corresponds to your device shows up, right-click the icon, and select Back Up, as shown in Figure 4–4.

Figure 4–4. *Selecting the Back Up option by right-clicking your device icon*

8. After the backup is complete, open a terminal.

9. Change the working directory of the location of the MobileSync backup by using `cd ~/library/ApplicationSupport/MobileSync/Backup/[backup GUID}`.

10. Once in that directory, type `mdhelper -extract`, and then hit Enter.

Once the parsing is completed, all the data is placed in a folder on the desktop, called Recovered iPhone Files.

Figure 4–5 is an example of the output of mdhelper. The parsing of the directory structure is not as shown on the device but is a close representation. This will allow the examiner to go through the data quickly and efficiently without expense.

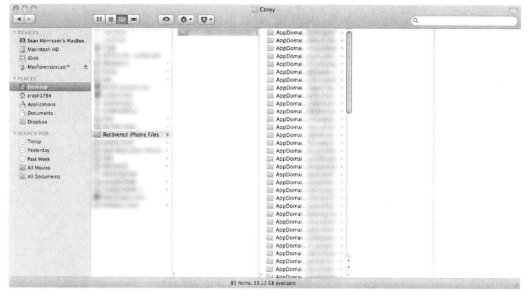

Figure 4–5. *The mdhelper output*

Available Tools and Software

Many tools can acquire logical images of the iPhone. The remainder of this chapter will be devoted to the logical extraction applications of the iDevices.

Lantern

The first application we will discuss is Lantern. Lantern is developed by Katana Forensics and is a Mac OS X application. Katana is a tool that was developed to be low cost. It costs law enforcement $399 and corporate examiners $499. The application can be acquired at www.katanaforensics.com. Installing the application is very easy by starting the downloaded .dmg after purchase and installing it into the application directory on a Mac. Lantern can acquire the logical portion of all iDevices, including iPhones (all generations), iPod touch (all generations), and iPad. Figure 4–6 shows the user interface, which is simple and easy to use.

Figure 4–6. *Lantern's user interface—simple and easy to use*

First, a case needs to be opened for acquiring a iDevice by clicking the New Case icon. A dialog box will appear, and the case number and the location of the case directory can be chosen, as shown in Figure 4–7.

Figure 4–7. *Choosing the case number and case directory*

Next, after the case has been opened, you can acquire the device by clicking the Acquire icon, which lights up after a case has been opened, as shown in Figure 4–8.

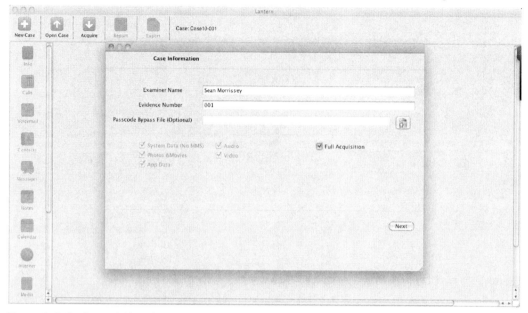

Figure 4–8. *Begin acquisition of the device by clicking the Acquire icon.*

In the acquisition dialog box, you can import the examiner's name, evidence number, and, if necessary, lockdown certificates. Then the acquisition either can be a full logical extraction or can be scaled down to databases, phone information, images, application data, and audio or video. Depending on the needs of the case, all or some of the data will be acquired. By clicking Next, the acquisition will start. Depending on the size of the iDevice acquired, the time for the acquisition can take from 5 minutes to 30 minutes. Figure 4–9 shows an acquisition in progress.

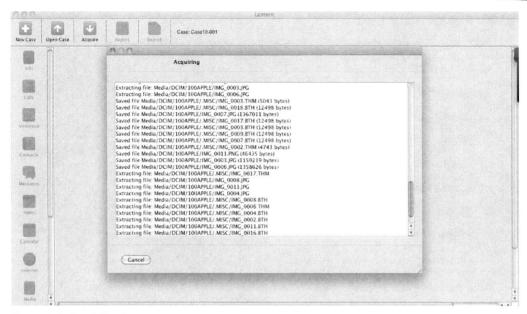

Figure 4–9. *Acquisition in progress*

The application will advise that the extraction is complete with a simple dialog box, as shown in Figure 4–10.

Figure 4–10. *Acquisition complete*

After the acquisition is complete, then the data can be viewed. Lantern breaks down the data into panes:

- Phone information

- Calls

- Voice mail

- Contacts

- Messages

- Notes

- Calendar

- Internet evidence

- Media

- Photos

- Dictionary

- Maps

- Voice memos

Phone Information

The first information pane is the phone information. This pane will give information such as ICCID, UUID, device name, phone number, IMEI, IMSI, WiFi MAC address, and serial number, as shown in Figure 4–11.

Figure 4–11. *Phone information*

Call Logs

The Calls pane lists all calls from the Call History database. This database can hold a maximum of 100 calls. Lantern can show the number; the date, time, and flag pertaining to that call; and incoming, outgoing, missed, and canceled numbers; as well as those that are tied to a voicemail, all shown in Figure 4–12.

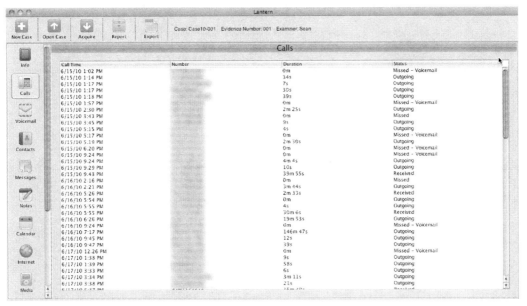

Figure 4–12. *Call logs*

Voicemail

The Voicemail pane shows the number associated with the voicemail; the duration, if it was listened to; and whether it was played by the examiner straight from the GUI. Figure 4–13 displays the Voicemail pane.

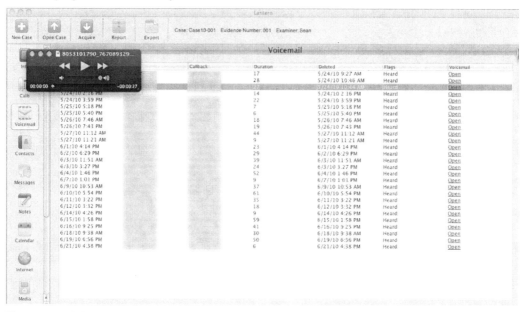

Figure 4–13. *Voicemail*

Contacts

The Contacts pane, otherwise known as the phone book, is unique in its design. It is the only application that shows all the data pertaining to a contact in one screen. This will parse out the largest and most important database on the device. There can be a plethora of data in regard to a contact, including the name, address, e-mail, phone numbers, birth dates, and other personal information. There also can be account numbers, passwords, and more information found in the notes section if the user places that kind of data there. The address book is one of many apps on the iDevice that can have data synced to and from a MobileMe account. So, it would be important to check whether there is an .me mail account; also look for an iDisk app, which can give you information to then possibly get a court order so that all possible artifacts can be gained and added to the investigation. Figure 4–14 displays the Contacts pane as shown within the Lantern application.

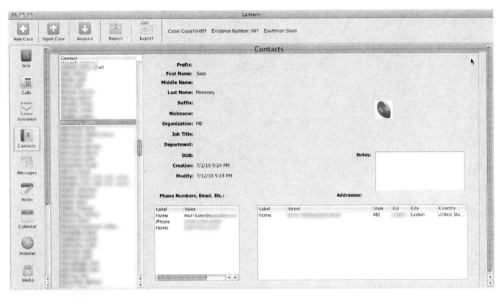

Figure 4–14. *Contacts*

Messages

Messages are a key area for examiners, and there is a lot of textual data in this area. Lantern parses both SMS and MMS data, and Lantern allows for keyword searching within this portion of the data, as shown in Figures 4–15 and 4–16.

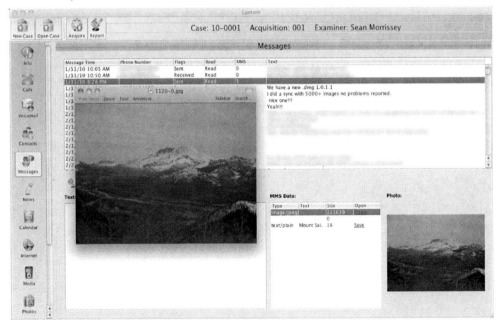

Figure 4–15. *SMS and MMS data*

Figure 4–16. *Keyword search option*

Notes

Notes is a electronic notepad on iDevices. This can contain anything that can be typed. These notes have MAC times and can be read from the GUI. Notes can also have data that was synced from a MobileMe account, not just from the phone. One can't determine the source, but as stated before, getting court orders for MobileMe can bear a lot of additional evidence. Figure 4–17 shows the Notes pane.

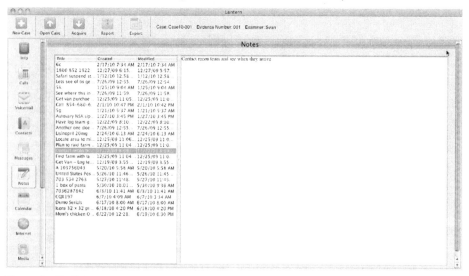

Figure 4–17. *Notes pane*

Calendar

The Calendar app is also one of those applications that is updated and synced from MobileMe. The app can also have multiple calendars within it. Lantern parses the appointments, determines whether they are recurring, and shows the MAC times of those events, as shown in Figure 4–18.

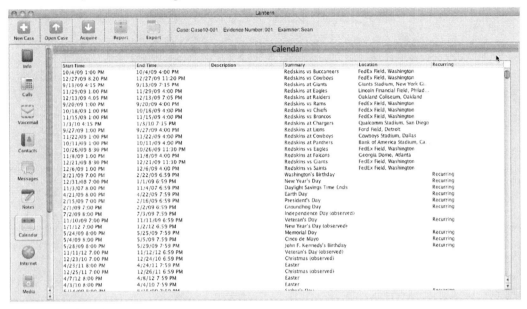

Figure 4–18. *Calendar*

Internet History

Internet history can be very important considering the nature of an investigation. Lantern can parse Internet bookmarks and history from the Safari application, as shown in Figures 4–19 and 4–20.

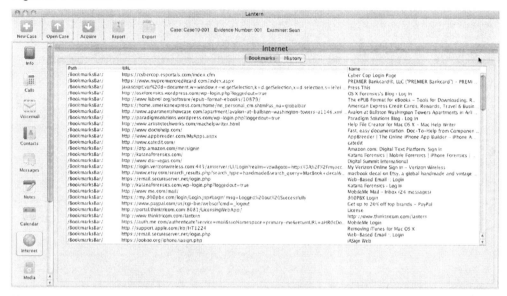

Figure 4–19. *Internet bookmarks*

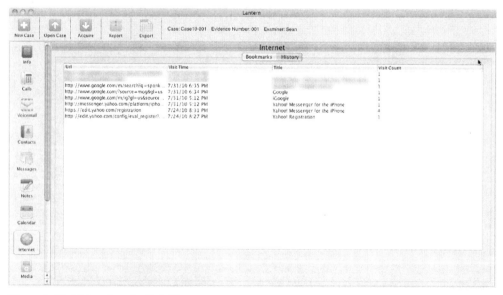

Figure 4–20. *History from the Safari browser*

iPod and Media

The largest amount of data is in the iPod or media portion of the iDevice. This contains audio and video data. Most of this data is innocuous, but those items that have no ID3 tags would be items worth examining. Lantern can easily show this, and all the media can be viewed from the GUI, as displayed in Figure 4–21.

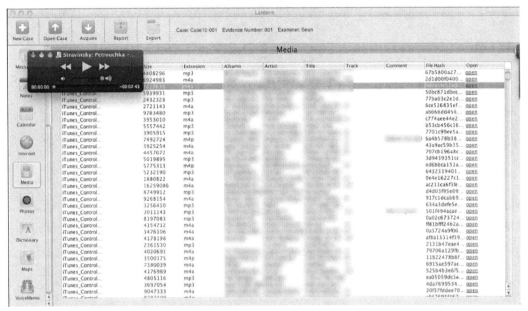

Figure 4–21. *Displaying the devices audio and video data*

Photos

Photos could be arguably the most important area for examiners, and rightfully so. This can put a person at a certain place at a certain time. All the images taken from the iPhone camera can have Exchangeable Image File Format (EXIF) and geographical geo-related data embedded. Lantern identifies those images and parses out all the EXIF data. The image can be viewed from within the GUI, and with the use of Preview, the geo-related data can be sent directly to Google Maps if the application is attached to the Internet. When an image is viewed within the app, the image is opened with the Preview app. The Preview application can show all EXIF and geo-related data. If Lantern is connected to the Internet, a Locate button from Preview can show the spot where the image was taken, as shown in Figures 4–22, 4–23, and 4–24.

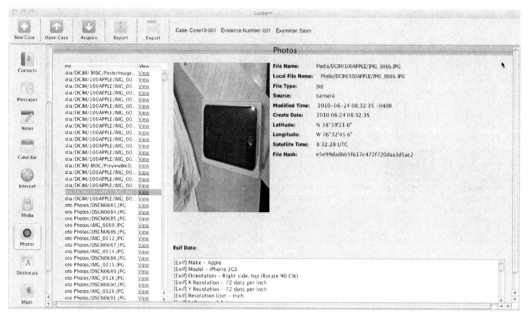

Figure 4–22. *The Photos pane*

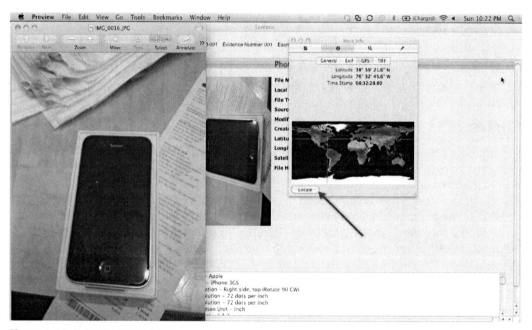

Figure 4–23. *Using the Locate button*

Figure 4–24. *Viewing the location where a photo was taken*

Dynamic Text Data

The Dynamic Text data on the phone can have data that has long been deleted. This is a key logger for the device. Every time a user types something in such as a text message, those words typed in get saved into this file. Entries inside this file can come from any application on the device, such as User Dictionary, as shown in Figure 4–25. Lantern parses this data in order of how it was typed. One can read remnants of e-mails, text messages, and anything that the .dat file is designed to keep. The ability to perform keyword searching is also available in this section.

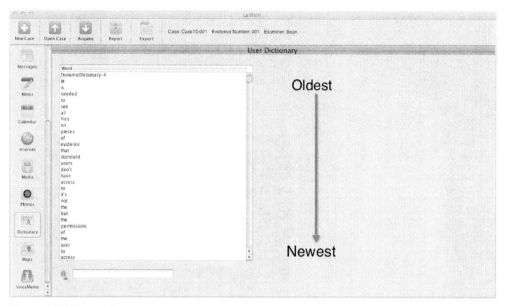

Figure 4–25. *User Dictionary pane*

Maps

The Maps pane contains data from map routes and queries from user input. Lantern can parse that data that can be exported to Excel and then port it to Google Maps for further analysis, as shown in Figure 4–26.

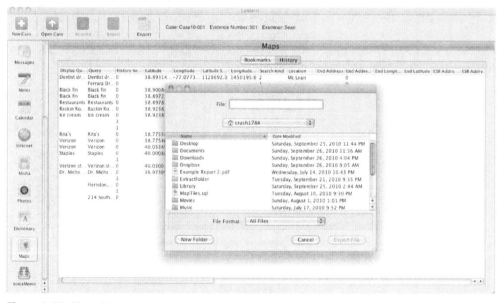

Figure 4–26. *Maps data*

Directory Structure and More Detail

For the examiner who needs to go into more detail when examining the device, Lantern reconstructs the directory structure of the iPhone. This will contain more artifacts, as shown in Figure 4–27.

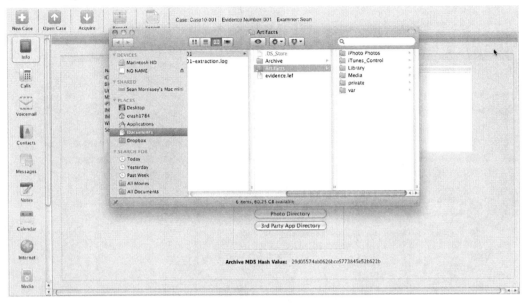

Figure 4–27. *More artifacts from the directory structure*

Susteen Secure View 2

Susteen Secure View 2 is a cell phone analysis tool that can acquire logical data from the iPhone. You can obtain the software at www.mobileforensics.com/Products/Secure-View-for-Forensics.php. The software is very easy to install, and the dongle is just as easy to activate. Two devices were used to test this application, a 2G iPhone and a 3GS iPhone. Susteen does not have support for the iPad or the iPhone 4.

Setting Up and Navigating the Interface

The interface of this application is quite easy to navigate, and the home screen is very simple for what examiners want to accomplish. Figure 4–28 shows the home screen.

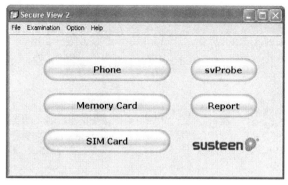

Figure 4–28. *Secure View 2 home screen*

To acquire an iPhone, choose Phone. Going through the process of starting an acquisition is straightforward and simple. Figure 4–29 displays the Phone Setup Wizard's connection screen.

Figure 4–29. *Connection type section of Phone Setup Wizard*

You will then be asked to select your phone's manufacturer and model, as shown in Figure 4–30.

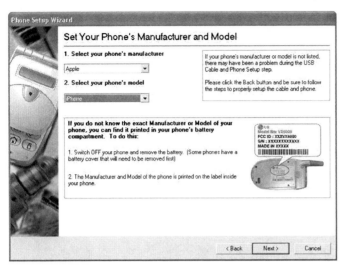

Figure 4–30. *Setting the phone's manufacturer and model*

Figure 4–31 shows that the setup is complete, so you are ready to start acquiring data from the phone.

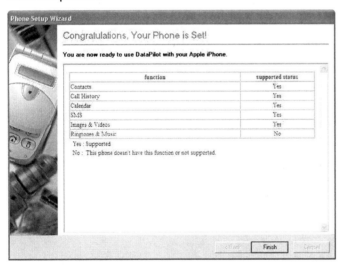

Figure 4–31. *Setup complete*

Once the setup with the phone is complete, the type of data that can be acquired is displayed, as shown in Figure 4–32.

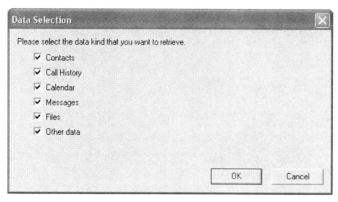

Figure 4–32. *Types of data to be retrievedl*

Acquiring Data

Prior to acquisition, the user can select the type of data retrieved. This screen doesn't give a lot of information that will be included or excluded. The Files and Other Data options are very vague. The rest of the categories are straightforward. After clicking OK, the acquisition begins.

The first test we conducted with the 3GS with version 3.1.3 was aborted because of connection problems. So, a test of the acquisition of geotagged photos and videos cannot not be shown in this report. Subsequent attempts by limiting the type of data acquired did not advance the acquisition to completion. We saw the same error of connection loss every time. However, the 2G iPhone with 3.1.3 was successful, as shown in Figures 4–33 and 4–34.

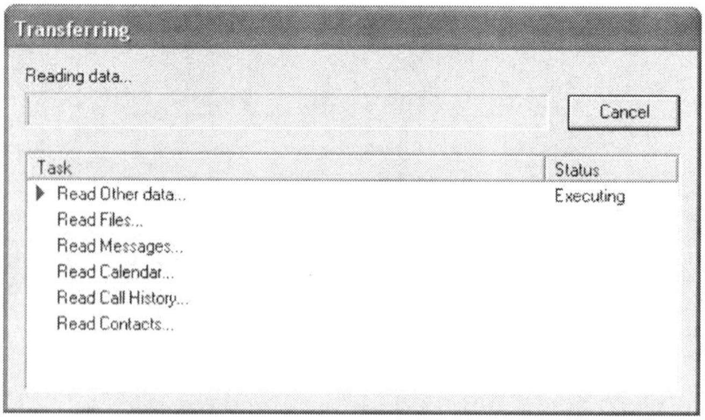

Figure 4–33. *Reading data*

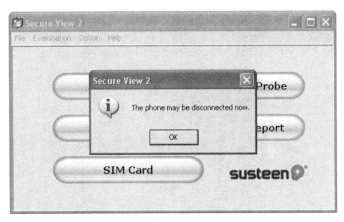

Figure 4–34. *Acquisition complete*

Reporting Data

After the acquisition is complete, a report is generated and displayed. The report has limited information, though. Other programs offer much more in the scope of information that is pulled from the iPhone. The report that is given by Secure View is user friendly in navigation but also redundant in its presentation. For example, the SMS messages are reported twice, once in a table form and another time in rows, as shown in Figure 4–35.

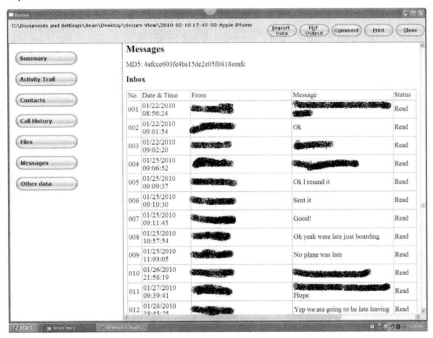

Figure 4–35. *Reporting of SMS messages*

One downfall of this program is its inability to acquire simple iPhone information. The program requests that the user insert the information that will then be added to the report. Figure 4–36 shows the data that could not be acquired by the device and the input necessary to continue.

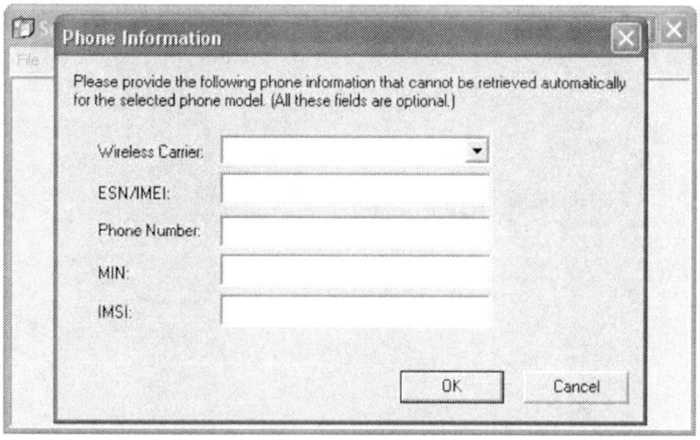

Figure 4–36. *Entering data that cannot be automatically retrieved*

As stated previously, the report is quite simple to read but lacks some information that can be acquired in other tools. For example, in the call history, the log doesn't show incoming or outgoing calls or the duration of them; Figure 4–37 does show this information.

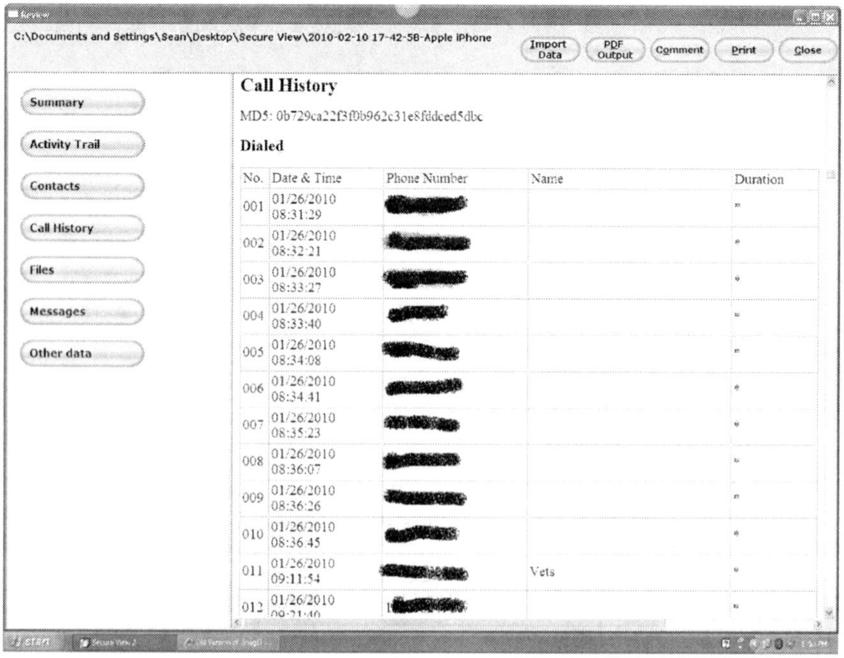

Figure 4–37. *Call history log*

The parsing of the history property list is not in the prettiest form, but it does show the URL and visit counts, as shown in Figure 4–38. However, the times are not translated and therefore would have to be done manually by the examiner.

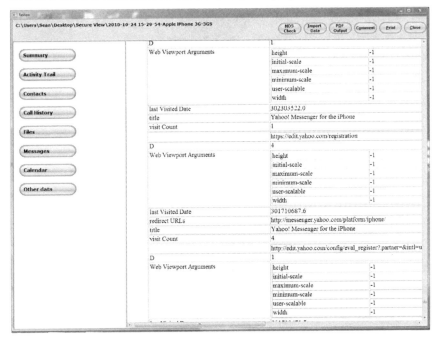

Figure 4–38. *Parsing of the history property list*

Secure View 2 does one thing that no other applications do, and that is acquiring the e-mail address settings that are on the Phone. These are e-mail accounts that the iPhone user has set up on the device. The results are, again, not in a very readable form, but they do detail the settings from Accountsettings.plist. This information is valuable to the investigator so that subpoenas can be served on those providers to possibly add valuable information to a case. Figure 4–39 depicts the data reported.

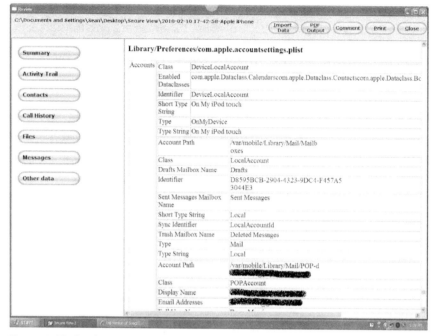

Figure 4–39. *Parsing the e-mail address settings on the phone*

Part of the report is called Files, where you are able to view the images from the device. The data extracted in Figure 4–40 is not just the photo itself but also includes a lot of EXIF data that was extracted, including any GPS data. Other programs were able to parse some or all of the EXIF data and the "pseudo" GPS data that gets placed with images taken from the 2G iPhone.

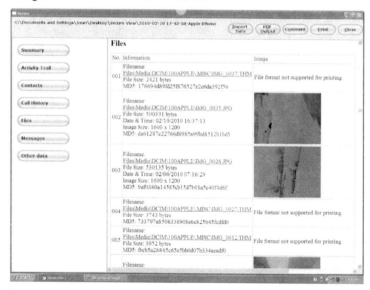

Figure 4–40. *Output of the Files report*

Paraben Device Seizure

Device Seizure from Paraben is cell phone forensic tool that supports more than just the iPhone. Many manufacturers jump to support the iPhone with their software whether or not they can actually parse all the data, and Device Seizure is one of them. Device Siezure fails to acquire devices and sometimes incorrectly reports data. But this is an inherent problem with most cell phone forensic tool developers, because they are so eager to announce support for Apple devices that they fail on execution.

For just over $1,000, Paraben's Device Seizure seems like a good deal, and for the actual cost and the number of supported phones, it is an affordable platform. The installation of Paraben is very time-consuming if all the drivers are selected for installation. Our copy had numerous problems with keys and reported that the dongles that were supplied failed and needed to be reprogrammed by Paraben, which created downtime. This is an inherent problem that comes with tools that require dongles. We used numerous iPhones to test this software—2G iPhones, 3G iPhones, and 3GS iPhones. Device Seizure was able to acquire iPhones but could not successfully acquire an iPad. Device Seizure has some good and bad to it when it comes to the iPhone.

Supported Devices

Here's how the support breaks down:

- iPhone 2G: Logical data
- iPhone 3G: Logical data
- iPhone 3GS: Logical data
- iPhone 4: No support
- iPad: Supported

The Good

Device Seizure, when it is able to acquire the logical data, does a pretty good job. It will parse the data into categories such as SMS, address book, call logs, and so on. Even when the tool cannot parse the information within the application, such as property lists and other databases, there is an option to export the file from Device Seizure and open it with tools such as iPod Robot's Plist Editor for Windows, SQLite Database Browser, and Irfanview. This allows for granular reporting in CSV, HTML, text, and XML outputs. This is demonstrated in Figures 4–41 and 4–42.

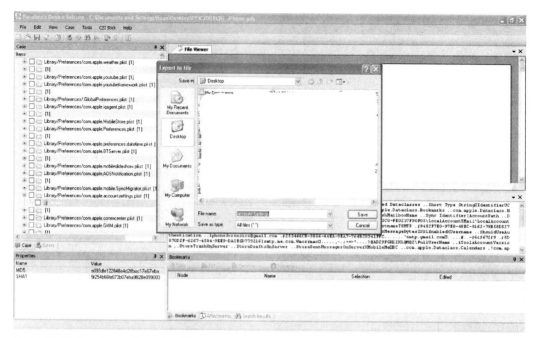

Figure 4–41. *Reporting with Device Seizure*

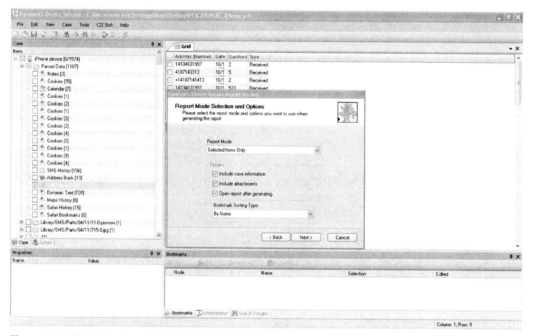

Figure 4–42. *Selecting the report mode*

The Bad

In some of the tables, such as the address book, Device Seizure was unable to parse the images associated with the contact and place them in the Address Book pane. In fact, Device Seizure couldn't parse the data at all, as shown in Figure 4–43.

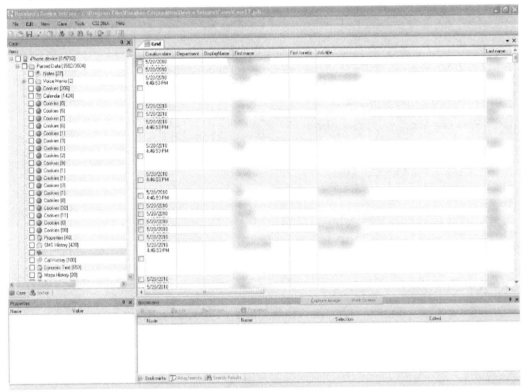

Figure 4–43. *Limitations of Device Seizure in parsing contacts*

The main difficulty is installing the program in relation to the problems with keys and dongles. Device Seizure will not work in a virtual machine, and it has conflicts with other forensic tools. In addition, the dongle needs to be connected to the Internet for any updates. For reprogramming of the dongle, the dongle needs to be shipped back to the company. Device Seizure 4.0 claims to recover deleted data; however, from an iPhone 3GS, it was unable to recover any deleted data. The data that it claimed to recover consisted of items that were undeleted in the databases.

Overall, Device Seizure is a well-priced cell phone forensics program. However, there are problems in reference to the iPhone, such as the incorrect parsing of information and the inability from within the program to decipher information. However, the ability to export to other tools makes up for that shortcoming. The tool does allow bookmarking and reporting of only selected items.

Oxygen Forensic Suite 2010

Oxygen Forensic Suite 2010 is available at www.oxygen-forensic.com, and it is rather pricey at $1,499. However, there is a 30-day or 30-runs fully functional trial version. It has support for phones up to 3GS and the iPad. The program requires the latest version of iTunes to communicate with the devices. The installation of Oxygen is one of the more difficult of the bunch. But the dongles make this a little easier. To acquire an iDevice, the phone wizard can automatically identify the device. The program will perform an iTunes backup and read files from the device.

Apple Devices Supported

Here's how the support breaks down:

- iPhone 2G: Logical data
- iPhone 3G: Logical data
- iPhone 3GS: Logical data
- iPod touch: Logical data
- iPad: Logical data

Oxygen Connection Wizard

To use Oxygen to connect to the iDevice in question, follow these steps:

1. Start the connection wizard. Figure 4–44 shows the wizard's first screen.

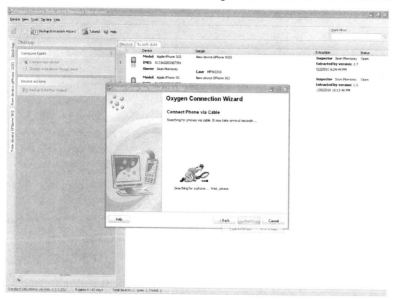

Figure 4–44. *Starting the Oxygen connection wizard*

2. Fill in the connection type, such as USB cable, Bluetooth, or infrared, as shown in Figure 4–45. For Apple devices, connect using the USB cable.

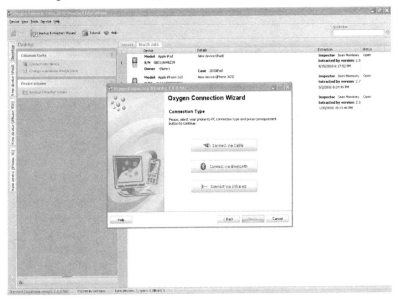

Figure 4–45. *Choosing your connection*

Oxygen Data Extraction Wizard

After finishing the connection wizard, the extraction wizard opens, as shown in Figure 4–46.

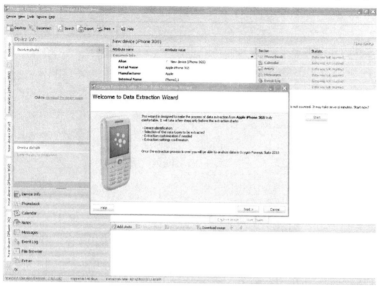

Figure 4–46. *Moving on to the extraction wizard*

The extraction wizard will inquire about the level of extraction, as shown in Figure 4–47.

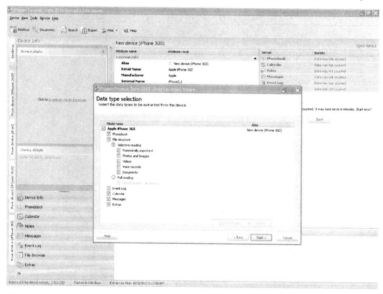

Figure 4–47. *Enter the level of extraction.*

Viewing Backup Data

After the extraction wizard, the program will then begin backing up data to its database, as shown in Figure 4–48.

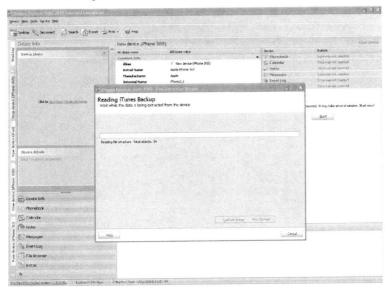

Figure 4–48. *Reading iTunes backup*

After the extraction, Oxygen then has a different section on the bottom left of the screen that the examiner can comb through to look at the artifacts, as shown in Figure 4–49.

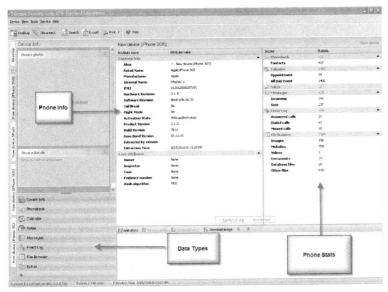

Figure 4–49. *Options for combing through artifacts*

Oxygen will parse device information, contacts, notes, messages, event logs (call logs), the file browser, and extras. The extras are modules that can be purchased from O2 for web browser data parsing, Skype parsing, WiFi data parsing, and geo-related event positioning (Google Maps locations on geotagged data). The latest add-ons include a plist and SQLite database viewers. It should be noted and will be shown in this book that these last two have numerous free or low-cost apps that can do the same thing on the Windows side. On the Mac, there are very good free apps that parse out plists and SQLite databases. Figures 4–50 through 4–55 show some of the data panes.

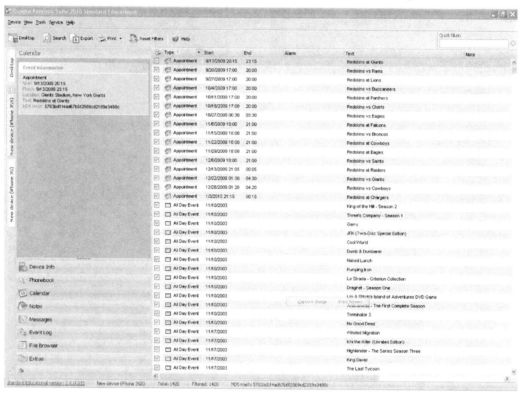

Figure 4–50. *Calendar data*

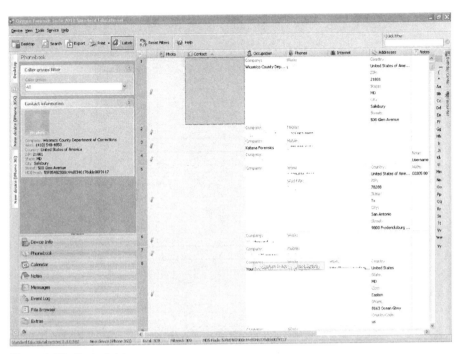

Figure 4–51. *Contact data*

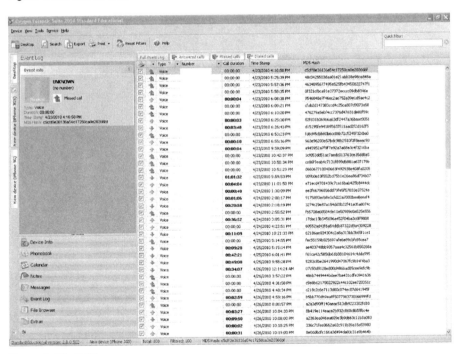

Figure 4–52. *Call logs*

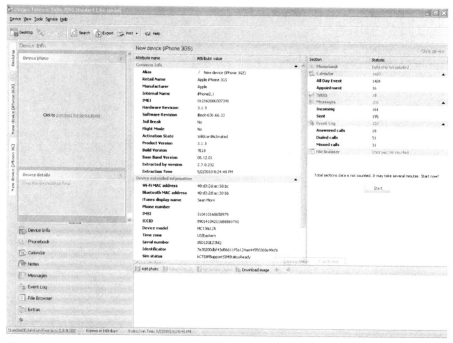

Figure 4–53. *Device information*

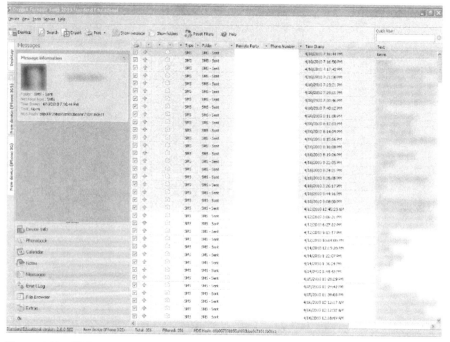

Figure 4–54. *SMS data*

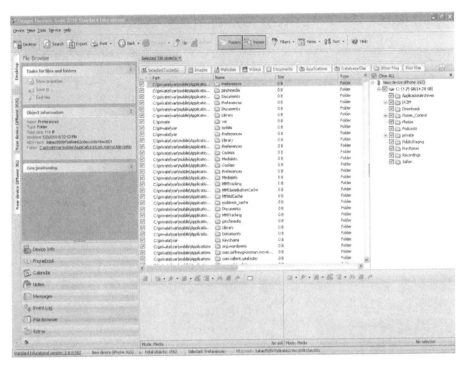

Figure 4–55. *Directory data*

Oxygen does a good job of extracting data from the Apple devices it supports. The retail cost with all add-ons is approximately $2,029. This is a Russian company, so support can be a factor depending on where you are. The only downside to Oxygen is the layout of the data and the price, and yes, it has a dongle. However, the presentation of the data is not intuitive, and there is some learning curve. Some of the nomenclature of the data could be different depending on your location.

Cellebrite

The Cellebrite Universal Forensic Extraction Device (UFED) first started as a consumer product that was primarily used by cell phone providers to transfer user data from one phone to another. It was a service that was needed when an individual changed carriers or phones. Cellebrite then developed the UFED device. Similar to the commercial device, however, this version could not write to another phone; this was replaced by writing that data to a USB flash device, SD card, or Windows computer. At a higher level, prior to the UFED physical Pro, the UME-36 was not much different from the UFED. Cellebrite is a hardware device, as compared to the other applications that are all software based. The UFED has Windows CR core 5.0 as its operating system as the engine that runs this device. The device is simple to use, which in itself is a cause of the diminishing importance of mobile forensic science.

Supported Devices

Here's how the support breaks down:

- iPhone 2G: Logical data

- iPhone 3G: Logical data

- iPhone 3GS: Logical data

- iPhone 4: Logical data

- iPad: Phone info and photos

- Password recovery: Only with lockdown plist

Setting Up Cellebrite

As previously stated, using Cellebrite is easy:

1. Plug the iPhone into the device, and select Extract Phone Data, as shown in Figure 4–56.

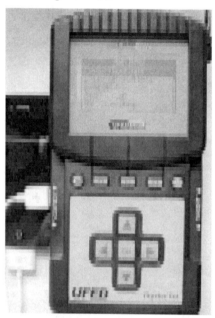

Figure 4–56. *Extracting Phone data*

2. Select the iPhone, iPod, or iPad device, as shown in Figure 4–57.

Figure 4–57. *Selecting iPhone, iPod, or iPad device*

3. Select the type of acquisition needed.

4. Specify where to put the data, whether it be a USB flash drive, SD card, or Windows computer, as shown in Figure 4–58.

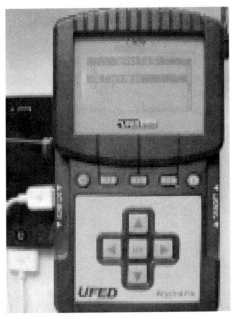

Figure 4–58. *Selecting where to put the data*

5. Then the acquisition dialog box asks which type of data you want require to extract, as shown in Figure 4–59. Specify an option.

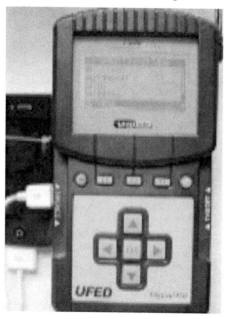

Figure 4–59. *Choosing the type of data to extract*

The Cellebrite will advise which cable to use, and then the acquisition begins. As with other applications, Cellebrite is no different, depending on the size of the device and the amount of data on the phone. The extraction can take from anywhere from 30 minutes to several hours.

After the extraction is completed, all the data is written to the location previously mentioned. The data will have an HTML report and other data such as images and video in separate folders. In a logical directory structure extraction, the data can be placed into Encase for further analysis. This will be explained in more detail in the next chapter. Figures 4–60 and 4–61 show a sample Cellebrite report.

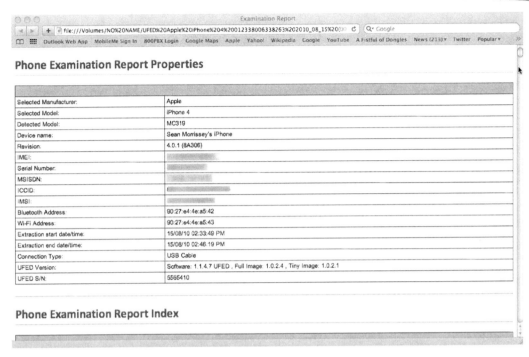

Figure 4–60. Phone Examination Report Properties screen

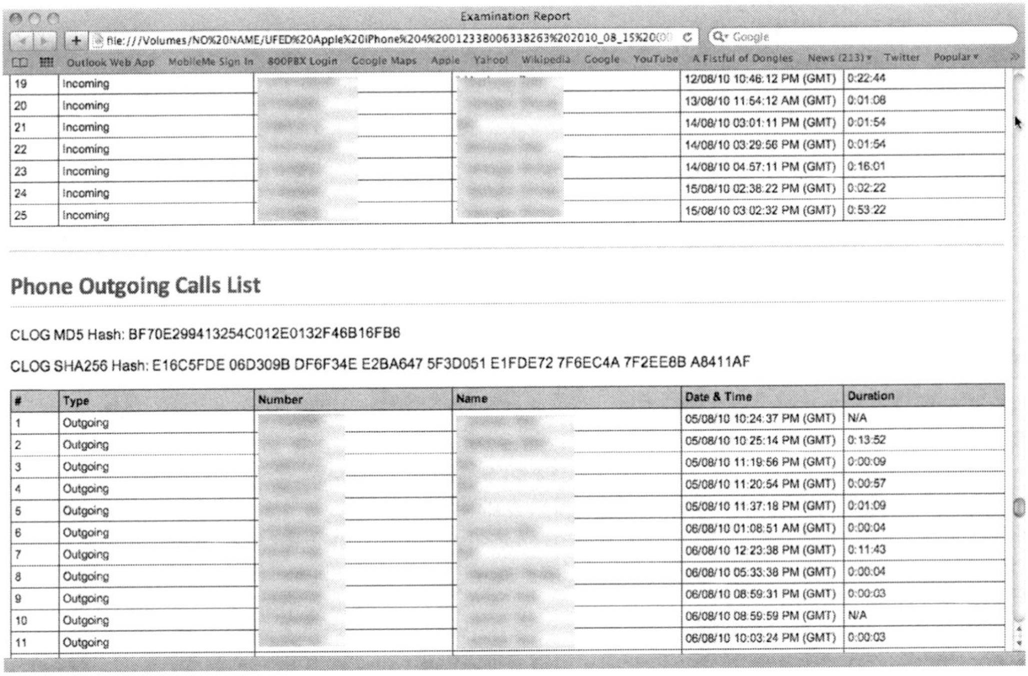

Figure 4–61. *Phone Outgoing Calls List screen*

Cellebrite can also extract images that have geotagged images. The report is connected to a system that has Internet access and can have the latitude and longitude coordinates mapped in Google Maps. The basic report does not parse other data such as notes, Internet history, and so on. The Physical Pro portion of this product does not really give any more data than the UFED. The problem that the Cellebrite UFED causes mobile forensics investigators is the push-button mode of analysis. No analytic thinking is done. The UFED Physical Pro has finally brought some of that thinking back into the space. The main barrier is the overall cost for the Physical Pro, approximately $8,000.

Comparing the Tools and Results

Let's say you have an iPhone 3GS and want to use one the mentioned tools to gather artifacts. The following demonstrates what you might get with each of these tools.

On the iPhone 3GS, you have this:

- Firmware 3.1.3
- 309 contacts
- 220 audio files
- 2 video files
- 10 iPhone images
- 2 iPhone videos
- 18 notes
- 1 voice memos
- 356 SMS/MMS messages
- 1421 calendar events
- 27 voicemails

Buyer Beware

Most mobile phone forensic developers are pushed by the law enforcement and intelligence communities to support more and more phone acquisitions. Needless to say, most software companies and the tools they make haven't fully measured up to the notion of support. Support means that all the logical data can be extracted and parsed. This is the pain that examiners deal with every day. Each company advertises support on any given phone, and that support is sometimes relegated to just the phone book. Forensic tools should be judged on the merits of what they claim and the cost of their tools. Just putting the word *forensics* on an application doesn't mean that it is or that it is worth several thousand dollars.

Paraben Device Seizure Results

On Device Seizure, these are your results:

- 2 hours to acquire
- 309 contacts
- 18 notes
- 1421 calendar events
- 100 calls
- 10 images
- 2 videos
- File system extracted but not logically reconstructed
- Third-party tools needed to parse app data
- Third-party tools needed to decode EXIF data

Oxygen Forensic Suite 2010 Results

On Oxygen Forensic Suite 2010, these are your results:

- 21 minutes to acquire.
- 309 contacts.
- 356 SMS/MMS (MMS no visible media).
  - 1 deleted SMS identified no content.
- 18 notes.
- 1419 calendar events.
- 100 calls.
- 20 images (duplicates found).
- 0 videos.
- Oxygen has developed internal SQLite and property list viewers. These aren't free; the top-of-the-line suite needs to be purchased. The performance of these viewers is below that of some freely available tools.
- File System is reconstructed for manual review but seems buried within the interface. Oxygen is a good tool, but its detraction is its inability to connect to iDevices. There is some inconsistency with this tool that reliability is its big detraction.

Cellebrite Results

On Cellebrite, these are your results:

- 15 minutes for backup selection only. 12 hours for full extraction fails numerous times. The extraction was completed by doing only one artifact type at a time.
- 309 contacts.
- 382 SMS (numerous duplicates located in the report).
- 100 calls.
- 12 images.
- 19 audio files.
- Two image files with the wrong extension. They were actually `.mov` files.
- Password extract does not work on Firmware 2.0+.

Susteen Secure View 2 Results

Unable to acquire a iPhone 3GS.

Katana Forensics Lantern Results

On Lantern, these are your results:

- 100 calls
- 309 contacts
- 356 SMS/MMS
  - 2 MMS
  - 1 deleted
- 27 voicemails
- 12 images
- 2 videos
- 1 voice memo
- 1421 calendar events
- Needs one third-party app to view additional databases
- File system is reconstructed

The Issue of Support

We've discussed all the logical extraction tools and shown our test results. It is only fair to acknowledge that some of these tools also support other phones and devices. But that begs the question, what constitutes support? It may be time for the community or an unbiased organization to provide guidelines for allowing tool makers to use the seal of "support."

Summary

It is important to note that the most expensive tools performed poorly as compared to tools that had better support for iDevices. It is good to have many tools in your tool kit, but in the times of shrinking budgets, it is better to know how these tools perform against a device. The examiner should be educated in how these tools perform so they can mitigate those deficiencies by either acquiring a new device or using some other free tools to complete an exam.

The goal is to retrieve all the data. It is better to get everything and find nothing instead of not getting everything and being embarrassed in court for not completing the task at hand.

Chapter 5

Logical Data Analysis

Apple's mobile devices can contain a huge amount of data. There is telephony-type data such as call logs, address books, and text messages. There is data from third-party applications that could be a subset of the 300,000+ apps that are on the App Store. In addition, with the iPad and iWorks, document editing and storage are now possible, and all this data can interact with other applications. Apple devices do more than ever before. People can create data with phones as well; for example, iMovie, iWorks, and many other applications allow users to communicate in different mediums. As with all things that are beneficial for society, these tools can also be used for criminal activity. Therefore, it is incumbent on investigators to look at all the data and know how it was placed onto the phone. This chapter will show how to set up a forensic workstation and comb through iPhone directories and artifacts.

Setting Up a Forensic Workstation

Prior to any analysis, you must set up your forensic workstation. The setup discussed in this chapter is merely one way to set up a Mac workstation, such as on a Mac Mini, MacBook Pro, or Mac Pro. We suggest getting as much RAM as you can afford in order to assist mainly in virtual machine performance.

1. Wipe the entire disk with zeros using the Disk Utility application on the Mac OS X installation disk.

2. Install Mac OS X.

3. Install all updates by downloading them from an Internet-accessible system, scanning them, and then installing them on the forensic workstation. You can access the updates from the Apple Support Downloads page at `http://support.apple.com/downloads/`.

4. Install a virus-scanning utility such as Norton AntiVirus for Mac on the workstation, and then download and install the following:

- iWork '09, Apple's Version of Office

- iLife '09, which actually comes free with any new purchase of a Mac

- Microsoft Office 2008/2011

- VMware Fusion V3+, $79 (www.vmware.com/products/fusion/)

- Parallels 5+, $79 (www.parallels.com/)

- Virtual Box, $0 (www.virtualbox.org/)

- CF Absolute Time Converter, which is a free absolute time converter (www.hsoi.com/hsoishop/software/)

- Froq, a SQLite database application (SQLite Database Editor/Viewer) (www.alwintroost.nl/products/mac/froq)

- FileJuicer, which is used to parse multiple file types (Artifact extractor) (http://echoone.com/filejuicer/)

- SQLite Database Browser, which is free (http://sourceforge.net/projects/sqlitebrowser/)

- Md5Deep, a free hashing utility (http://sourceforge.net/projects/md5deep/)

- Dc3dd and dc3dd GUI, a free imaging utility (http://sourceforge.net/projects/dc3dd/)

- Hfsdebug, a free volume information utility (www.osxbook.com/software/hfsdebug/)

- Lantern Unix Time Converter, a free time conversion tool (www.katanaforensics.com)

- Lantern iPhone Forensic Application, which costs $399 to $499 (www.katanaforensics.com)

- iPhone Backup Extractor, a free tool to parse iDevice backups (http://supercrazyawesome.com/)

- mdhelper, a free iPhone backup tool to parse iDevice backups (http://ericasadun.com/ftp/Macintosh/)

- Subrosasoft's MacForensicsLab, which is a Mac forensic analysis application (http://subrosasoft.com/)

For Windows within the virtual machine, download and install the following:

- Windows XP or Windows 7 (Vista is not recommended)

- A Window-based cell phone forensic tool such as Oxygen

- Encase 6.17+ (www.guidancesoftware.com/)

- FTK Imager (www.accessdata.com/downloads.html)

- iPhone Explorer (www.macroplant.com/iphoneexplorer/)

- Time Lord, a free time conversion utility
(http://computerforensics.
parsonage.co.uk/timelord/timelord.htm)

- Skype Analyzer, a Skype log parser
(http://belkasoft.com/bsa/en/Skype_Analyzer.asp)

- FTK 1.8+ (if you have fewer than 5,000 files, no dongle is
needed) (www.accessdata.com/downloads.html)

- HxD, a free hex editor (http://mh-nexus.de/en/hxd/)

- SQLite Database Browser
(http://sourceforge.net/projects/sqlitebrowser/)

- iPod Robot PlistEditor, which is free
(www.icopybot.com/blog/free-plist-editor-for-windows-10-
released.htm)

After your workstation is completed, return to the Mac side and then back up your
complete drive to Time Machine. Restoring your complete OS is a snap after wiping it.

As discussed in Chapter 4, you can acquire data from an iDevice using tools from
numerous vendors. However, there is a plethora of information that these types of tools
miss. Examiners should manually review the data while examining an iPhone. Using a
third-party tool or a command-line utility on the Mac platform is the ideal option for this
type of examination. Mac-based tools and applications such as Property List Editor,
Preview, Quicklook, and TextEdit can help you view the data from iDevices. Or, with
tools such as mdhelper and Lantern, you can import the logical data to a Windows-
based forensics tool.

Once a backup of the iPhone or iPod touch created with iTunes Backup has been
acquired and converted using mdhelper, you can then analyze the data. The backups
are in the following directory, /Users/[username]/Library/Application
Support/MobileSync/Backup/[UUID]/. Note that this type of conversion doesn't bring
over any device information; that data is still in the backup folder. But there is a property
list called info.plist that details the device's information. You can extract the following
information from this file:

- Device name

- ICCID

- IMSI

- Phone number

- OS version and build

- Serial number

Figure 5–1 shows an `info.plist` file viewed with Property List Editor.

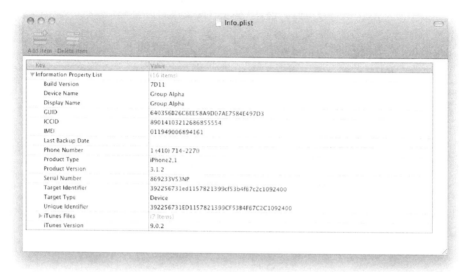

Figure 5–1. *An* `info.plist` *file viewed with Property List Editor*

NOTE: This data, especially the serial number, can matched to an individual's Mac or Windows computer. For instance, the images that were synced by iTunes and the device have most of their EXIF data stripped when placed into Apple's `.ithmb` files in devices with firmware older than 3.2, and the originals are still on the synced machine. In 3.2+, the firmware has the same type of images, but they are now stored differently. The EXIF data is still stripped, but if an investigator can match the serial number of the device to a suspected system, they can connect the dots in reference to images.

After the device information has been gathered, the remaining information can now be analyzed. Return to `/Users/[username]/Desktop/Recovered iPhone Files/`. The files above the home domain are all application data. The home domain holds the following directories and the data that can be acquired.

This first directory is `AddressBook`, which contains contact data. This is the largest database on the iPhone, and numerous applications and databases use it. There are two SQLite databases in this folder, `AddressBook.sqlitedb` and `AddressBookImages.sqlitedb`. The free SQLite Database Browser application can aid in reading the data contained in these SQLite databases; you can obtain it from SourceForge at `http://sourceforge.net/projects/sqlitebrowser/`. Once you've installed this application, open `AddressBook.sqlitedb` with SQLite Database Browser. Table 5–1 details the tables of the `AddressBook` database and the artifacts that can be located within.

Table 5–1. *The AddressBook Database and Its Artifacts*

Table	Artifacts
ABGroup	Groups
ABGroupMembers	Members of groups
ABMultiValue	Phone numbers and e-mail addresses for contacts
ABMultiValueEntry	Addresses for contacts
ABPerson	Contact information: name, address, organization, department, job title, notes, created date, modified date

You can extract these tables via the command line using SQlite commands or by using GUI tools such as SQlite Database Browser or Froq. For example, the complete table of separate columns can be exported to an Excel spreadsheet, as shown in Figure 5–2.

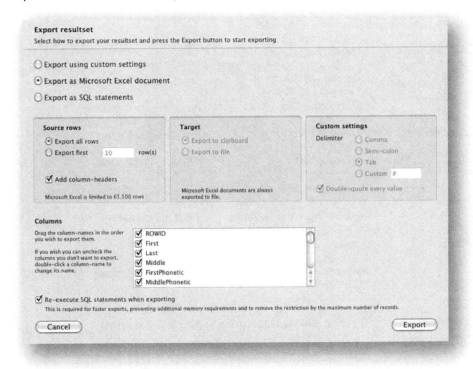

Figure 5–2. *Exporting the AddressBook database*

Forensics tools have come along way over the past few years. Most can decipher these databases and present the data in a comprehensible manner. For example, Lantern does this and presents all contact information to the examiner. Froq (www.alwintroost.nl/?id=82) is another good tool for the Mac that you can use to examine the SQlite databases; it has some very nice exporting function as well. Froq can export just the columns an investigator needs.

When manually traversing the file structure, all databases that can be viewed by either Froq or SQLite Database Browser have a header of sqlite3 when viewed by a hex editor.

Library Domain

Let's go through the Library directory and look at the data and the tools you can use to view and parse the data. Additional information from the Library directory appears in the Recovered iPhone Files directory. Table 5–2 outlines the artifacts and the tools used to recover the data.

Table 5–2. *Retrieving Additional Information in the Library Directory*

Directory	Artifacts	Tool to Be Used
AddressBook	AddressBook.sqlitedb	Froq, SQLite Database Browser
Caches	Consolidated.db Safari/Thumbnails	Froq, SQLite Database Browser
Calendar	Calendar.sqlitedb	Froq, SQLite Database Browser
Call History	call_history.db	Froq, SQLite Database
ConfigurationProfiles	PasswordHistory.plist	Property List Editor
Cookies	Cookies.plist	Property List Editor
Logs	ADDataStore.sqlitedb	Froq, SQLite Database Browser
Keyboard	Dynamic-text.dat	TextEdit, Lantern
LockBackground.jpg	Image	Preview
Maps	Bookmarks.plist Directions.plist History.plist	Property List Editor
MobileInstallation	ApplicationAttributes.plist	Property List Editor
Notes	Notes.db	Froq, SQLite Database Browser
Preferences	Numerous property lists	Property List Editor
Remote Notification	Clients.plst	Property List Editor

Directory	Artifacts	Tool to Be Used
Safari	Bookmarks.plist History.plist SuspendedState.plist	Property List Editor
SMS	Sms.db	Froq, SQLite Database Browser
Voicemail	.amr	QuickTime
Webclip	.png info.plist	Preview, Property List Editor
Webkit	Databases	Froq, SQLite Database Browser
System Configuration	Autowake.plist Network.identification.plist Wifi.plist Preferences.plist	Property List Editor

Table 5–3 shows items from the iOS directory and the artifacts that can be located.

Table 5–3. *Artifacts Retrieved from the iOS Directory*

Directory	File(s)	Artifact
AddressBook	AddressBook.sqlitedb	Contact information
Caches	Consolidated.db Safari/Thumbnails	Cell tower geodata, screenshot images
Calendar	Calendar.sqlitedb	Event data
Call History	call_history.db	Call history data
ConfigurationProfiles	PasswordHistory.plist	Passcode history
Cookies	Cookies.plist	Internet cookies
Logs	ADDataStore.sqlitedb	Application usage
Keyboard	Dynamic-text.dat	Keyboard logger
LockBackground.jpg	Image	Wallpaper background
Maps	Bookmarks.plist Directions.plist History.plist	Map bookmarks, map route directions, map route history
Notes	Notes.db	Notes
Preferences	Numerous property lists	System/app data

Directory	File(s)	Artifact
Safari	Bookmarks.plist History.plist SuspendedState.plist	Safari bookmarks, Internet history, suspended web pages
SMS	Sms.db	SMS and MMS messages
Voicemail	.amr files	Voicemails
Webclip	.png info.plist	Web icons
WebKit	Databases	WebKit data from numerous sources, which use HTML5

AddressBook

As stated previously, the AddressBook is the largest and most central database in the iOS system. There are two databases in the AddressBook directory:

- AddressBook.sqlitedb: Contact information

- AddressBookImages.sqlitedb: Contact images

Table 5–4 lists the various artifacts found in the AddressBook database.

Table 5–4. *The AddressBook Database and Its Artifacts*

Table	Artifacts
ABGroup	Groups
ABGroupMembers	Members of groups
ABMultiValue	Phone numbers and e-mail addresses for contacts
ABMultiValueEntry	Addresses for contacts
ABPerson	Contact information: name, address, organization, department, job title, notes, created date, modified date

Many applications and developers use this database. Applications such as Lantern and other forensic tools are able to extract the data. Some tools can present all the data; some present a portion. For example, Lantern shows the AddressBook.sqlitedb and AddressBookImage.sqlitedb data in a one-screen presentation, as shown in Figure 5–3.

Figure 5–3. *Lantern displaying* AddressBook *data*

The same databases can also be manually examined with SQLite Database Browser, as shown in Figure 5–4.

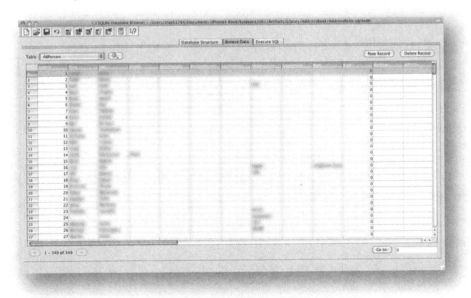

Figure 5–4. AddressBook.sqlitedb *shown in the SQLite Database Browser*

The ABThumbnailImage table holds the data of images that have been used as an avatar image for that contact. Using SQLite commands, you can extract these images manually, or you can use a forensic tool to show them, as shown in Figure 5–5.

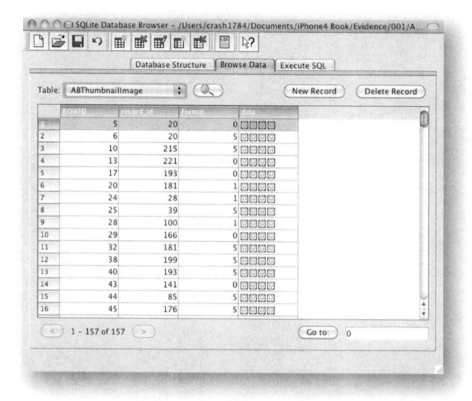

Figure 5–5. *The* ABThumbnailImage *table*

Caches

The Caches directory holds some important information about an iOS device and particularly the iPhone. Some of the directories in this folder are as follows:

- Com.appleWebAppCache
- Locationd
- Safari

The com.appleWebAppCache folder stores ApplicationCache.db. Within this is the data needed for web apps. Web apps are applications that are accessed from the Internet. These were the first type of applications seen on first-generation iPhones prior to the App Store. Exporting this data using SQLite commands can assist in viewing this data.

The Locationd directory has different artifacts depending on the version of iOS, because this data has changed over time in location and file type. Previous to iOS 4, the data was in the plist format and was not in the logical data extraction. In iOS 4 devices, there is a database in SQLite database format in this directory. There are two databases in this folder:

- Consolidated.db: Cell tower and Wifi geolocation data

- Clients.plist: Applications and services that use geolocation data

The consolidated.db file can hold a tremendous amount of geolocation data. The database holds goelocation data for every cell tower that the iOS device communicates with. This data, along with corresponding data from carriers, can link a phone to a specific location on a given date and time. Clients.plist is a database that also holds information in reference to Wi-Fi hotspots that the device has come into contact with, with MAC addresses, geolocation, and date/time values. All this goelocation information is crucial in investigations where it is imperative to place an individual in the area of a crime or at the crime scene itself. The consolidated.db and Clients.plist data will be discussed in greater detail in Chapters 7 and 10. Figure 5–6 is an example of the consolidated.db CellLocation table.

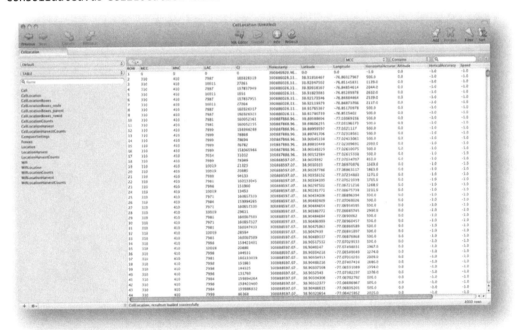

Figure 5–6. *The* consolidated.db CellLocation *table*

The Clients.plistproperty list contains data in reference to applications that use geolocation. The following is some of the data that can be gleaned from this plist:

- Application name

- Last date and time the app was started

- Last date and time the app was terminated

For example, in the Maps application, let's look at how the data is stored. The property list can be viewed using the Property List Editor application, as shown in Figure 5–7.

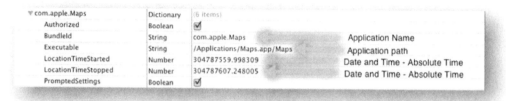

Figure 5–7. *Maps data displayed in Property List Editor*

Using a time converter such as CFAbsoluteTimeConverter, you can decode the dates and times. This can be very important in reference to an application being used during a crime. Using the data from Figure 5–7, Figures 5–8 and 5–9 show utilizing CFAbsolutrTimeConverter to convert the data.

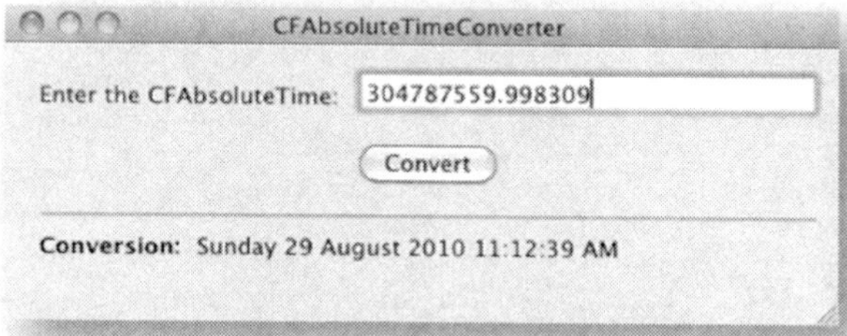

Figure 5–8. *The CFAbsoluteTimeConverter*

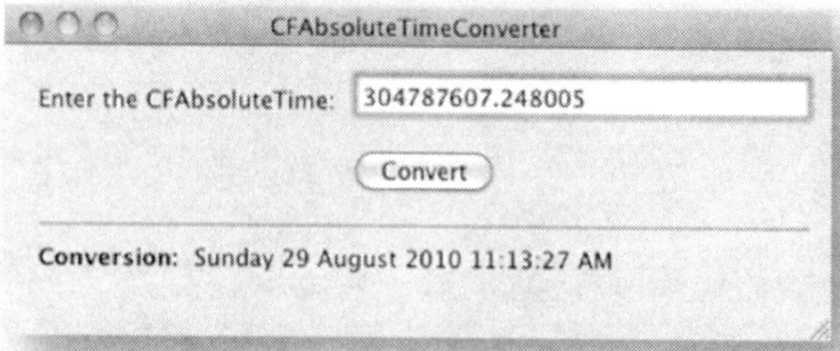

Figure 5–9. *Another example of the CFAbsoluteTimeConverter*

Call History

The call history is contained in `call_history.db`. This database contains a maximum of 100 calls. The call history maintains a log of all incoming, outgoing, and missed calls. It also lists the date and time of the calls, the duration of the calls, and the phone numbers that were dialed or received. Figures 5–10 and 5–11 show the database and the embedded data, which includes the following:

- *Rowid*: This is the record number for the call. These numbers do not get reused unless the phone is not restored from a backup.

- *Address*: This is the phone number of the incoming or outgoing call.

- *Date*: This is a Unix epoch data and time value that needs to be converted using a forensic application or a converter.

- *Duration*: This is the duration of the call in seconds.

- *Flags*: This shows whether it is an incoming, outgoing, or missed call.

- *Country code*: For example, (310) is the United States. You can find a list of country codes at `http://en.wikipedia.org/wiki/List_of_mobile_country_codes`

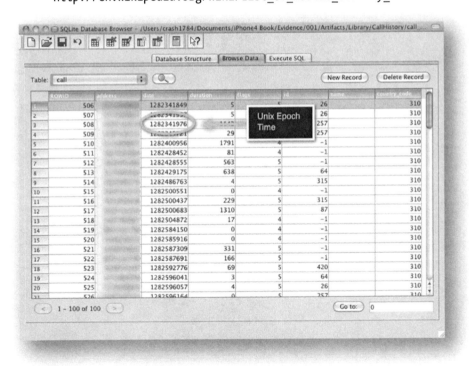

Figure 5–10. *The* `CallHistory` *database*

Figure 5–11. *The embedded data from the* `CallHistory` *database as displayed by Lantern*

Figure 5–12 shows the way the call history looks from a forensic tool with all the data parsed correctly.

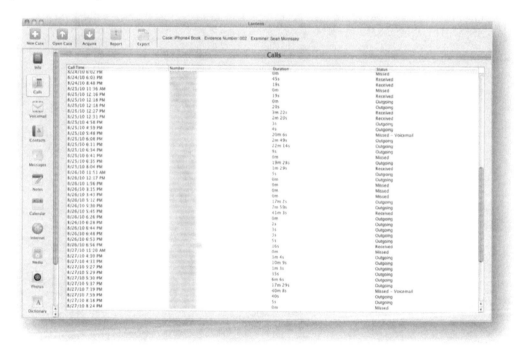

Figure 5–12. *Call history with all data parsed correctly*

Configuration Profiles

The `SystemProfiles` directory contains system- and user-created settings for the iOS device.

An important plist to look at is `MCDataMigration.plist`. This property list details the use of a passcode, a system restore, or a data migration.

Cookies

Cookies are defined as pieces of text stored by a web browser in Mobile Safari. Cookies contain data from the browsing history of a user. Internet cookies in the Mobile Safari browser aren't different from its bigger cousin, OS X. The data is stored in its XML plist format and can be viewed with Property List Editor. This is a dynamic plist and can expand over time; in addition, the user can delete cookies.

This is the data stored in this plist:

- The domain of the web site placing the cookie
- The expiration date of the cookie

To view this data, you can use Property list Editor by installing the Developers Kit. The 3.0 version of the Developers Kit (otherwise known as Xcode) is the best tool that can parse this type of data in a concise and easy-to-read manner. To utilize this app, sign up for the Mac Developers Connection (MDC). It is a free program, and you can then download Xcode. The MDC is at `http://developer.apple.com/products/membership.html`. The Developers Kit is at `http://developer.apple.com/mac/`. Once the Developers Kit is installed, navigate to `/Developers/Applications/Utilities/Property List Editor`. Drag and drop the app to your Dock for easier use.

You can view the `cookies.plist` file using Property List Editor. Figure 5–13 demonstrates the contents of this `.plist` file.

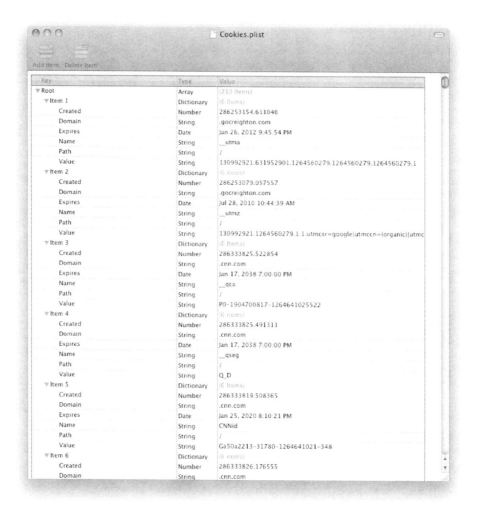

Figure 5–13. *The* `cookies.plist` *file*

The data that is given in this property list is the created date and time of the cookie and the domain where cookie came from.

Keyboard

You'll see the `dynamic-text.dat` file. This file is sometimes referred to as a *key logger* for the iPhone, which is mostly true. Words get populated in this database by the user from keyboard inputs from numerous applications on the iPhone. Since this is a dynamic file, the data continues to grow. A keyword search of this database can garner interesting information regarding the nature of the investigation. On the Mac, this file can be opened with TextEdit, as shown in Figure 5–14.

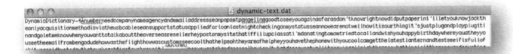

Figure 5–14. *The* `dynamic-text.dat` *file opened with TextEdit*

TextEdit can do some simple keyword searching if you select the **Edit ➤ Find** menu, as shown in Figure 5–15.

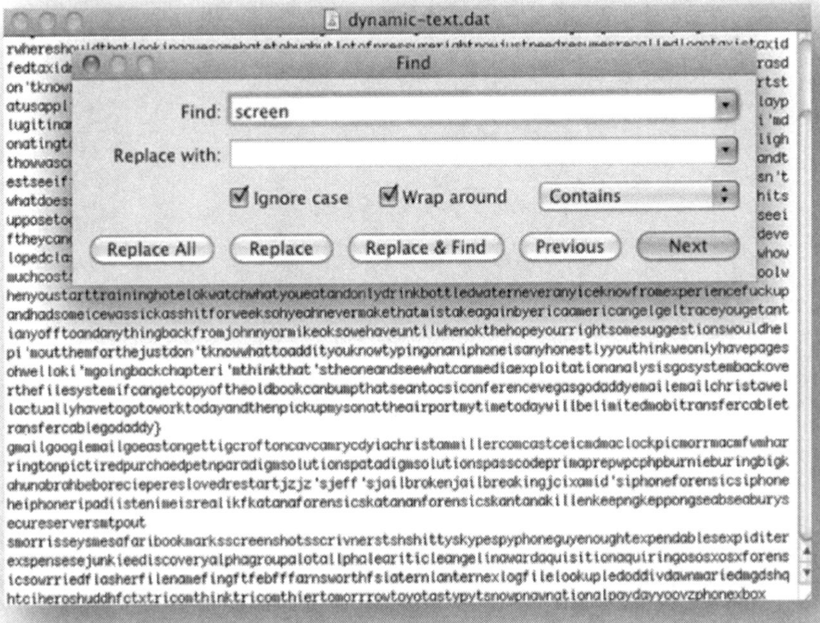

Figure 5–15. *Using keyword search in TextEdit*

Forensic tools such as Lantern parse this data in a more intuitive fashion; the data is shown from the oldest words on top to the newest words on the bottom, as shown in Figure 5–16. Sometimes sentences can be reconstructed from preciously deleted data such as SMS.

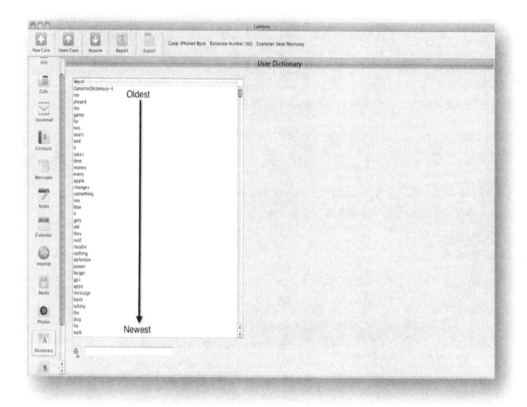

Figure 5–16. *Lantern displays data from oldest to newest.*

Logs

In the Logs directory, there is one file that, depending on the version of iOS, is a property list or a SQLite database. The ADDataStore file contains information on application usage from the device. This has been helpful in several investigations. The database is shown in Figure 5–17 using Froq. This database contains historical information on application usage. The oldest date is on rowid 1, and the newest date is the last rowid.

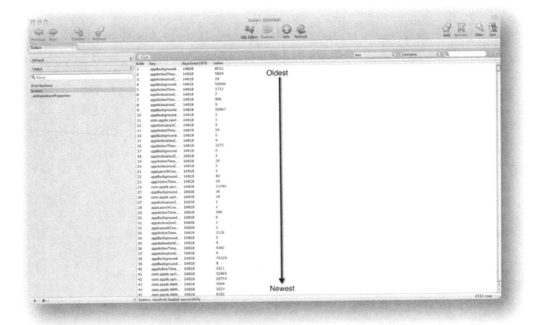

Figure 5–17. *Froq displays historical information application usage.*

The data is stored by key, days since 1970, and value.

The keys contains the following data:

- appBackgroundActiveTime.com.[application name]
- appActiveTime.com.Apple.[application name]
- appLaunchCount.com.Apple.[applicationname]

The Days Since 1970 field contains Unix time in days since January 1, 1970, with a value counted in seconds. (See Figure 5–18.)

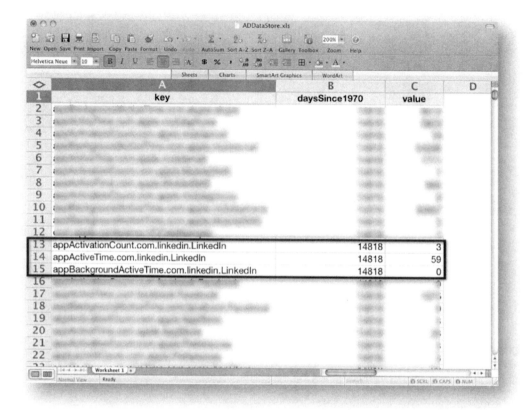

Figure 5–18. *Days since 1970 displayed in seconds*

The application LinkedIn was used three times on July 28, 2010, for 59 seconds. If the application was running in the background, that time would be annotated also.

Maps

On the iPhone there is an application called Maps. This is mainly powered by Google Maps, but it gives the user the ability to search for locations, points of interest, and plan routes. The users can also bookmark locations as favorites. In the Maps directory are some property list that can give investigators a lot of GPS and route information.

The first property list is Bookmark.plist. This property list contains data from the Maps application. When a user adds bookmark to Maps, this populates bookmarks.plist file, as shown in Figure 5–19.

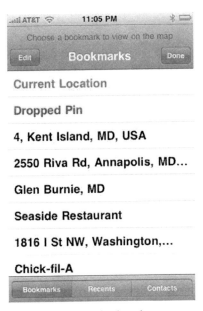

Figure 5–19. *Maps bookmarks*

The bookmark.plist file stores that data for easy retrieval by the OS. Property List Editor is the tool of choice for viewing this and all property lists.

Map History

The history.plist file located in the Maps directory will give you a list of previous searches using the Maps app, as well as routes that were generated. As you see in Figure 5–20, there are starting and ending GPS coordinates and names of locations.

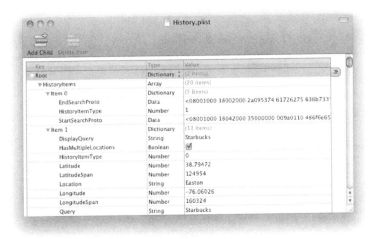

Figure 5–20. *Starting and ending GPS coordinates and names of locations*

Notes

notes.db is a database that accumulates the text that is written using the Notes app (see Figure 5–21). Using Froq or SQLite Database Browser will help you examine data from the file. The Note table holds the following data: the created and modified dates, the title, and a summary of all notes.

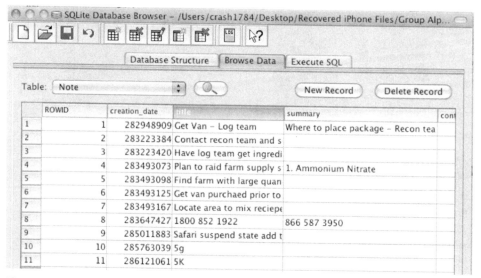

Figure 5–21. *The Notes table and summary of data*

Preferences

The Preferences folder contains a wide range of data that is usually ignored, but manual examination is an important component in a thorough examination. Table 5–5 shows the corresponding property list and the possible artifacts that can be located.

Table 5–5. *Manually Examining the Preferences Folder for Possible Artifacts*

Property List	Artifacts
com.apple.accountsettings.plist	E-mail accounts and settings
com.apple.AppStore.plist	Last application search
com.apple.AppSupport.plist	Country code of App Store used
com.apple.commventer.plst	ICCID and IMSI and international roaming setting
com.apple.compass.plist	True north or magnetic north settings
com.apple.locationd.plist	Apps that use location services

`com.apple.Maps.plist`	Latitude, longitude, and address of last pin dropped
`com.apple.MobileBluetooth.devices.plist`	List of paired Bluetooth devices
`com.apple.mobilephone.settings.plist`	Call forwarding numbers
`com.apple.mobilephone.speeddial.plist`	UID from `AddressBook` database, name and phone number of all favorites
`com.apple.mobilesafari.plist`	Recent searches
`com.apple.mobiletimer.plist`	Lat and log of times in different cities and time zones worldwide
`com.apple.preferences.datetime.plist`	Time zone settings
`com.apple.prefernces.network.plist`	Status of Bluetooth and Wi-Fi networks
`com.apple.springboard.plist`	List of standard and user-added applications
`com.apple.stocks.plist`	List of tracked stocks
`com.apple.weather.plist`	List of cities to track weather and the last update
`com.apple.youtube.plist`	List of all bookmarks and the last search term in YouTube

Subfolder SystemConfiguration

`com.apple.network.identification.plist`	Network settings of all networks that the iPhone was connected to
`com.apple.wifi.plist`	List of Wi-Fi networks that the iPhone was connected to include all SSIDs and the last date and time connected

Safari

The mobile version of Safari has always been on the iPhone since its first version. As with all browsers, you can acquire Internet history data from this location. There are three property lists: Bookmarks, History, and Suspended State.

You can create bookmarks by the user or sync them from the iTunes, as shown in Figure 5–22. The property list will give the URL and web site name.

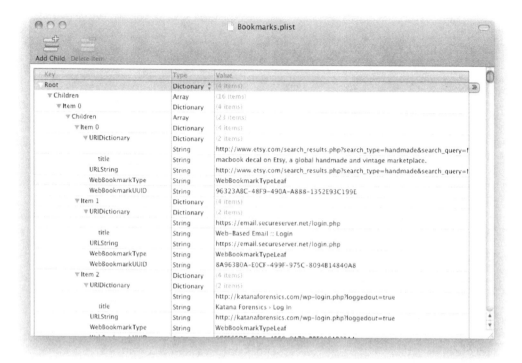

Figure 5–22. *Property list displays the URL and web site name*

Next is the Safari History property list. Each entry in `history.plist` contains the URL of the site visited, the site name, the visit count, and the date and time of the last visit. Figure 5–23 gives a sample of the `history.plist` entries.

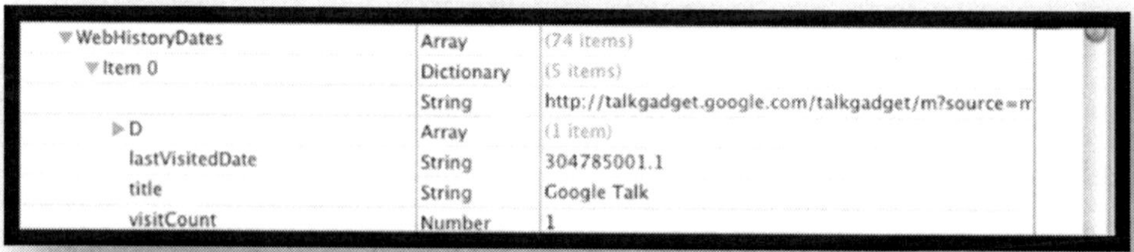

Figure 5–23. *A sample of the* `history.plist` *entries*

As Figure 5–23 shows, item 0 has the following values:

- *String*: The full path of the URL.

- *Last visited date*: 304785001.1. This is in absolute time; it's Sunday August 29, 2010, at 10:30:01 a.m.

- The web page title: Google Talk.

Suspended State

The Suspended State property list comes from suspended web pages in the Safari application. There can be a maximum of eight web pages that are stored in this property list. This sometimes can be useful information because users can keep these pages for fast switching from one page to another.

Figure 5–24 shows a suspended web page on an iPhone.

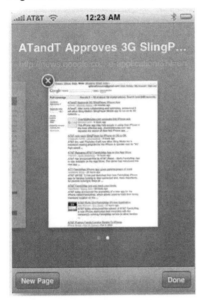

Figure 5–24. *A suspended web page as displayed on the iPhone*

The property lists tracks these web pages, as shown in Figure 5–25:

- The URL
- The title of the web page
- The date and time that site was viewed

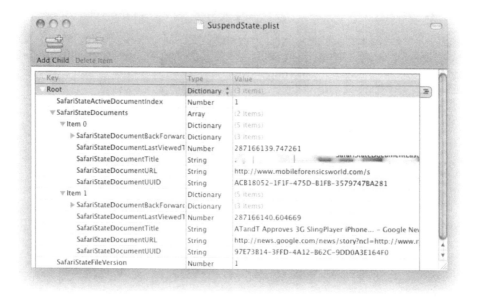

Figure 5–25. *Tracking web pages*

SMS and MMS

Located in the /Library/SMS directory, this SMS database is the container for text and media messages that were sent or received. The message table holds the date and time of each text, the phone number associated with the texts, and the content of the texts, as with other databases in the iPhone, in Froq, or in SQLite Database Browser. Figure 5–26 shows the view of this data.

ROWID	address	date	text	flags	replace
1	1	1279157908	Hello	3	0
2	2	1279158008	Fine how are yo	2	0
3	3	1279158331	So what are doi	2	0
4	4	1279164051	Apple sent an e	3	0

Table: message   New Record   Delete Record

Figure 5–26. *Sent and received messages data displayed*

The data in the SMS database is as follows:

- *ROWID*: This is the record ID for the text or media message.

- *Address*: This is the phone number that the message came from or sent to.

- *Date*: This is the time in Unix epoch time.

- *Text*: This is the content of the message. This may be blank, which indicates an MMS message.

- *Flags*: These are incoming or outgoing message identifiers:

    - 3: Sent SMS or MMS

    - 2: Received SMS

    - 4: Received MMS

    - 33: Unsent SMS or MMS

SMS message are also tracked in this database. However, the media content of the messages are in the same directory but in the subfolder /Library/SMS/Parts, as shown in Figure 5–27.

Figure 5–27. *SMS messages tracked and displayed*

In the SMS.db file there is another table for the MMS, called msg_pieces.

The data in this table will correspond to the message table and the Parts subdirectory, as shown in Figure 5–28.

ROWID	message_id	data	part_id	preview_part	content_type
		198 Another test p	0		1 text/plain
5	6	158	1	1	
6	7	158	1	-1	image/jpeg
7	9	804	0	0	
8	10	804 Calgary, Canad.	1	-1	text/plain
9	11	804	0	-1	image/jpeg

Table: msg_pieces   New Record   Delete Record

Figure 5–28. *The* message *table and the* Parts *subdirectory*

Figure 5–28 shows the msg_pieces table. It contains the following data:

- *ROWID*: This is the record for the MMS.

- *Message_id*: This is the message ID number of the MMS that corresponds to the ROWID number of the message table.

- *Data*: This will show any text sent along with the MMS.

- *Part_id*: This corresponds to the file name of the media, such as 804-0.jpg.

- *Preview_id*: This corresponds to the file name of the media, such as 804-0-preview.

- *Content_type*: This is the type of media, such as JPEG, PNG, GIF, MOV, AIF, and so on.

In the directory structure, the media can be manually located, as shown in Figure 5–29.

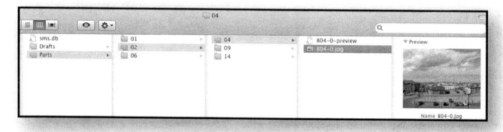

Figure 5–29. *Media manually located in the directory structure*

Voicemails

It wasn't until iPhone OS version 3.0 that voicemails were beginning to be backed up by the phone. The voicemails are all in an .amr file type that can be listened to by QuickTime. The number of the .amr file name corresponds to the ROWID of the database. Voicemail in Voicemail.db gives the sender and callback numbers and the date and time of the voicemail left by the caller, all displayed in Figure 5–30.

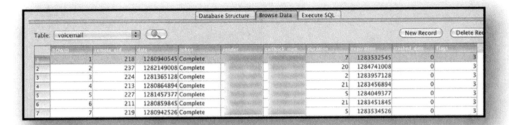

Figure 5–30. *Voicemail data displayed*

The voicemail.db is located in the /Library/Voicemail directory. These values are as follows:

- *ROWID*: This is the record number for the voicemail that corresponds to the actual .amr file.

- *Date*: This date is recorded in Unix epoch time.

- *Sender and Callback_num*: This is the number of the caller leaving the voice message.

- *Duration*: This is the duration of the complete voicemail.

- *Expiration Date:* This is in Unix epoch time.

- *Trashed date*: This value is in absolute time This is the date the user deleted the voicemail. Voicemails appear to be deleted to the user but are just moved to another part of the interface.

- *Flags*: This denotes the status of the voicemail.

    - 2: Unheard voicemails

    - 3: Heard voicemails

    - 11: Deleted voicemails

WebClips

The WebClips folder holds all web apps that are used on the iPhone. Web applications were the first type of applications used on the iPhone. They are still used today, and many popular web apps come from Google, such as iGoogle and Google Voice. Each web clip has an associated icon and info.plist. Figure 5–31 displays the WebClips folder. It contains the following:

- The URL of the web app

- The name of the web app

- The location of the icon used for the home page

Figure 5–31. *The* WebClips info.plist *data*

Figure 5–32 displays the icon for that web clip.

Figure 5–32. *Web clip icon*

WebKits

The WebKits folder contains information in databases from mobile web page. WebKits were designed to speed up the experience for the user accessing data from the web using HTML5 technology. Gmail is one of those web sites that drops a lot of information into a SQLite database. There is a subfolder called http_mail.google.com_0. The naming conventions of these files are as follows: 0000000000000002.db. As discussed earlier, use a SQLite application to view this data. Table 5–6 and Table 5–7 show the data that can be retrieved in this database.

Table 5–6. *Cached Messages*

Message ID	Message ID of the E-mail
Conversation ID	Used the thread e-mails.
isUread—whether the message was read or not	0–read 1–unread
isStarred—whether the message was starred in the GUI	0–no star 1–starred
isinbox—whether the message in still in the inbox	0–not in inbox 1–is in the inbox
Subject	The subject line of the message.
SnippetHMTL	Short snippet of the actual content of the e-mail.
Address_to	The e-mail address that the e-mail was sent to.
Address_cc	Any other e-mail addresses that were copied.
Address_bcc	Any other e-mail addresses that were blind copied.
Address_replyTo	The address that the sent message has as a reply e-mail address.
ReceiveddateMS	Date of the e-mail; this is in Unix Epoch time.
Body	This can possibly have the complete message in this cell; however, this is in HTML and can be carved any looked in any browser.
hasAttachment	This indicates whether the message has an attachment to it and the title of the attachment to include its file type as well. 0–No attachment 1–the message has an attachment

Table 5–7. *Cached Conversation Headers*

Conversation ID	From the Cache Message Table
isUread	Whether the message was read or not. 0–read 1–unread
isStarred	Whether the message was starred in the GUI. 0–no star 1–star
isinbox	Whether the message in still in the inbox. 0–not in inbox 1–is in the inbox
Subject	The subject line of the message.
SnippetHMTL	Short snippet of the actual content of the e-mail.
senderListHTML	Sender, or "me" and can tell the number of emails in the thread in parentheses.
numMessages	Number of messages in the thread.
dateMS	Date of the e-mail; this is in Unix Epoch time.
ModifyDateMs	Modification date of the e-mail in Unix Epoch time.
userLabelIds	This annotates whether the message has a user created label attached to this message.
has Attachment	This indicates whether the message has an attachment to it. 0–No attachment 1–the message has an attachment

Another directory that can contain other data is https_www.google.com_0. As you can see in Figure 5–33, it uses the same naming convention as the one found in https_mail.google.com_0.

Figure 5–33. *The* `https_www.google.com_0` *directory*

From the `0000000000000003.db` file, you can find a rather extensive contact list. This can come from Google contacts or a syncing computer. From the `Contacts16` table, the following can be viewed: name, e-mail address, and phone numbers.

> **NOTE:** It was once thought that no e-mail could be retrieved from the iPhone. That is because the mail from the Mail application of the iDevce was inaccessible from conventional forensic tools. However, as users install web apps and not those from the App Store, those artifacts will be present on the logical image of the phone.

System Configuration Data

The SystemConfiguration directory has a wealth of information that can be very important, such as network data and system preferences. These can give you various IP addresses and hotspots that the device encountered over time.

■ Autowake.plist: These are items that wake the device to grab information such as e-mail and push notifications, shown in Figure 5–34.

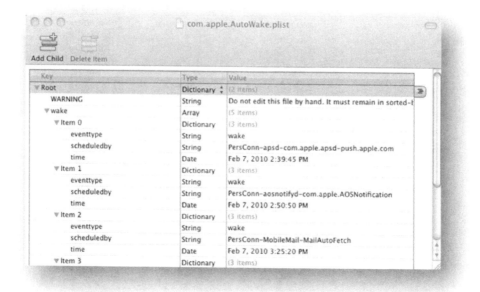

Figure 5–34. *Autowake.plist*

■ Network.identification.plist: This holds all the settings to include IP addresses of all the networks that the device connected to. Apple does this as part of its new feature that allows the iPhone to remember the settings and automatically connect to a network without user intervention, as shown in Figure 5–35.

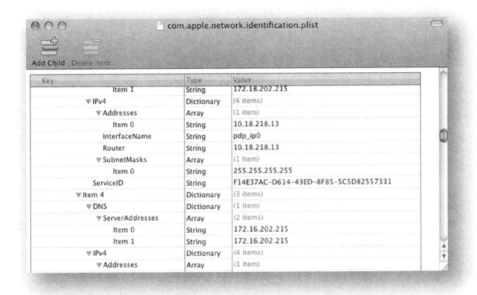

Figure 5–35. *Network.identification.plist*

- `Wifi.plist`: This is a list of all networks and their SSID information, as shown in Figure 5–36.

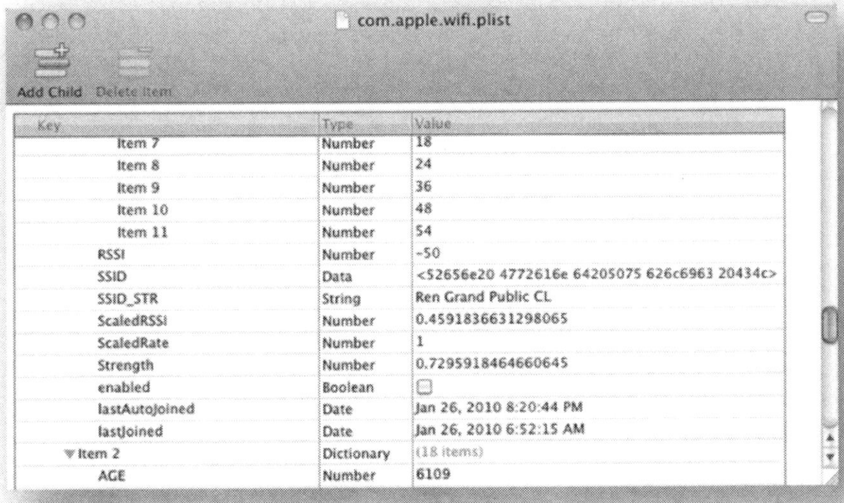

Figure 5–36. *Wifi.plist*

- `Preferences.plist`: This gives the name of the iPhone or iPod touch, as shown in Figure 5–37.

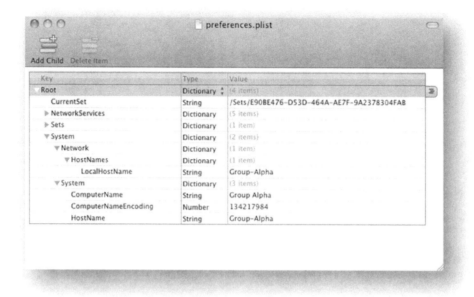

Figure 5–37. *Preferences.plist*

Media Domain

The Media Domain directory holds the images and recordings found on the iPhone. Since iPhone 3.0, additional data has been located in this directory, as shown in Table 5–8.

Table 5–8. *Media Domain Directory*

Directory	Artifact	Tool Used to View
Media	.m4a, .png, .jpg, .mov, .m4v, .mpg files	QuickTime, Preview

Media Directory

In the Media directory are all the images taken with the iPhone camera and the voice memos created with the iPhone. The first subdirectory is DCIM. In this directory you can find one or more folders. Application such as Time Lapse will create their own folder for the images that are created with the iPhone. The default folder in DCIM is 100APPLE. The images that are taken from the iPhone 3G and 3GS will contain GPS data as long as location services are being used. 2G phones will appear to have GPS data, but these are triangulation from cell towers. Preview is an excellent application to see all the data from these images. By default the Mac will open all images with Preview. Once they're opened, there is a menu item that can show all EXIF and GPS data. From the Preview toolbar, navigate to **Tools ▶ Inspector**, as shown in Figure 5–38.

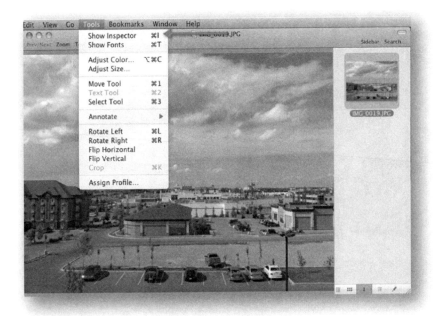

Figure 5–38. *From Preview, navigate to Tools and then Inspector.*

From the Inspector, you'll see all the EXIF data, the most important of which is the date and time the image was taken. The GPS data includes latitude, longitude, altitude, and compass direction, as shown in Figures 5–39 and 5–40.

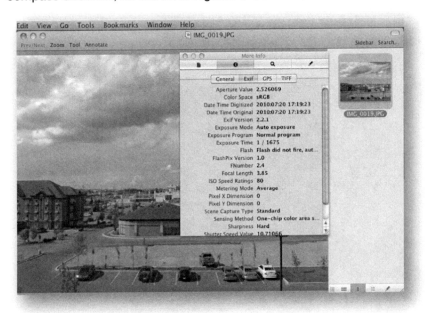

Figure 5–39. *Previewing EXIF data*

Figure 5–40. *Previewing GPS data*

A global map and crosshairs is shown in the GPS data box. If you export this image to a nonforensic system, you would just have to hit the Locate button at the bottom left, and the GPS coordinates will be sent to Google Maps, which will place a marker where the picture was taken, as shown in Figure 5–41. (You would take this data to a nonforensic system because the forensic workstation should never make contact with the Internet.)

Figure 5–41. *GPS coordinates sent to Google Maps and marked*

Why is this data important to investigators? These images taken with the iPhone can put an individual at a given time and place, which can greatly assist in investigations and interviews.

> **NOTE:** The GPS coordinates from iPhone OS 2.0 to 2.2 weren't very accurate. Pictures taken indoors have degraded GPS coordinates that appear to have been downgraded to cell tower triangulation. 2G phones do not have GPS onboard. Pictures will still appear to have coordinates in the EXIF data. However, these are cell tower triangulation coordinates.

Another analysis tool for examining photos from the iPhone is part of the iLife suite of tools: iPhoto. iPhoto has two things that can assist, such as geolocation and facial recognition software, built into the tool. All the images can be exported to iPhoto and examined. Figure 5–42 shows how iPhoto works with images that were imported and its ability to present geolocation data in a user-friendly way that any juror could see and interpret.

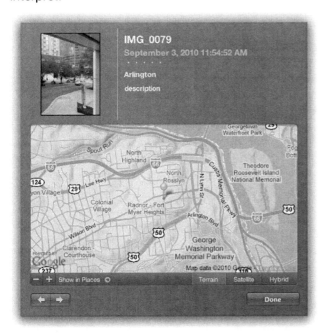

Figure 5–42. *Using iPhoto to display photos and data in a user-friendly way*

For investigations that require you to quickly sort images by people, iPhoto can automatically sort images by people's faces, as shown in Figure 5–43.

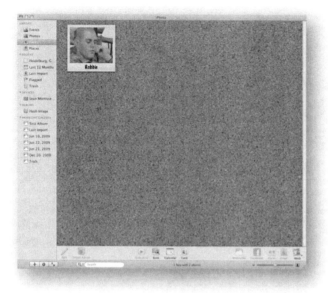

Figure 5–43. *Using the Faces tool to sort photos by a person's face*

In the firmware before 4.0, there also is a folder called .Misc. This contains thumbnails of all images from images created by the iPhone camera. These are used by the Camera app to show the thumbnails of the previous photos taken. For example, in Figure 5–44, circled in red is the thumbnail that is generated by the Camera application. The same is created in 4.0 phones; however, the path to the thumbnails is different, /Media/PhotoData/DCIM/100APPLE.

Figure 5–44. *Thumbnail generated by the Camera application*

In the firmware for iOS 4.0, there are two new databases that are related to images:

- `Photos.sqlite`
- `PhotosAux.sqlite`

Photos.sqlite Database

This database contains metadata in reference to images and movies created by the iPhone camera. In the photo table, the following are the types of data stored:

- *Primary key*: This is the record number for the image.

- *Title*: This is the file name, such as `IMG_0001`.

- *Capture Time*: This is the date and time the image was taken. This value is in absolute time.

- *Width*: This is the width in pixels.

- *Height*: This is the height in pixels.

- *Directory*: This is the directory where the image was created, for example `DCIM/100APPLE`.

- *File name*: This file name will also have the file extension, such as `IMG_0001.jpg`.

- *Duration*: This is for movies taken with the camera. This value is in seconds.

- *RecordModDate*: This is in absolute time.

PhotosAux.sqlite Database

The `PhotosAux.sqlite` database will contain all geotagged data from the images taken with the iPhone camera. The data is structured in the AuxPhoto table as follows:

- *Primary key*: This corresponds to the primary key in the `photos.sqlite` database.

- *Latitude*: This is the latitude coordinate.

- *Longitude*: This is the longitude coordinate.

Recordings

This directory will hold all the voice memos that were taken using the Voice Memo application. These recording can be played with QuickTime. The file name gives the date and time of which the recording was created. For example, 20091220 172138.m4a corresponds to December 20, 2009, as shown in Figure 5–45.

Figure 5–45. *Voice memos*

iPhoto Photos

There are two primary structures of how iPhoto pictures are stored on the phone. This is reflected in the change from iOS 3.1.3 to 3.2+. All phones prior to 3.1.3 are structured the same. Newer ones have the new directory structure. First let's look how the pictures were stored previously. Vendor tools such as Lantern can parse out the Apple .ithmb files that have been on iPods for years. The MobileSync database doesn't contain any of these artifacts. These are photos that get synced from iPhoto through iTunes and get compressed and placed into .ithmb files. The downside of this is that most EXIF data gets stripped to include all GPS data. So, if there are photos of relevance found on an iPhone or iPod touch, it is paramount to locate the syncing computer to find the original images.

In devices prior to 3.2, the structures of the synced photos were stored in .ithmb files. An Apple-proprietary compressed file that can hold many photos, as shown in Figure 5–46.

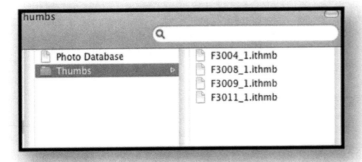

Figure 5–46. *Compressed photos*

There are Windows command-line tools and Mac GUI tools that can convert these files. For Windows, you can use `ithmbconv.exe`, a free tool. For the Mac, you can use File Juicer (not free) or Keith's iPod Photo Viewer, also free.

File Juicer is a simple and fast application that can convert the `.ithmb` file. All the images can be viewed with Preview. It is a low-cost app ($17.95) and consists of just drag-and-drop functionality. You can find it at `http://echoone.com/filejuicer/`.

In 3.2 and newer, the `.ithmb` files were removed, and the structure looks more like iTunes. They are no longer compressed and still void of any metadata. The structure is in the venerable iTunes-type directory structure in folders with names such as F01. The file name for each image is named like iTunes media files with a four-character file name, as shown in Figure 5–47.

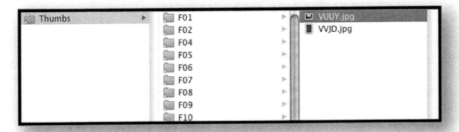

Figure 5–47. *Each image is stored and displayed like an iTunes media file.*

Multimedia

As with synced photos, photos synced from a Mac or Windows computer using iTunes are not found in the iTunes Backup or from the extraction done with mdhelper. These artifacts are found on the syncing computer or from the iPhone or iPod touch. Because these devices can download both video and audio straight from iTunes. Not only can commercially created media be synced, but the user-created audio and video can be placed here as well. Some vendor tools can retrieve this information. A Mac-based tool can be easily listened and viewed with iTunes and QuickTime. The directory structure of the iTunes data on iDevices has not changed over the years. There are folder names such as F00 and the four-character file name and the extension of the artifact such as .m4a, .m4v, and .mp3, as shown in Figure 5–48.

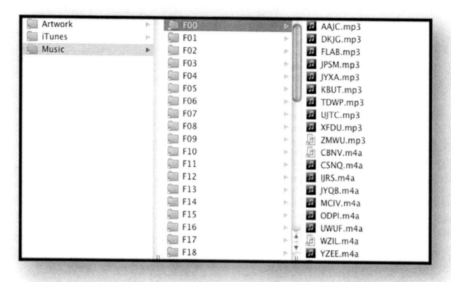

Figure 5–48. *The directory structure of the iTunes data on iDevices*

Third-Party Applications

At the time of this writing, the App Store has about 300,000+ applications for download. These applications are created by an army of developers from around the world. So, the data that can be garnered comes in different formats—from text files to property lists to SQLite databases, and so on. We will discuss some of the more popular apps and the kind of data that you can acquire from them.

This analysis is the most time-consuming because you have to examine it manually. Besides the more than 300,000 applications that can be purchased from the App Store, there are also applications that can be placed onto an iPhone from other sources. However, these phones need to have been jailbroken. For example, the Cydia Store can be accessed by jailbroken phones. These are generally applications that were denied acceptance to the App Store.

This third-party application data can be a wealth of information. What is stored is determined by the developer of the application and the type of data the app retains. Some of the data is in text files, property lists, and even SQLite databases. All the applications have a GUID number that is unique to that application. Within those folders, you can see a PNG file, which is the icon for that application, and a property list, which gives information about that application.

Social Networking Analysis

Social networking is the newest craze on the Internet and on smartphones. This genre of applications has become the new vehicle for communication. This is mainly textual data, but some of the apps also are vehicles for uploading photos and multimedia files. These apps should be explored for possible artifacts that may be beneficial to an ongoing investigation. Some of the applications discussed in this section will be Skype, Twitter, LinkedIn, AOL AIM, and Facebook.

The iPhone Twitter application has two important directories, `Documents` and `Library`. In the `Documents` folder, the following subdirectories exist:

- `Com.atebits.tweetie.application-state`

  - `App.state.plist`: Account information and tweets in order of follower.

- `Com.atebits.tweetie.compose.attachments`

  - Documents with hash numbers as file names that are actual attachments sent with tweets. These can be viewed with the Preview application.

- `Com.atebits.tweetie.streams`

  - There can be several property lists that hold numerous tweet handles (user names) and tweets with date and time values in absolute time. Additional information can be viewed as well, as shown in Figure 5–49.

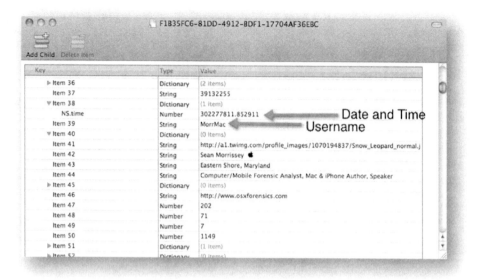

Figure 5–49. *Property lists display user names and times of tweets*

Skype

Skype allows users to make phone calls via a Wi-Fi connection from either an iPod touch or an iPhone; it's located in the `/Library/Skype/Application Support/[username]/` folder. Some of the artifacts that can be captured are the following:

- Phone call logs
- Account information
- Chat logs

Figure 5–50 shows what the directory structure of a Skype application looks like.

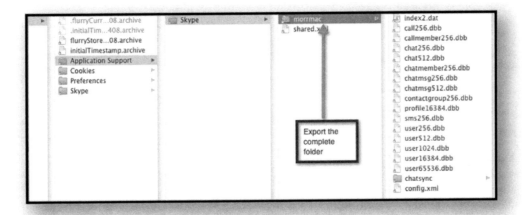

Figure 5–50. *The directory structure of a Skype application*

To analyze these artifacts correctly, there are two window tools that can assist in this type of parsing:

- *SkypeLogView, from Nirsoft*: This free tool can parse chat logs and create HTML reports, such as the one shown in Figure 5–51.

Figure 5–51. *SkypeLogView parses chat logs and creates HTML reports.*

■ *Skype Analyzer, from Belkasoft*: This is not a free tool but parses Skype calls and chat logs. This tool can also export to various file types. Figure 5–52 shows an example.

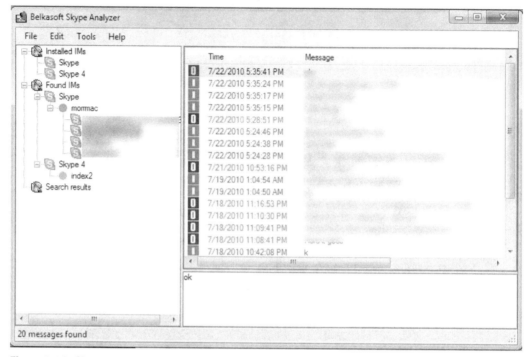

Figure 5–52. *Skype Analyzer from Belkasoft*

Facebook

One of the most popular application is Facebook. It has million users, which can lead to a wealth of information that can be useful in an investigation. However, on the iDevice, most of the artifacts are on the server side and not stored locally on the device. Some of the data that is present is as follows, as shown in Figure 5–53:

■ com.apple.facebookfacebook.plist

   ■ User's full name

   ■ Last Facebook read date and time

   ■ User's e-mail address

   ■ User's ID Facebook ID number

- Friends.db: List of friends associated with this application

    - Name

    - Address

    - Phone numbers

    - E-mail addresses

    - Facebook ID number

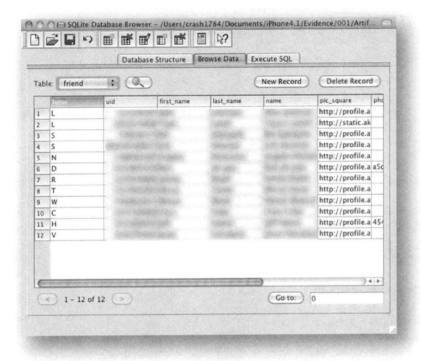

Figure 5–53. *Facebook data stored on iDevices*

AOL AIM

AOL is another chat client for the iOS. AIM has always been seen in OS X systems as a part of iChat. The following are the artifacts that can be garnered from any device that has this application installed, as shown in Figure 5–54:

- Account information

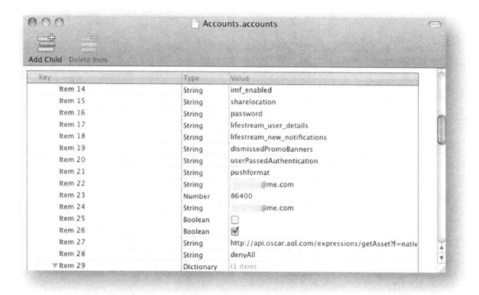

Figure 5–54. *AOL Instant Messenger artifacts*

- Chat logs with file names such as
  `[username]@me.com.conversations.+12073177913.history`. These chat logs can be opened with TextEdit or through the command line using the `strings` command.

LinkedIn

LinkedIn is a popular social networking service that could be a valuable list of connections in an investigation. These contacts can be downloaded to the `Addressbook.db`, and the images can also be imported to the `AddressbookImages.db` files. The types of data in the Member Property List are listed here and displayed in Figure 5–55:

- Name

- E-mail addresses

- Location

- Job title
- Created date

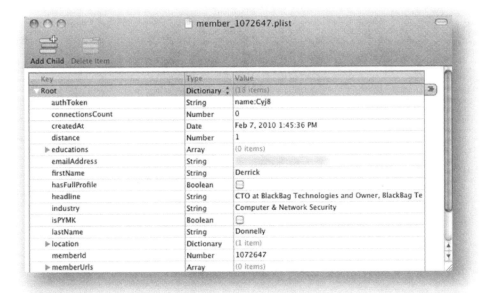

Figure 5–55. *LinkedIn artifacts*

Twitter

One of the newest fads in communications is microblogging, such as with sites like Twitter. Twitter is used by people who have things in common to receive information quickly; it is also used as a new form of marketing, and some criminal organizations have used this form of communication to share information quickly and efficiently. There are many types of Twitter applications—some free, some paid for. The artifacts that can be garnered from the Twitter application are account information, account information of contacts that are followers and followed individual, and tweets.

MySpace

One of the first social networking sites, MySpace has been the subject of many investigations. For example, in Maryland John Gaumer was arrested and convicted of the murder of Josie Brown. Not only was there cell phone evidence from call records, but it also came from Gaumer's MySpace account. From the iPhone there are some artifacts that can be retrieved, as listed and shown in Figure 5–56:

- Date of birth
- Gender
- Last date and time of sign-on

- User ID

- First and last name

- Cached images

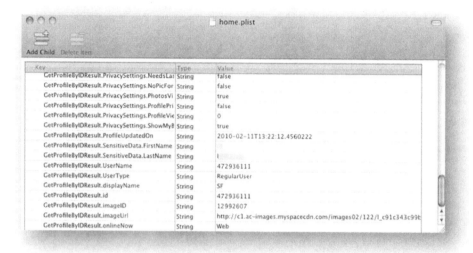

Figure 5–56. *MySpace artifacts retrieved from iPhone*

The information gathered in this property list can assist in furthering an investigation via subpoena and search warrants. As with MySpace and Facebook, it's always good to not forget about artifacts located on the provider's servers.

Google Voice

One of the biggest controversies that surrounded the App Store was the rejection of Google Voice. As a result, Google in its infinite wisdom has bypassed the App Store process and made Google Voice available to iPhone users as a web application. This could be the model of apps that get rejected and don't want to end up as pirated software on the hacker's sites. The application is quite simple and, with the addition of WebKits, makes the interface cleaner and more user friendly. The good news for examiners is that a lot if information gets cached onto the iPhone for better performance. The artifacts are in the same location as the Gmail artifacts: Library/WebKit/Databases. First you must look at Database.db, which gives the application that corresponds to the web app and the file name for that database, for example. Figure 5–57 shows this database and how to correlate the data.

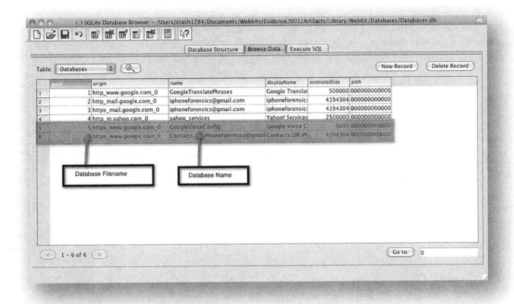

Figure 5–57. *Web app and file name display*

In the WebKits directory, there can be several subfolders that store SQLite databases. Each folder is used by a corresponding web application. Within these are file names that have several zeros and a number. Each number corresponds to the GUID number in the database, as shown in Figure 5–58.

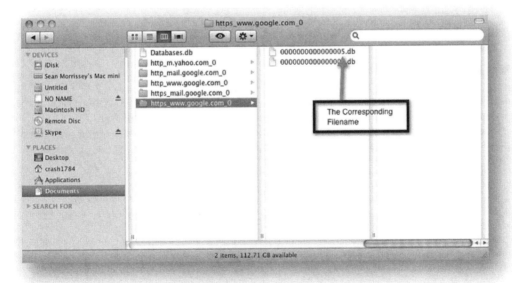

Figure 5–58. *Database and corresponding file name*

As shown in Figure 5–58, the database 5.db is the Google Voice configuration database. Inside this database is the forwarding number. Each Google Voice account has a forwarding number where all calls from numerous other numbers are forwarded. That number resides in this database and is depicted in Figure 5–59.

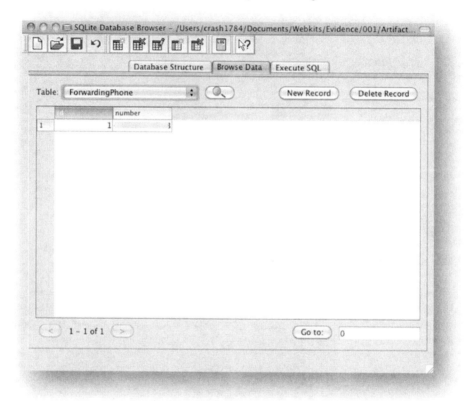

Figure 5–59. *Google Voice forwarding number*

Another artifact in the WebKit folder consists of ID numbers linked to Google Voice from the list of contacts from a Gmail account. That database is contacts.db@ [username]@gmail.com. This database can hold contact information from that specific Gmail account such as name, e-mail address, phone numbers, and so on, as shown in Figure 5–60.

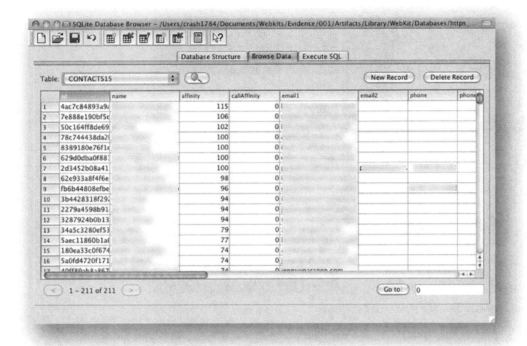

Figure 5–60. *Gmail account contact information*

Web apps are those developed by Google to bypass Apple's review process and still function as if they were an app on the device. It is possible that we will see more and more web apps that are developed with WebKit and then see more and more artifacts in this directory.

Craigslist

In 2009, Philip Markoff was dubbed the Craigslist Killer. In this case, Markoff found his targets from the use of Craigslist. The iPhone also has an app for Craigslist; it's called Craig Phone. The app is very similar to the web-based service. The user can browse the categories and even post items, as shown in Figure 5–61.

Figure 5–61. *The Craig Phone app for iPhone*

The artifacts are in the applications directory and can show a wealth of information; there are artifacts that show searches, with dates and times, as shown in Figure 5–62.

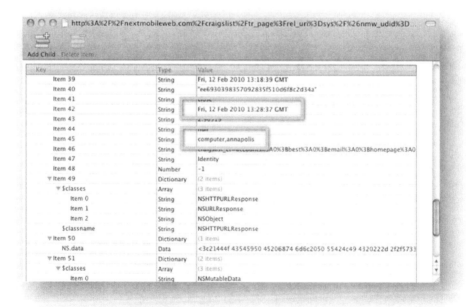

Figure 5–62. *Artifacts from Craigslist*

Analytics

Some third-party applications have embedded analytical databases within their structure to mine different amounts of user information. A couple of these miners are Medialets and Pinch Media, shown in Figure 5–63. Both of these tools create SQLite databases that can collect data and send that information to the collectors, which are the creators of the databases, and return the analysis to their benefactor and other organizations. Some of the data that is mined are as follows:

- Latitude and longitude

- Gender

- Birth month and year

- iPhone OS

- Generation of iPhone or iPod touch

- Jailbroken phones and applications

Looking for this type of data can assist you if other data has been deleted and the user doesn't have the ability to delete this data. The user has to know that the application is mining and then delete that application. This information can be valuable because it can reveal data that was previously deleted or reveal that the user didn't use the Maps application, which would not give an investigator any GPS data. However, within the analytical data, there could be GPS data. Sometimes these databases can be empty as well. So, it can be hit or miss, but it is still a good idea to look at these databases.

Figure 5–63. *Pinch Media, a third-party mining application*

iDisk

Not really third party since it comes from Apple, iDisk is an Apple application that syncs with a MobileMe account (see Figure 5–64). iDisk can hold a multitude of artifacts. Documents, spreadsheets, audio and video files, and DMG files can be uploaded to MobileMe via iDisk and then be downloaded to any iDevice. The iPhone, iPod touch, and iPad all have iDisk applications. This is part of the third-party application manual review that should not be ignored. MobileMe is also a content-sharing application on the Web. Knowing that this application exists is a good indicator that other data resides on Apple servers. Again, the power of subpoenas can aid in generating more leads and evidence in any given investigation.

Figure 5–64. *iDisk*

Google Mobile

Google Mobile is an application that can use voice recognition to conduct web searches. This was the only Google application that was accepted by Apple. (Other apps such as Google Voice did not make the cut and caused Apple to become the center of government investigations. Google, however, found it no longer had to create apps for the App Store and could use the new HTML5 and the web app approach to foster some of its other services such as Google Talk and Google Voice.)

In the Google Mobile directory, the following artifacts are possible, as shown in Figure 5–65:

- Cookies

- Search history, which is in a database that can be viewed with Froq or SQLite Database Browser

   - Date and time created and accessed

▪ Text of the query

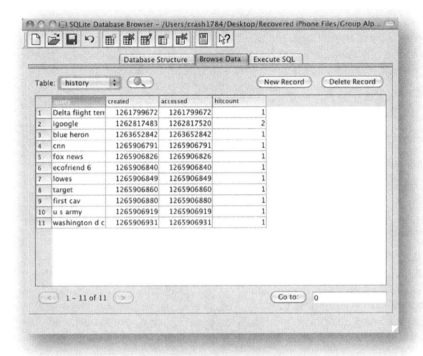

Figure 5–65. *Possible artifacts from the* `Google Mobile` *directory*

Opera

One mainstream browser did make it through the Apple gauntlet, Opera. Opera Mini is browser that can be used on iPhones and iPod touch. The artifacts are minimal:

▪ Images of bookmarked web pages

▪ Files that contain web history that can be viewed with the strings command or TextEdit

Bing

With the war between Apple and Google, it didn't come as a surprise that Microsoft's Bing would come to the iPhone and iPod touch. Bing has also made it the default web search engine for Safari. The Bing application has two SQLite databases of interest:

- `BIBookMarks.sqlite`

  - List of prepopulated and user-created bookmarks

- `BISearchHistory.sqlite`

  - Access date and time of the search in absolute time

  - The string of text used in the search

Documents and Document Recovery

With the arrival of the iPad, there came the ability to transfer and view Pages documents, Numbers spreadsheets, and Keynote presentations. There are also other office applications available such as Documents To Go. Applications such iWorks, Documents To Go, and Office2 are able to sync files over USB via iTunes. The documents can be examined using forensic tools such as EnCase, which can view the metadata of each file, as shown in Figure 5–66.

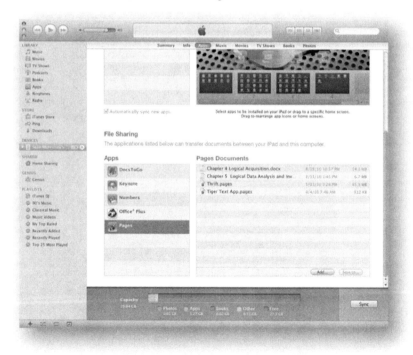

Figure 5–66. *Analyzing Pages files*

Pages has support for both Microsoft Word and Apple Pages documents. Complete documents are held in the `Documents` directory. These can be analyzed like those compound documents located in dead-box exams. Users don't just have to sync documents; they can create them as well from the iPad, as shown in Figure 5–67.

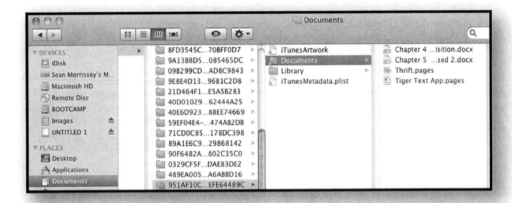

Figure 5–67. *Documents on the iPad*

In the application support folder there is a subfolder called `Documents`. Within that folder there can be multiple subfolders that are numbered. Each numbered folder will contain a preview image and any media that is placed within that document, as shown in Figure 5–68.

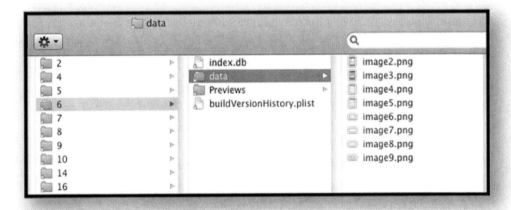

Figure 5–68. *Numbered folders with preview image and any media*

Numbers, Apple's version of Excel, can support Excel and its own numbers file types. Numbers documents are also located in the third-party application folder. As with the Pages documents, these can be analyzed just like other spreadsheets. The structure of the Numbers directory is the same as Pages, and the subfolders have the same function. As with its word processing counterpart, users can create spreadsheets from the device.

The Documents to Go app can store a multitude of file types including Word documents, Excel and PowerPoint files, PDFs, and images. Documents can be user-created and synced from iTunes. These can be synced wirelessly and retrieved from online services such as MobileMe or Google Docs. This application is very versatile and can store a lot of data.

Figure 5–69 shows the directory structure of this application.

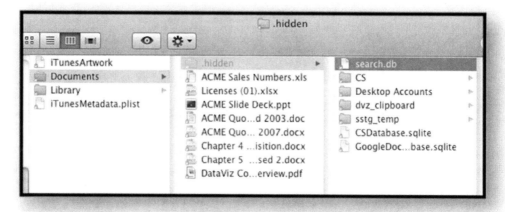

Figure 5–69. *The directory structure of Documents to Go*

The Documents folder will hold all the files that are contained in this app. There is a .hidden folder that contains more data such as the following:

- Search.db: This database holds a list of all files.

- CS: This folder contains a TXT file that is a log for the syncing with services such as MobileMe and can contain other files as well.

- Desktop Accounts: This contains even more files, but this comes from the desktop sync, not iTunes.

- CSDatabase.sqlite: This contains user account information from syncing services.

- GoogleDocDatabase.sqlite: This contains Google Doc account information, document folder information, and file information.

All these folders should be examined for relevant artifacts. This application can store items from multiple sources and multiple file types. As with all compound documents, data can be hidden in them as well.

Antiforensic Applications and Processes

There are some applications that have been developed with good intentions of securing user's data. However, these applications can take a more sinister twist. Several applications are available in the App Store that assist users in deleting free space on their device. Figures 5–70 and 5–71 are snapshots of some applications available from the App Store from iTunes.

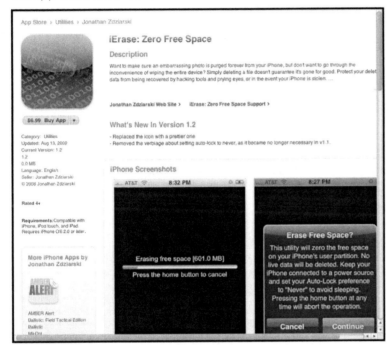

Figure 5–70. *iErase*

iErase is an utility that overwrites the free space on an iPhone and iPod touch.

Figure 5–71. *Shredit and Shredit HD*

Shredit is another wiping utility that has the capability to wipe the free space on a device to Department of Defense and Department of Energy standards. Shredit is an application that has a long history with Macs back to OS 7. Shredit HD was developed for iOS 3 and newer.

Image Vaults

Some applications offer the ability to encrypt images on the device and lock these files with strong passwords. However, there are some that are advertised to do the encryption and some that don't. You can even find the password in plain text in a property list.

Picture Safe

One application that I hope that bad guys use is Picture Safe. Figures 5–72 and 5–73 are snapshots of Picture Safe. This application does not encrypt images, and the passcode is in plain text in its property list. This app is very unsecure and can easily be traversed and the images viewed with Preview. The one thing that it does do is strip all the EXIF and geolocation data.

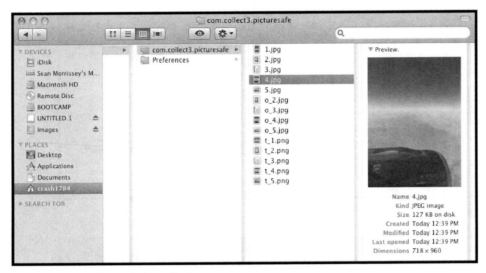

Figure 5-72. *The Picture Safe application*

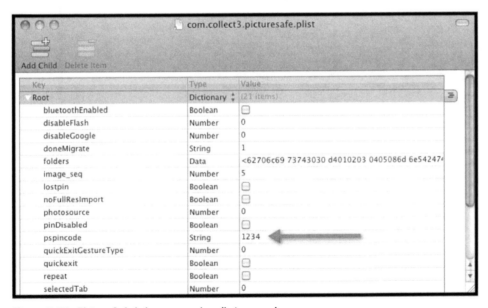

Figure 5-73. *Picture Safe is insecure and easily traversed.*

Picture Vault

Picture Vault is an app that actually does as advertised. This app does encrypt the images, and nothing is left in the plist for readable passcodes. Although Picture Vault used a four-number pass code, which was very visible in the plist, Picture Vault is secured with a strong password capability. Picture Vault is shown in Figures 5–74 and 5–75.

Figure 5–74. *The Picture Vault app*

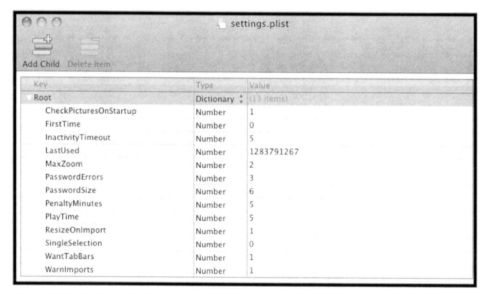

Figure 5–75. *The Picture Vault plist*

Incognito Web Browser

Incognito is an application that allows a user to not cache any web browser history, shown in Figure 5–76. However, this history may not be left behind, but there is a cookies.plist file that is populated. This list is just like any other browser cookies.plist, which would hold the following information (see Figure 5–77):

- Domain information
- Created date in absolute time
- Expiration date

Figure 5–76. *The Incognito app*

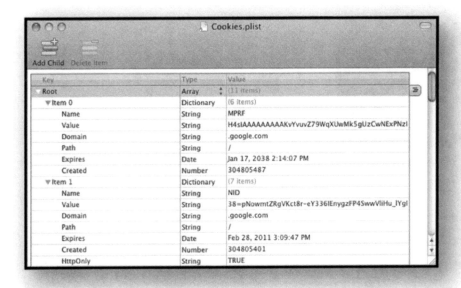

Figure 5–77. *The* `cookies.plist`

Invisible Browser

This web browsing application is designed for the iPad. This app, as with Incognito, doesn't save a lot of information. Even though it appears to have the same type of database found in WebKits, these files don't hold any historical information. However, there is the `cookies.plist` file, which does have the same type of data found in the plist in Incognito.

tigertext

A new app for the iPhone is called tigertext, shown in Figure 5–78. The premise of the application is that if both the sender and receiver use tigertext, all their communications will be deleted.

Figure 5–78. *The tigertext app for iPhone*

The settings of this app are listed as follows and displayed in Figure 5–79:

- User name
- Password
- Cell phone number
- Length of time until the texts are deleted
- Settings for deleting history upon closure of the app
- Settings for deleting the text after reading the message

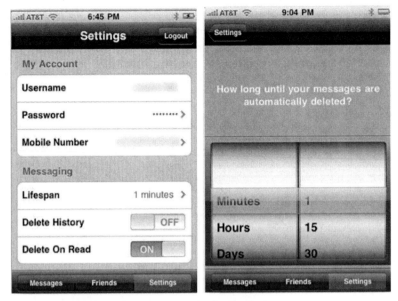

Figure 5–79. *Settings allow users to customize tigertext*

When a text is sent from a phone to another, the life span timer begins to start. This timer stops if the application is closed, but if the delete history button is switched to on and the timer hasn't completed its countdown, the app is shut down. The text is still there until the app is restarted and the counter is allowed to finish. Once the message is completed, paws appear in the place of the original text, as shown in Figure 5–80.

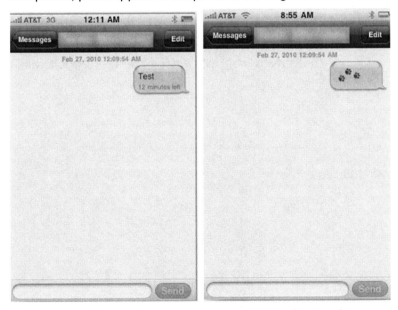

Figure 5–80. *A completed and deleted message is replaced with paw prints.*

So, the question remains, are the messages really deleted like in the SMS database? The answer is yes; they are deleted from their own SQLite database. Let's look at the database that is created by this application, as displayed in Figure 5–81. It's located within the Application folder of the logical image, at /Private/var/mobile/Application, as shown in Figure 5–81. The file name is tigertext.sql.

Figure 5–81. *The database created by tigertext!*

Open the database with either SQLite Database Browser or Froq. There are two tables of interest, friends and messages. The friends table will give the examiner the following information, as shown in Figure 5–82:

- Display name
- Address
- Phone number
- Date and time last modified

Figure 5–82. *The friends table in the tigertext database*

The message table, shown in Figure 5–83, can provide the following information if the application was allowed to delete the messages. The following data can possibly be retrieved:

- Sender user name
- Sender phone number
- Recipient's phone number
- Text message
- Date and time sent and set for deletion
- Settings for delete on read
- Whether the text was deleted
- Whether the text was read

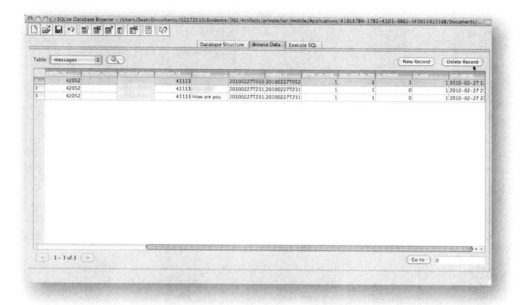

Figure 5–83. *The* message *table from tigertext*

After an examination of the database, Figure 5–84 shows the before and after of a message after the text was deleted by the application, and the paws remain.

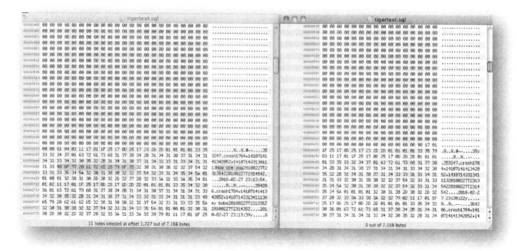

Figure 5–84. *Before and after snapshot of the tigertext app*

A search on the complete database confirmed that the text was actually deleted from the database.

Jailbreaking

Jailbreaking an iPhone has become a subject of great controversy until the Library of Congress issued an opinion on making jailbreaking legal. What the Library of Congress didn't consider in its opinion is the effect that this has on law enforcement's use of forensic tools. There are reported problems after imaging some of these phones. In Chapter 9, we will discuss the remedy to this problem.

Summary

The telephone data and third-party applications that are on the iDevices can be a treasure trove of information. In the world in information gathering, the iPhone has become a status symbol among terrorists and higher-level gang members who tend to have higher-end phones like the iPhone. It's an excellent tool for bad guys to use to network and communicate. An iPhone investigation isn't just getting the call logs and the text messages; there is a complete user history in the application data—from social networking, which is the fastest growing technology, to the advent of mini-blogging.

As you saw in this chapter, a lot of this data resides on the logical portion of the phone and is in plain text. Some applications can also geolocate, which will help pin down people's locations at specific times. Again, this data is on the phone and easily located and parsed. Bad guys will always finds ways to exploit these apps to further their ambitions. Always look at the applications on a phone, because you have no idea what you can find or what your missed.

This chapter dealt with the huge swath of data that is resident in the logical space on the iDevice. It would be a major undertaking to show how all data lives from more than 300,000+ applications that are now part of the App Store. You should always have at least an iPod touch handy to populate data from and see how information is placed on the device and therefore educate yourself based on the investigation at hand.

Chapter 6

Mac and Windows Artifacts

In this book, we've put a lot of emphasis on the iPhone and not a lot on the data that could be left behind on a Mac or Windows computer. Most investigators forget to grab any Mac or Windows computers or to specify within their search warrants that important data is on the desktops; these computers can have historical data and passcode-bypass certificates. Not everyone syncs their iPod touch or iPhone as often as in the past, because more and more information is able to be added to these devices without ever syncing with a desktop computer. However, when a new update is released from Apple, Apple has made it necessary to connect to a computer and update the device. During the update process and without user intervention, iTunes automatically creates a backup of the device prior to installing the new firmware. So, both on a Mac and on a Windows computer, there will be historical data left behind.

Artifacts from a Mac

You can find a few types of mobile artifacts on a Mac, such as property lists, the MobileSync database, and lockdown certificates.

Property List

Property lists include `/Library/Preferences/com.apple.ipod.plist` and `/User/Library/Preferences/com.apple.ipod.plist`. The library property list contains all the iPods and iPhones attached to a given Mac. The user library property list contains only those iPods and iPhones connected by that user. The data that is in this property list includes the last date and time connected, firmware version, IMEI, serial number, and number of times (use count) the iPhone was connected to the Mac. This data, displayed in Figure 6–1, is important to link a computer with an iDevice.

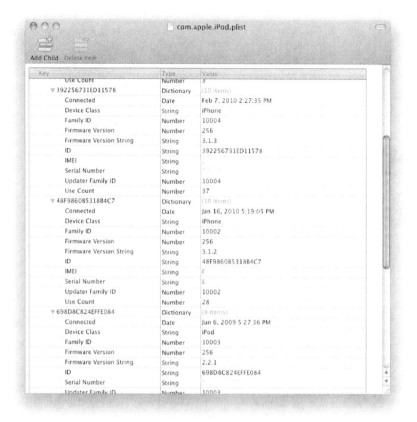

Figure 6–1. *Displaying the library property list*

The MobileSync Database

The MobileSync database is located in
/User/Username/Library/ApplicationSupport/MobileSync/Backup/[Device UUID]. The
MobileSync backup folder could have multiple backups from assorted iDevices that
have been synced to that computer. Figure 6–2 shows six devices were synced to this
example computer.

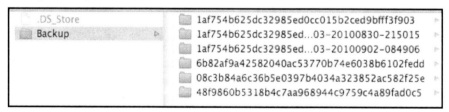

Figure 6–2. *Backups from multiple devices*

Apple Changes to Backup Files Over Time

Apple has made several changes to backup files and versions over time. The first change was with an extension of .mdbackup files. These files contained the data of the original file that was on the phone and its metadata. These .mdbackup files were seen from firmware 1.0 to 2.2 phones; Figure 6–3 shows some examples.

```
c4b37848cdbfc374e2...bc457e940.mdbackup
c5ac8af87a3850c95f...8d699ccfae.mdbackup
c6cba79ffe134520d0...e5934765d.mdbackup
c9da3d93bafd25a755...15568254.mdbackup
c22fa6d0608745dcbe...7ccd50447.mdbackup
ca63accd6d9ec43337...1ab9850cb.mdbackup
cd2f115fb55fb3045a...d6ec836dfc.mdbackup
```

Figure 6–3. *Examples of* .mdbackup *files*

When Apple released the 3G iPhone and iOS 3.0, the .mdbackup files changed to a set of two files for every piece of data backed up from the phone. The files with an extension of .mddata contained the data for the phone, and the files with the extension of .mdinfo contained the metadata in reference to the corresponding .mddata file. Figure 6–4 shows the two types of file extensions.

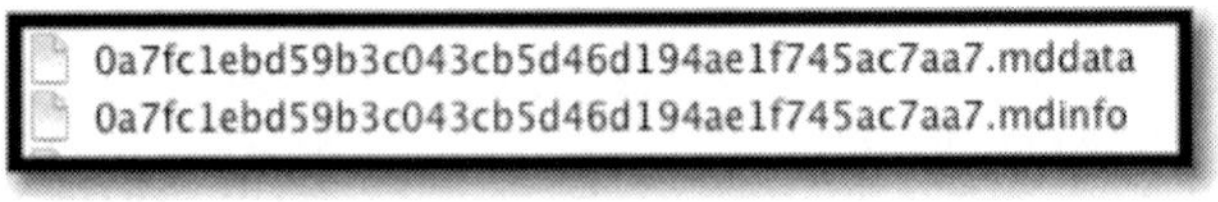

```
0a7fc1ebd59b3c043cb5d46d194ae1f745ac7aa7.mddata
0a7fc1ebd59b3c043cb5d46d194ae1f745ac7aa7.mdinfo
```

Figure 6–4. *Two file types for every piece of backed-up data*

With the iPhone 4 and iOS 4, Apple again changed the structure of the backup files. These files still have hashes as file names without an extension. This file type, like its predecessor .mddata, contains the data. Figure 6–5 shows the structure of iPhone 4 and iOS 4 backup files.

```
0a17684edfc1e7a3c8b0f3f0656509b9056286e3
0a509521c2daf30081adc6cf28690fa4e1d8c34e
0a209028622bd04ebe086bc820c979e71e867d79
0adc639ea39591b37f180f8dc545096d53750578
0b4bb5b184c6c4987005da650421182f9acccf99
```

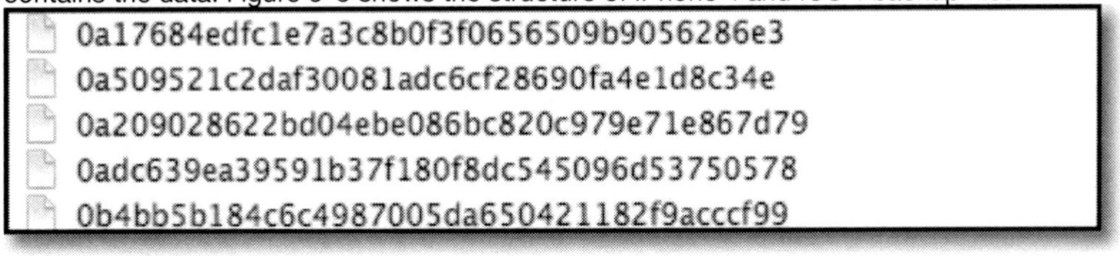

Figure 6–5. *iPhone 4 and iOS 4 backup file structure*

The file name and full path are located in a new database, manifest.mbdb. To view this data, you can open the file in TextEdit, as shown in Figure 6–6.

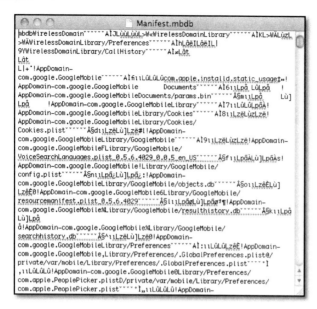

Figure 6–6. *Viewing the data by opening the file in TextEdit*

Lockdown Certificates

The last item to investigate on a Mac is the location of the lockdown certificates. The lockdown certificates are actually property list files that, if copied from the suspect's system, can allow the investigator to bypass the passcode on the device. The location of the property lists on OS X is `/private/var/db/lockdown`.

Artifacts from Windows

Windows has similar mobile artifacts related to iOS devices. These include the `iPodDevices.xml` file, MobileSync backups, and lockdown certificates.

iPodDevices.xml

The `iPodDevices.xml` file is located at `C:\Documents and Settings\All Users\Application Data\Apple Computer\iTunes\iPodDevices.xml`. This file gives similar information as in the Mac `iPod.plist` file. As with the Mac, this file can assist in tying the device and the computer together. This is important when finding photos that were synced to a device in order to then locate the computer that holds the original images. As stated earlier in the book, the synced photos don't contain EXIF data, but finding the originals will. The following are pieces of information found in `iPodDevices.xml`:

- Last data and time connected
- Firmware version
- IMEI
- Serial number
- Use count (the number of times the device was connected to the system)

Figure 6–7 shows a list of the output using EnCase.

```
1) iPhone artifacts\C\Documents and Settings\All Users\Application Data\Apple Computer\iTunes
\IPodDevices.xml

Devices

39Z256731E D11578

Connected
2010-02-07T23:59:10Z
Device Class
iPhone
Family ID
10004
Firmware Version
256
Firmware Version String
3.1.3
ID
392256731ED11578
IMEI
011949006894161
Serial Number
869233V53NP
Updater Family ID
10004
Use Count
2
```

Figure 6–7. *Listing of output using EnCase*

MobileSync Backups

MobileSync backups on a Windows system, synced through iTunes, are located at the paths in Table 6–1, based on the version of Windows. The formats of the backups are the same as on the Mac.

Table 6–1. *The Location of MobileSync Backups on a Windows System*

Operating System	Full Path to iDevice Backups
Widows XP	C:\Documents and Settings\[Username]\Application Data\Apple Computer\MobileSync\Backup
Windows Vista	C:\Users\[Username]\AppData\Roaming\Apple Computer\MobileSync\Backup
Windows 7	C:\Users\[Username]\AppData\Roaming\AppleComputer\ MobileSync\Backup

Lockdown Certificates

Lockdown certificates have the same benefits as those found on the Mac. They can assist in bypassing passcodes. Table 6–2 shows the locations of these property list files based on the version of Windows.

Table 6–2. *The Location of the Property List Files Based on Windows OS Version*

Operating System	Path to the Certificate .plist File
Windows XP	C:\Documents an Settings\[username]\Application Data\Apple Computer\Lockdown
Windows Vista	C:\Users\[username]\AppData\roaming\Apple Computer\Lockdown
Windows 7	C:\ProgramData\Apple\Lockdown

Analysis of the iDevice Backups

Both mdhelper as discussed in Chapter 4 and other tools can parse the MobileSync database. The mdhelper tool is a Mac binary, but the MobileSyncBrowser (MSB) tool is cross-platform. You can purchase MSB at http://homepage.mac.com/vaughn/msync/. The application costs $20. It is not a forensic tool but can assist in viewing the backup files in an iPhone emulator interface.

iPhone Backup Extractor

One of a few free (but closed source) Mac tools is iPhone Backup Extractor, which can be downloaded at http://supercrazyawesome.com/. This application will also work with the latest iOS 4 version of Backups. iPhone Backup Extractor is an extremely easy tool to use; just follow these steps:

1. After launching the app, you will see a Read Backups button, as shown in Figure 6–8. This button will allow you to read the backup from the folder where backups are typically located on your examination system, depending on the operating system version. Figure 6–9 shows the device name and date of the backup.

Figure 6–8. *Using the Read Backups button*

Figure 6–9. *Viewing the device name and backup date*

2. Copy the Backup folder from the suspect system, and then paste it in a location that would be normally stored on your forensic machine. For more guidance, see Table 6–1, which explains the location of backup files. The dialog box will ask which iDevice backup to examine and then which type of files to extract. The top files named are third-party applications, and the iOS files are the databases and phone data, as shown in Figure 6–10.

Figure 6–10. *iOS files appear below the third-party applications in this view.*

3. The output is stated by the examiner, and the selected data will be extracted for viewing, as shown in Figure 6–11.

Figure 6–11. *Listing of output using EnCase*

JuicePhone

Another great free (closed source) application is JuicePhone. JuicePhone is a Mac app and is also compatible with iOS4 backup files. JuicePhone can be acquired from www.addpod.de/juicephone. As with iPhone Backup Extractor, this tool is not intended to be a forensic tool. It is important to know that it is a tool that converts the backup files to a folder structure that an examiner can then look through and search for artifacts. Upon the startup of the application, JuicePhone automatically locates and shows available backups for conversion.

Figure 6–12 shows the startup screen of JuicePhone.

Figure 6–12. *JuicePhone startup screen*

The JuicePhone screen gives a lot of information about the backup:

- Device name
- Model of device
- Size of the backup
- Date of the backup
- Firmware version of the device that was backed up
- iTunes version that was used to create the backup
- Serial number of the device
- UUID of the device
- Number of third-party applications

JuicePhone has two ways to convert the backup: Custom and Complete. The Custom conversion will give you options about which applications to convert. The Complete conversion will convert all applications, the home folder, and Keychain.

This application will by default place all the converted files on the desktop, or the user can specify a different location. Manual examination of the files can be done after conversion. All the techniques discussed in this book will assist in that manual recovery.

mdhelper

mdhelper is a free command-line binary that can be downloaded at
http://ericasadun.com/ftp/Macintosh/. This application supports only those iOS
versions prior to 4.0. The developer has stated that she is exploring adding support for 4.0
in the future. After downloading that binary, follow these steps:

1. Place the file in your $PATH. For example, copy the file into /usr/bin. This will
allow the command to be used.

2. Next, open the Terminal application.

3. From Terminal, change the directory to back up the files, as shown in Figure 6–13.

Figure 6–13. *Changing directory to back up the files*

4. Hit Enter.

5. Next type mdhelper -extract, as shown in Figure 6–14.

Figure 6–14. *Typing* mdhelper -extract

6. Hit Enter.

7. After the extraction has completed, you should see the result shown in Figure 6–
15.

Figure 6–15. *Resulting screen from previous steps*

The output on the screen will tell you the device name and the number of total files
recovered.

The default location for the recovery is on the desktop and is called Recovered iPhone
Files.

The recovery is of all third-party applications and home domain files. This, as with all other backup recovery tools, covers all the relevant databases, property lists, and all other iDevice data. Figure 6–16 shows the resulting backup. mdhelper will work with iPod touch and iPad devices as well.

Figure 6–16. *The resulting backup displayed when using mdhelper*

Oxygen Forensics Suite 2010

Oxygen Forensics Suite 2010 retails for $2,000. In Chapter 5, we discussed that this application can analyze logical data from iDevices. Oxygen also has a Backup Extraction Wizard that can extract backup files from all versions of iOS. The extraction is done within the interface, and the outputs are placed in the same areas as with its live acquisition of iDevices. Figure 6–17 shows the wizard interface, and Figure 6–18 shows the finished extraction in the analysis window.

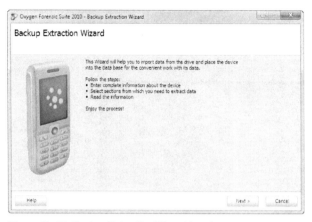

Figure 6–17. *Backup Extraction Wizard interface*

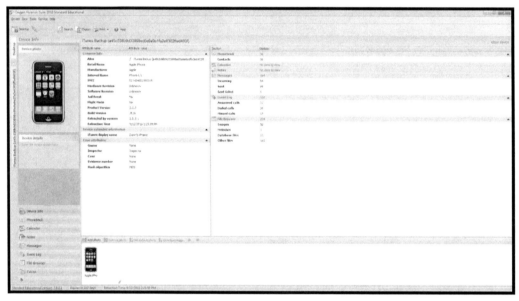

Figure 6–18. *The finished extraction in the analysis window*

Windows Forensic Tools and Backup Files

As you know, you can use a Mac to analyze the backup files quickly and efficiently, and the procedures that were covered in Chapter 4 apply to backups as well. You can use tools such as Preview, SQLite Database Browser, Property List Editor, md5deep, and hfsdebug.

What you might not know is that you can take the converted backups to a Windows forensic tool; however, you should be cognizant that Windows tools can't present the information better than on a Mac. First let's look at Guidance Software's EnCase. You'll need a virtual machine for these steps.

1. Start your virtual machine software, either VMware or Parallels.

2. Set up your shared folders from the Mac to the virtual machine.

3. Start the EnCase application.

4. Pull the extracted backup files into the EnCase as a logical evidence file, as shown in Figure 6–19.

Figure 6–19. *Extracted backup files in EnCase*

5. From here, some of EnCase processes can be completed, such as Internet history search, hashing, graphic review, bookmarking, and report generation.

6. For databases that are located with the backup, an external files viewer such as SQLite Database Viewer can be set up for those artifacts.

7. For property lists, switch the view to Doc to see those artifacts. If you do not like that type of output, another external viewer, PList Editor, can be associated with plists as well.

FTK Imager

FTK Imager is a free download from Access Data, which is at www.accessdata.com/downloads.html. FTK Imager is one of the best tools for just about anything. You can use this tool in conjunction with other free tools to finish examining the backup files.

1. Start your virtual machine.

2. Start FTK Imager.

3.   Add the contents of a folder to FTK Imager.

4.   Use other free tools from Imager to complete the exam, such as SQLite Database Browser, PList Editor, and Infanview.

FTK 1.8

Normally you would need a licensed copy and a dongle to use the FTK tool; however, If the total number of files from the backup does not exceed 5,000 files, a dongle is not necessary, so most backup files meet this requirement. FTK 1.8 can be downloaded from www.accessdata.com/downloads.html, and it's extremely easy to use. First you need to find out how many files are in the backup directory.

1.   Navigate from the Finder to the backup directory.

2.   Right-click and select Get Info, as shown in Figure 6–20.

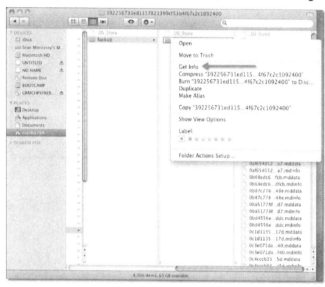

Figure 6–20. *Get Info option*

3.   Locate the number of items (files) that are in the folder, as shown in Figure 6–21.

Figure 6–21. *Locate the number of items.*

4. Start your virtual machine.

5. Start FTK 1.8.

6. Start a new case.

7. Go through the wizard.

8. Add the contents of a folder to add the backup files as evidence.

9. Use the processes in FTK to complete your examination.

10. You can view databases and property lists with external free programs, such as SQLite Database Browser, PList Editor, and Infanview.

Tips and Tricks

If you have trouble bringing in backup files from a Mac to a Windows tool, both EnCase and FTK support .dmg files (disk images). Using the disk utility, you can create a .dmg file, place the contents of the backup into this disk image, and then bring the backup into a Windows forensic tool. The following are the steps to create the disk image:

1. Ascertain the size of the backup files. Repeat steps 1 to 3 of the previous instructions for bringing in backup files into a Windows tool.

2. From the Finder window, locate the size of the backup, as shown in Figure 6–22.

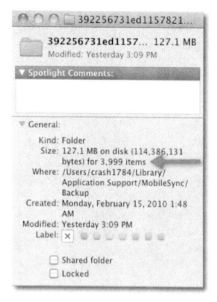

Figure 6–22. *Locate the size of the backup.*

3. Navigate to /Applications/Utilities/Disk Utility.app.

4. Double-click the app.

5. In the menu bar, select **New ➤ Blank Disk Image**.

6. From the dialog box, use the following settings, and always have the size of the image larger than the total size of the backups by choosing Custom, as shown in Figure 6–23.

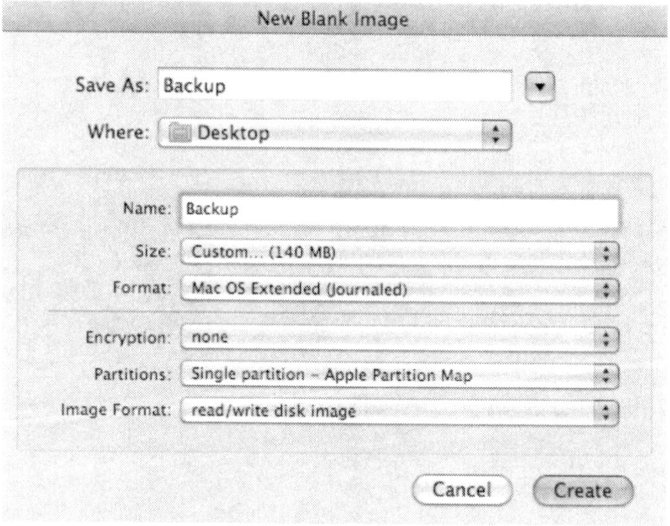

Figure 6–23. *Choose Custom to make the size of the image larger than the total size of the backup.*

7. Select Create.

8. After the image is created, it is automatically mounted, and the contents of the backups can be copied into the `.dmg` file that was just created.

9. Bring the `.dmg` file into either FTK or EnCase.

Summary

In this chapter, you learned there are numerous ways to extract and convert the iDevice backups. The iPhone, iPod touch, and iPad all can back up their data in case of catastrophic failure or in case the iDevice needs to be restored. This creates a history of the iDevice. Even though more and more items can be downloaded to the devices without having to sync to iTunes, a lot of backups are often located on Macs and Windows computers. Examining the backup files is no different from the logical extractions. The backups have all the same files except for any music, photos, and video synced from iTunes.

Chapter 7

GPS Analysis

The Global Positioning System (GPS) was first created and utilized by U.S. Department of Defense and consisted of 24 geosynchronous satellites. This, coupled with a GPS-enabled device, allowed an individual or weapon system to receive a value that would fix its location. These values were broken into latitudinal and longitudinal numbers and further delineated into degrees, minutes, and seconds. As we discussed in Chapter 1, the iPhone 3G brought GPS to the iPhone. GPS on the iPhone 3G was really Assisted GPS, meaning that radio tower triangulation was first utilized to ascertain the location of the device, and then the GPS receiver would then more accurately point to where the device was located. Therefore, with the iPhone 3G, the accuracy of this device was not very good. With firmware updates, though, the accuracy improved. The iPhone 3GS was a marked improvement in the accuracy of the device. In this chapter, we will discuss the artifacts located on an iDevice in reference to GPS.

Maps Application

Geo-location data is important to forensic examinations to place the device or individual at a specific place at a specific time. This can be invaluable information to assist in solving crimes and also to possibly locate perpetrators of crimes. The Maps app, which was designed to formulate point-to-point directions, has been on the iPhone since the iPhone 2G. In this version, these were not turn-by-turn directions as we know them from modern GPS devices.

Using the Maps application, the user can locate points of interest (POI) from the device that can give more detailed information for that location and to retrieve directions on how to get to that location. The next few figures will show how the Maps application can be used.

Specifically, Figure 7–1 shows the main interface of the Maps application. This window allows for searching by any keyword and also to get directions to a certain location.

Figure 7–1. *Maps application main interface*

Figure 7–2 shows a hit from a search for *Metro*; by tapping the blue left arrow of a hit, the screen switches to show more details of that location.

Figure 7–2. *Maps application searching for Metro*

The detail location screen can give a lot of information in reference to that search item. From this screen, a user can bookmark the location and get directions as well, as shown in Figure 7–3.

Figure 7–3. *Maps application location information*

If Directions To Here is tapped, a route will be calculated by Google, as shown in Figure 7–4. There is a Start button that starts the route, but each step is not automatic; the user has to hit Next for each waypoint.

Figure 7–4. *Maps application showing a route and start of directions*

This type of user input can be useful while conducting an exam. From either a physical or logical extraction, the following path is the default location for the Maps application: /Library/Maps. You'll find three property lists: History.plist, directions.plist, and bookmark.plist. The history.plist details all the queries that were conducted on the Maps app. The following information can be gathered from history.plist:

- The text of the query, *Metro*, was the input of the query on the app, as shown in Figure 7–5.

- Next there are values for latitude and longitude. Place these values into Google Maps to get the location from where the query was made. These types of artifacts can assist in possibly showing some premeditation of a crime by searching for and gaining directions from to and from a crime scene. This facilitates the ability to re-create directions to that location, as shown in Figure 7–6. The following are the latitude and longitude values from history.plist in Figure 7–5:

  - *Latitude*: 38.94725

  - *Longitude*: -76.86958

- Location of the query.

- Zoom level of the map.

- Longitude span, which assists in HTML markup in software tools.

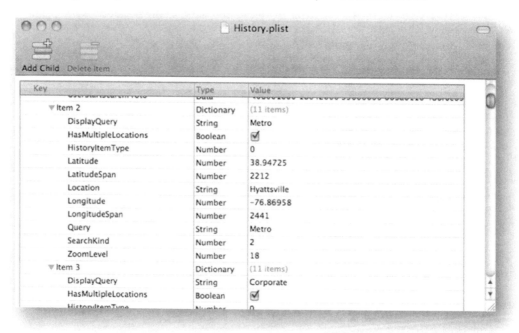

Figure 7–5. Bookmarks.plist

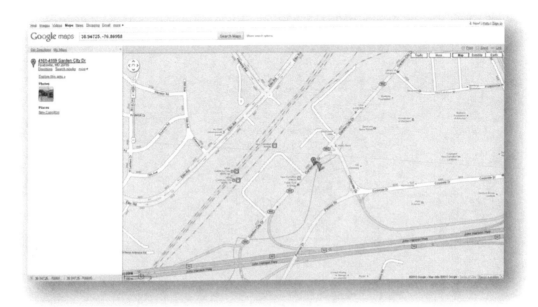

Figure 7–6. *Geodata as entered into Google Maps and the resulting location*

Numerous logical tools can extract data from areas that the mobile user has access to and can display such data. For example, Lantern parses these values and presents them on its GUI, as shown in Figure 7–7.

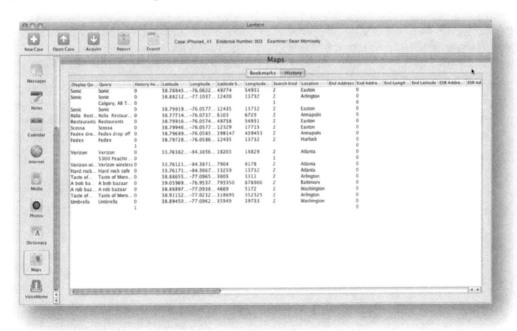

Figure 7–7. *Lantern maps history data*

Lantern also has the ability to export these values to a CSV via its export function, which then can be opened with applications such as Microsoft Excel, as shown in Figure 7–8.

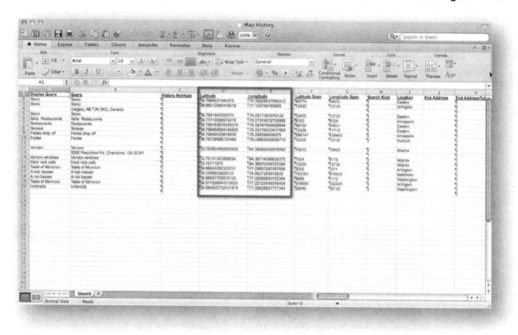

Figure 7–8. *Maps application data that has been exported by Lantern*

In Figure 7–8, the values from this Excel spreadsheet can easily be copied and pasted into Google Maps for rendering of these locations. As stated previously, you can ascertain the location of where the user of the phone was when the query was made.

The next property list from the /Library/Maps directory is bookmark.plist. Within the Maps application, locations can be stored as bookmarks for easy reference and retrieval. Most logical forensic tools can grab this information. Figure 7–9 shows a view of this plist from the Property List Editor application,

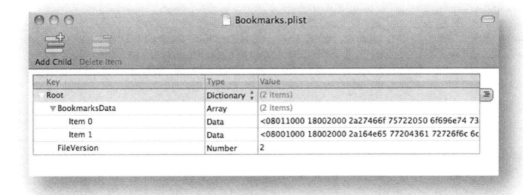

Figure 7–9. *Maps application* Bookmarks.plist *using Property List Editor*

As you can see, the plist has two bookmarks; however, the data is indiscernible. Now take this same plist, and open it with the TextEdit application, as shown in Figure 7–10.

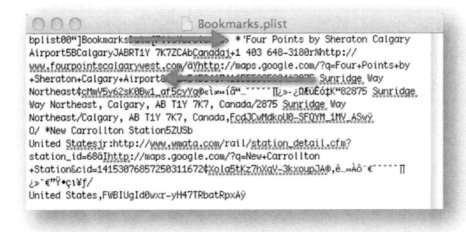

Figure 7–10. *Maps application* Booksmarks.plist *seen using TextEdit*

PROPERTY LIST EDITOR VS. TEXTEDIT

Property List Editor is a native Mac application that is part of the Xcode (otherwise known as the Developer Tools). Property List Editor can take the XML-formatted data and present it in a graphical user interface that can be easily read. TextEdit application is the Mac version of Windows' Notepad. It is a useful tool to view a variety of OS X or iOS file types. TextEdit will show only ASCII characters and sometimes is the only application to view a particular file.

As shown in Figure 7–10, after the asterisk (*) there is a location, for example, Four Points by Sheraton Calgary Airport. This is followed by a telephone number, a URL, and a Google search string. After the data, you can see a "cid" value. The cid is cellular identification. This is used by Google to reference a location against its internal database, which has a CID value for all locations. Figure 7–11 shows an example of the CID.

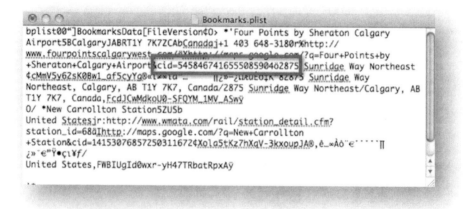

Figure 7–11. *Bookmarks.plist cid values*

Another property list from the /Library/Maps directory is Directions.plist. This property list contains data on point-to-point directions requested by the user from the Maps application. Figure 7–12 shows how the data looks when viewed with Property List Editor.

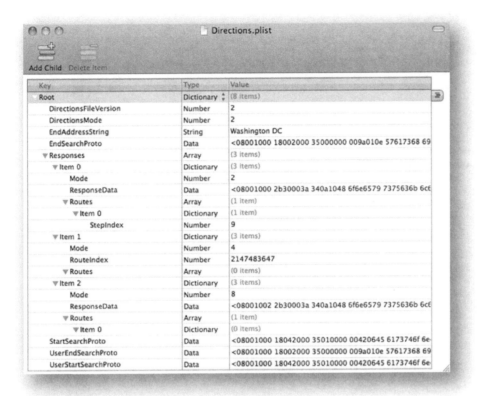

Figure 7-12. *Maps application* `Directions.plist`

As shown in Figure 7–12, the only discernable value is Washington, DC. Figure 7–13 shows that both beginning and ending points can be using TextEdit to view the file.

Figure 7–13. `Directions.plist` *seen using the TextEdit application*

These points of interest can be placed into Google Maps or a test device, and a route can be generated. This can be valuable information for investigations that involve an individual and to retrace the route that a suspect could have traveled. The only thing that can't be determined is who was using the phone at that data and time.

DETERMINING OWNERSHIP OF THE PHONE

Determining the ownership of a phone is like in traditional computer forensics when trying to place a particular person behind a keyboard. As in mobile forensics, one can gather all the data from the device, but it is still incumbent for the investigator to place the phone into the hand of a suspect. For example, asking a suspect, "Is this your phone?" If the suspect says yes, that needs to be notated in a report. If the suspect says no, well, then the investigator needs to document where the device was located, such as in the suspect's room, on his person, in his vehicle. This combined with subscriber information from a carrier will also assist in connecting a phone to a person.

Figure 7–14 shows retracing a route.

Figure 7–14. *Route re-created from the* `Directions.plist` *and using Google Maps*

Geotagging of Images and Video

Geotagging of images in the beginning was reserved for high-end digital cameras. Cell phone manufacturers saw the benefits of adding GPS to phones and then added the ability to add GPS data to the EXIF values on an image. Exchangeable Image File (EXIF) format is data that is generated from a camera and embedded into the graphical file. This is otherwise known as *geospatial metadata*. Now these values can consist of the following:

- Latitude

- Longitude

- Altitude

- Compass heading

- Accuracy data

On an iPhone, the concept of geotagging arrived with the iPhone 3G and iOS 3. Both the iPhone 2G and iPhone 3G had the ability to geotag images. Images that were taken with the iPhone camera are stored in the `/Media/DCIM/100APPLE` directory. The iPhone 2G did not have a GPS receiver but derived its geospatial data from cell tower triangulation. Figure 7–15 shows an image taken with a iPhone 2G with iOS 3, with the resulting geodata.

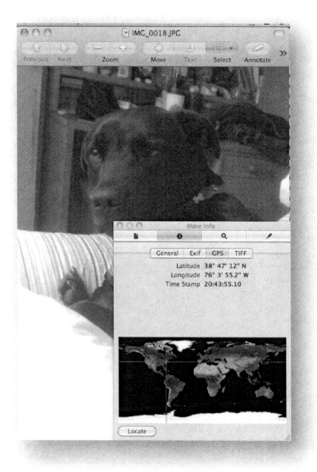

Figure 7–15. *Preview application showing geotag information from the Inspector function*

Just a reminder, the iPhone 2G uses cell tower triangulation when embedding geotag EXIF data into images. To demonstrate the accuracy of the iPhone 2G, Figure 7–16 shows the geotagged location, and the arrow shows that the actual location is off the map.

Figure 7–16. *iPhone 2G geotagged EXIF data placed into Google Maps*

In the further development of newer iPhones and firmware, the accuracy of the devices improved. Also, the amount of geospatial data improved as well. In the iPhone 2G, all that was given was the latitude and longitude. This was enhanced by adding values such as the altitude, satellite time, and compass heading from the onboard compass on the iPhone 3GS. Figure 7–17 shows the geodata on an image taken on the iPhone 4, by utilizing the Preview application.

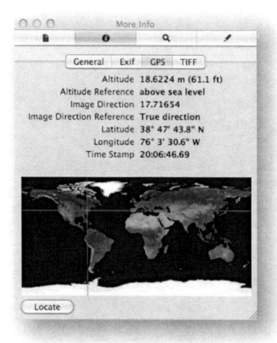

Figure 7–17. *Preview Inspector GPS data and the Locate button*

As shown in Figure 7–17, the values that can be shown are as follows:

- *Altitude*: In feet.

- *Altitude reference*: Above or below sea level.

- *Image direction*: Compass heading from O to 360 degrees from the compass application, as shown in Figure 7–18 (using different values than in Figure 7–17).

Figure 7–18. *Compass application interface*

- *Image direction reference*: This can be two settings, again also from the compass application, as shown in Figure 7–19.

Figure 7–19. *Compass application North Pole settings*

- *Latitude*: In degrees, minutes, and seconds.
- *Longitude*: In degrees, minutes, and seconds.
- *Time stamp*: In satellite time—hours, minutes, seconds, milliseconds.

There are logical tools that can aid in reporting geodata and using Google Maps to show the location of images. However, these applications need access to the Internet to allow the data to be presented. Forensic tools should not be connected to the Internet at any time. Depending on the licensing of the tool from its developers, two copies of an application is needed: one that never connects to the Internet (the forensic workstation) and one that is connected to the Internet to use functions from web-based applications such as Google Maps. There is a free tool that can assist in this without purchasing two copies. It is called CocoaSlideShow. This is a free Mac tool and can be downloaded at http://code.google.com/p/cocoaslideshow/.

Figure 7–20 shows the menu bar of CocoaSlideShow.

Figure 7–20. *CocoaSlideShow menu bar*

- *Set Directory*: This points to the directory where the images where will be imported.

- *Add Files*: Single or multiple files can be added to the app.

- *Flag*: Single files can be flagged/bookmarked.

- *Slideshow*: This is not needed.

- *Google Map*: This will render the location of the geodata of an image.

- *Rotate Left*: This will rotate the image: not needed.

- *Rotate Right*: This will rotate the image: not needed.

- *Remove*: This removes files from the application.

- *Move to trash*: *Do not use this*. It will delete the image.

The following will detail how to use this application and add geodata to reports:

1. Start the CocoaSlideShow app.

2. Click the Set Directory icon.

3. Navigate to the directory where the iDevice images are located. For example, Lantern reconstructs the directory structure of the iDevice. In the Extraction folder, navigate to [Case File Directory Name]/ Evidence/[Extraction Number/Name]/Artifacts/Media/DCIM/100APPLE.

4. Select Open.

   All the images will be presented in the left pane, and the view pane is on the right.

   As the image is highlighted from the left page, and if there is geodata, the Google Maps icon will change from a grayed-out status to Red, as shown in Figure 7–21.

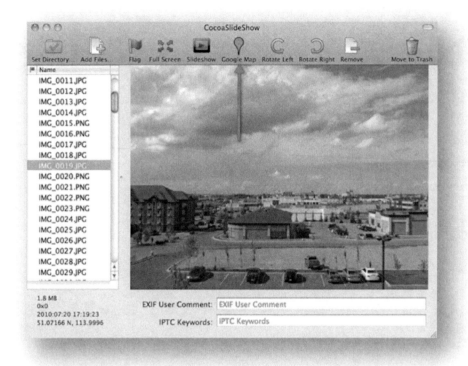

Figure 7–21. *CocoaSlideShow and the Google Map button*

5. To see the location of the embedded geodata, click the Google Maps icon, and the view pane will switch from image view to Google Map view, as shown in Figure 7–22.

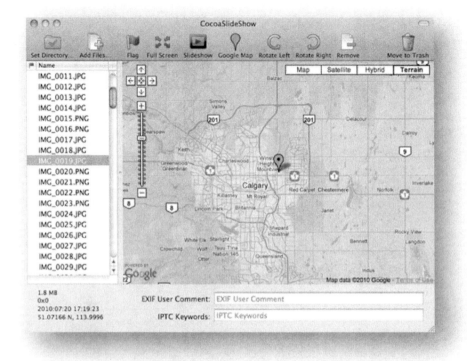

Figure 7–22. *CocoaSlideShow utilizing Google Maps*

6. A screenshot can be taken with applications such Snagit and Grab; download Snagit at www.techsmith.com/snagitmac/. Snagit has some functions that can be used for presentation such as blur, arrows, and text, which can be added to the screenshot. Also, there is a keyboard shortcut that will allow for screen captures. The shortcuts are as follows:

   - *Shift+Command+4*: Article will show up on the desktop, and you can manually select and area of the desktop for capture. The image is automatically saved on the desktop.

   - *Shift+Command+3*: This will take a screenshot of the complete desktop. The image is automatically saved on the desktop.

   - *Shift+Command+4+spacebar*: This will generate a camera icon. When an active window is selected, click your touchpad, and the imaged is saved as in the previous two items.

Images can be exported as an KML file and imported into Google Earth. First download the Google Earth application onto the Mac. The location for Google Earth is www.google.com/earth/download/ge/agree.html. The following are the steps to flag the image and export those selected as a KML file:

1. From the CocoaSlideShow application menu, select **Edit ➤ Select All**.

Then all the images will be highlighted.

2. Select **Image ➤ Export KML File**. Then save the file to the location of your choice. Also thumbnail images can be added to the KML file, as shown in Figure 7–23.

Figure 7–23. *KML Export function*

3. Open the Google Earth application.

4. From the menu bar, select **File ➤ Open**.

5. Navigate to the CocoaSlideShow.kml file.

6. Select Open.

All the images with GPS data will have yellow pins on the map. Also, in the Places window, all the images are displayed and can be selected individually, as shown in Figure 7–24.

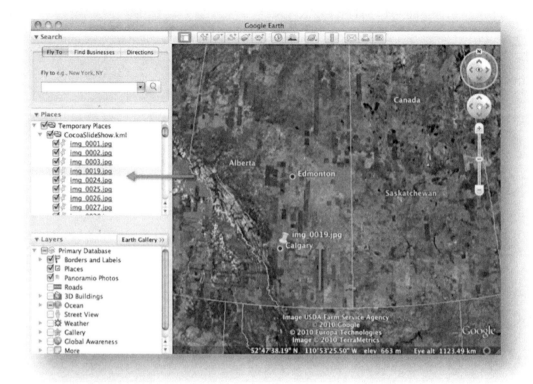

Figure 7–24. *KML export brought into Google Maps*

With the saved thumbnails, it is then possible to view the image associated with that location (Figure 7–25). This is a helpful way to present images and locations to investigators and prosecutors. This is good to use in showing the original image and the mapped location and is useful in a courtroom presentation.

Figure 7–25. *Image as seen in Google Maps from the KML export*

For geotagged videos, most forensic tools can't detect the geodata that is embedded within movie files taken with the iPhone camera. The reason for this is because of the placement of the data toward the end of the file, which is not in a standard EXIF location. This is demonstrated by looking at a MOV file using a hex editor, as shown in Figure 7–26.

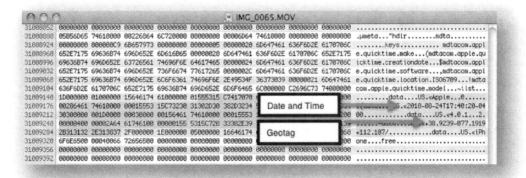

Figure 7–26. *Video geotag data seen with a hex editor*

The values from the Figure 7–26 can be placed into Google Earth, and a location can be determined. Since the addition of video creation from the iPhone camera, there has been geodata within them. The iDevices create MOV files, which can be viewed using the QuickTime application. These files are located within the same directory that the images are located in, /Media/DCIM/100APPLE. To view the geodata from a MOV file, follow these steps:

1.   Open the MOV file with the QuickTime app.

2.   From the menu bar, select **Window ➤ Show Movie Inspector**.

From the Movie Inspector box, you can see the latitude and longitude values for that movie, as shown in Figure 7–27.

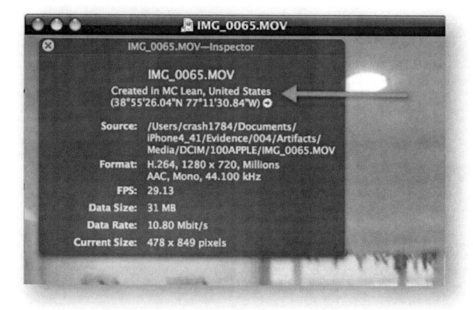

Figure 7–27. *QuickTime geodata from inspector*

Cell Tower Data

Cell tower data also has geospatial data. This data covers all cell towers that the iDevice comes into contact with. This list can be very extensive and can assist in investigations of placing a phone in a general area from a cell tower on a given date and time. These data points have changed file types over time. They were first seen as property lists and now are SQLite databases. Some were not in the logical portion of the extraction, but now on the iPhone 4, you can see that data.

The next item of investigative interest is in the root/Library/Caches/locationd directory. On an iPhone 4, you can now find the location and tower data in the logical directory structure. The files that are in this folder are as follows:

- Consolidated.db
- gyroCal.db
- clients.plist

On iPhone 3GS and older, several property lists deal with cell towers and GPS coordinates:

- Cells.plist: This gives the latitude and longitude for the cell towers that the phone has associated with its area code range (shown in Figure 7–28).

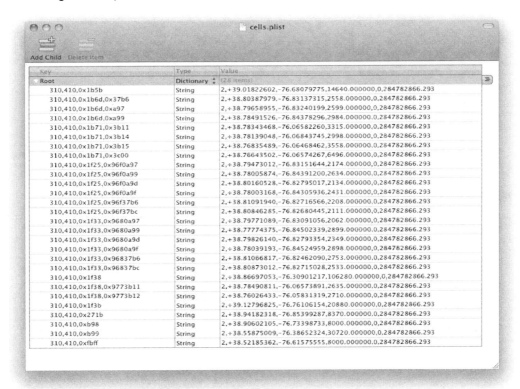

Figure 7–28. *Cell tower data from* `consolidated.db`

- Clients-b.plist: This property list has a list of blacklisted applications and the date and time that the list was generated. This is a list of installed applications on the phone and had been reported that this information gets transmitted to Apple (shown in Figure 7–29).

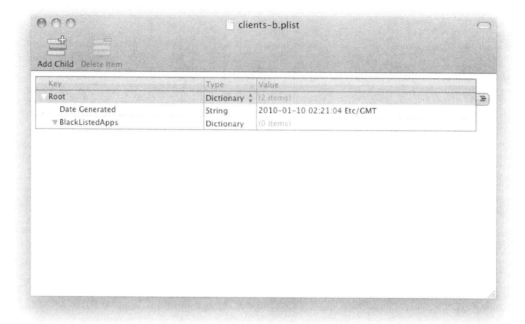

Figure 7–29. *Blacklist applications*

- H-cells.plist: This property list appears to give not only the latitude and longitude from where the cell phone was in relation to the cell tower but also the compass heading from it (see Figure 7–30). The compass heading is very important so you can get an azimuth from the cell tower to the iPhone. All these values—latitude, longitude, and azimuth—combined can give an approximate location of the iPhone. A date and time value is also given in the property list. So the following data, combined with other values, can possibly be used to re-create route taken by the device:

  - Latitude

  - Longitude

  - Course (compass heading)

  - Speed

  - Horizontal and vertical accuracy

  - Date and time—absolute time

  It is easy to see how cell phone companies can also get that type of information from legal paper sent to the provider. Then comparing the two sets of data can be invaluable.

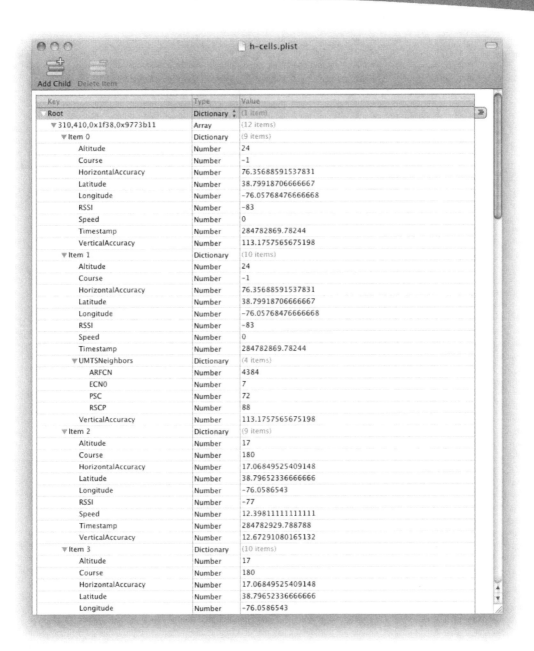

Figure 7–30. *h-cells.plist data*

- H-wifi.plist: This property list gives a historical list of GPS coordinates, in reference to WiFi connections that the iDevice has been in contact with. The plist contains the following values (see Figure 7–31). This is can be compared to data from a war-driving application.

  - Age/time

  - Altitude

  - Course (compass heading)

  - Horizontal accuracy

  - Latitude

  - Longitude

  - Speed

  - Timestamp absolute time

  - Vertical accuracy

Key	Type	Value
▼ Root	Dictionary	(14 items)
▼ 0:13:7f:8c:3e:21	Dictionary	(10 items)
Age	Number	0
Altitude	Number	9
Course	Number	178
HorizontalAccuracy	Number	17.06849525409148
Latitude	Number	38.7790975
Longitude	Number	-76.06024941666666
RSSI	Number	-92
Speed	Number	21.40088888888889
Timestamp	Number	284783053.461732
VerticalAccuracy	Number	23.16414931941728
▼ 0:13:7f:8c:3e:22	Dictionary	(10 items)
Age	Number	0
Altitude	Number	9
Course	Number	178
HorizontalAccuracy	Number	17.06849525409148
Latitude	Number	38.7790975
Longitude	Number	-76.06024941666666
RSSI	Number	-93
Speed	Number	21.40088888888889
Timestamp	Number	284783053.461732
VerticalAccuracy	Number	23.16414931941728
▼ 0:14:6c:d6:82:72	Array	(2 items)
▼ Item 0	Dictionary	(10 items)
Age	Number	0.129
Altitude	Number	24
Course	Number	-1
HorizontalAccuracy	Number	76.35688591537831
Latitude	Number	38.79918706666667
Longitude	Number	-76.05768476666668
RSSI	Number	-51
Speed	Number	0
Timestamp	Number	284782869.78244
VerticalAccuracy	Number	113.1757565675198
▼ Item 1	Dictionary	(10 items)
Age	Number	0.147
Altitude	Number	24
Course	Number	-1
HorizontalAccuracy	Number	76.35688591537831
Latitude	Number	38.79918706666667
Longitude	Number	-76.05768476666668

Figure 7–31. *H-Wifi.plist*

- Cache.plist: This gives the last GPS fix for the iPhone (see Figure 7–32).

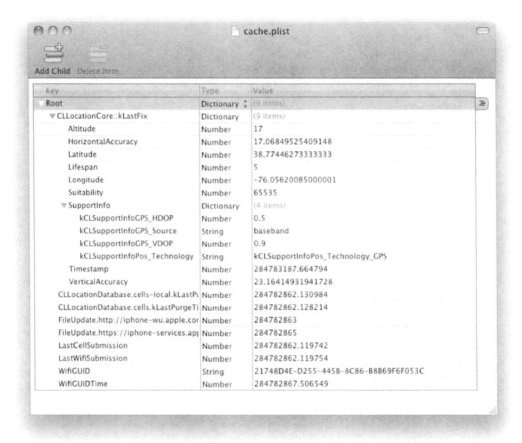

Figure 7–32. *Last reported GPS fix for the device*

GeoHunter

Katana forensics engineers have created technology called GeoHunter, which can take these property lists and convert them into viewable reports, as in Figure 7–33.

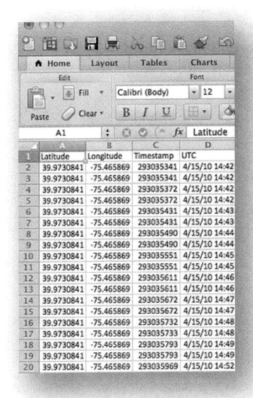

Figure 7–33. *GeoHunter output*

These values can then be converted to KML files for use into Google Maps. There is a web page that is free, which will convert the values from a CSV or XLS file and convert the values to a KML file. The following is how to use these sites:

1. Go to http://www.earthpoint.us/ExcelToKml.aspx.

2. From the web page, find and select Choose File, as shown in Figure 7–34.

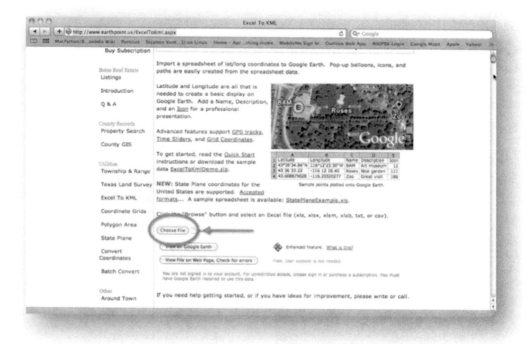

Figure 7–34. *Earthpoint web interface*

3. Navigate to the CSV or XLS files; for this example, the output form GeoHunter is chosen.

4. Select View on Google Earth.

   A KML file is generated and downloaded to your downloads directory on the Mac.

5. Double-click the KML file, and Google Earth will open and the points can be traversed, as shown in Figure 7–35.

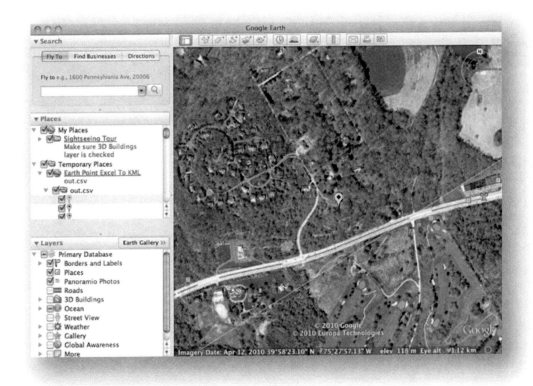

Figure 7–35. *Earthpoint output*

Another great site is GPS Visualizer at www.gpsvisualizer.com/
map_input?form=googleearth.

This has even more enhanced features such global support, and this shows all towers
associated with a given location and shows location data, as shown in Figure 7–36.

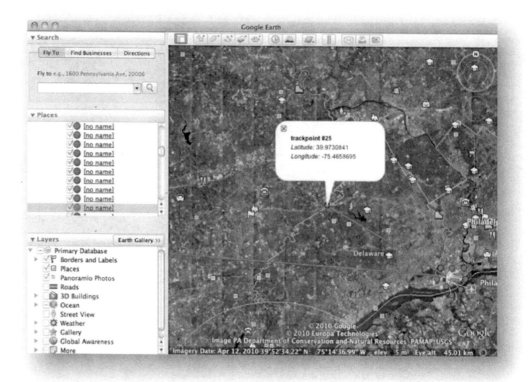

Figure 7–36. *GPS Visualizer*

In regard to the iPhone 4, we earlier discussed the files that were in the `locationd` folder. The first is `consolidated.db`. This is a SQLite database that contains the tables listed in Table 7–1.

Table 7–1. *consolidated.db Table*

Table	Artifacts
Location Harvest	Usually empty table
WiFi Location Harvest	Usually empty table
WiFi	Usually empty table
Cell	Usually empty table
TableInfo	Table information, version, iDevice serial number
CompassCalibration	Calibration information
CellLocationLocal	Cell site geo-location information
CellLocationLocalCounts	Nonevidentiary
CellLocationLocalBoxes	Nonevidentiary
CellLocationLocalBoxes_node	Nonevidentiary
CellLocationLocalBoxes_rowid	Nonevidentiary
CellLocationLocaBoxes_parent	Nonevidentiary
WifiLocation	WiFi MAC address and geo location
CellLocationCounts	Cell provider, application access, and geo-location information
CellLocationHarvestCounts	Cell towers connected to
WiFiLocationHarvestCounts	WiFi locations connected to
CellLocation	Cell site geo-location data
Fences	Nonevidentiary
Location	Nonevidentiary

For the items of relevance such as cell location, WiFi Location, and cell location local, these tables can be viewed with Froq, and the appropriate columns can be exported as XLS, CSV files, and KMLs (created in the manner that was previously discussed in this chapter using online applications).

Another artifact from the Locationd folder is clients.plist. This property list contains all the application that use GPS on the device.

Navigation Applications

There are numerous GPS applications for the iPhone. Most notable are Tom Tom and Navigon. Both of these apps are GPS turn-by-turn applications that are designed to function much like their GPS-only counterparts.

Navigon

Navigon is one of many navigation aids that is available for download from the App Store. This application does keep a lot of data in the logical part of the extraction. The artifacts are located in the /private/var/com.navigon.NavigonMyRegionUSEast folder. The region can vary from areas of the globe. The following are some the artifacts that can be gathered:

- Favorites.targets: Open the file with TextEdit, or use the Strings command. All favorites that were entered into the applications can be viewed as textual data with locations.

- Recent.targets: Again, open the file with TextEdit, or use the Strings command. The data here will consist of locations for routes requested within the application.

- com.navigon.NavigonMyRegionUSEast.plist: This can show the last city name and last location in latitude and longitude. Also, date/time values and the track log are given (see Figure 7–37 and 7–38).

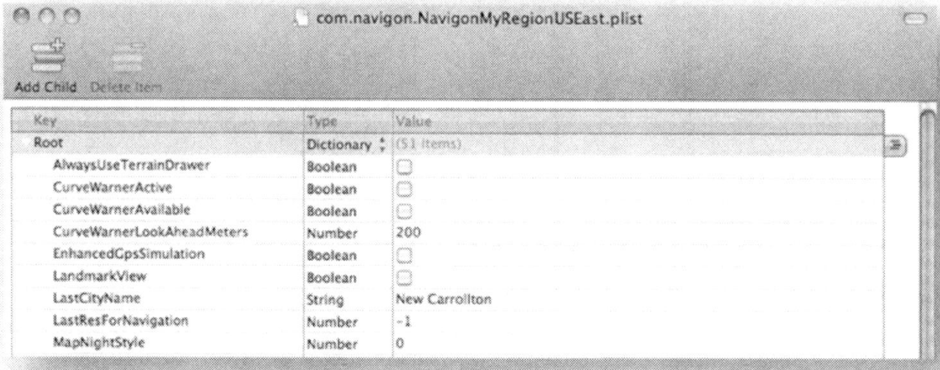

Figure 7–37. com.navigon.NavigonMyRegionUSEast.plist

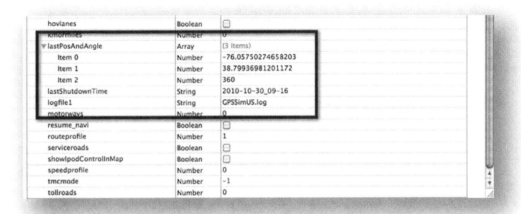

Figure 7–38. *com.navigon.NavigonMyRegionUSEast.plist continued*

The log file is GPSSimUS.log and can be opened in TextEdit. It contains several types of data:

- *$GPGGA*: Global Positioning System fixed

- *$GPRMC*: Recommended minimum specific GPS/transit data

Here is an example of GPGGA data:

$GPGGA,090431,4229.8662,N,8325.9111,W,1,4,1.00,0.00,M,,M,,*47

The data is broken down as follows:

- 090431: Time (given in UTC, so 09:04:31)

- 4229.8662, N: Latitude

- 8325.9111, W: Longitude

- 1: Fix quality

    - 0: Invalid

    - 1: GPS fix

    - 2: DGPS fix

- 4: Number of satellites

- 1.00,: Horizontal dilution of precision (horizontal accuracy)

- 0.00 M: Altitude

- M: DGPS reference station ID

- *47: Checksum

Here is an example of GPRMC values:

`$GPRMC,090430,A,4229.8730,N,8325.9141,W,27.00,166.19,580509,,,S*73`

This breaks down as follows:

- 090430: Time
- A: Navigation warning: A = OK V = warning
- 4229.8730, N: Latitude
- 8325.9141, W: Longitude
- 27.00: Speed in knots
- 166.19: Compass heading
- 580509: Date of fix
- S: Magnetic heading
- *73: Checksum

To view these codes in Google Earth, there is another free tool, GPSBabel, located at www.gpsbabel.org.

In the interface of the GPSBabel app, several fields are required (as shown in Figure 7–39).

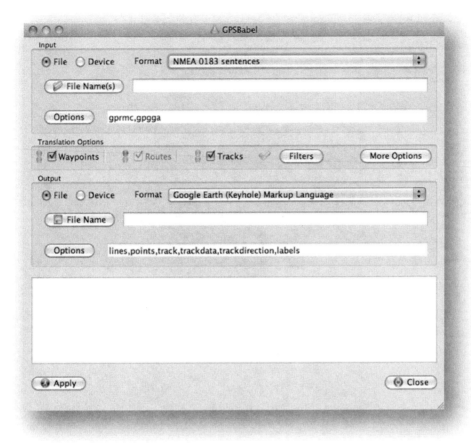

Figure 7–39. *GPSBabel*

- Input Type: File
- *Format*: NMEA 0183 sentences
- *File Name(s)*: The `.log` file from Navigon app
- *Option*: gprmc or gpgga
- *Translation Options*: Waypoints and tracks
- *Output*: File
- *Format*: Google Earth (Keyhole) Markup Language
- *File Name*: Location to save the KML file
- *Options*: Lines, points, track, track data, track direction, labels

1.   Select Apply. The KML file will then be created.

2.   Open Google Earth.

3. Select **Open** ➤ File, and navigate to the location of the saved KML file.

4. View the data.

Figure 7–40 shows an example of the Google Earth output.

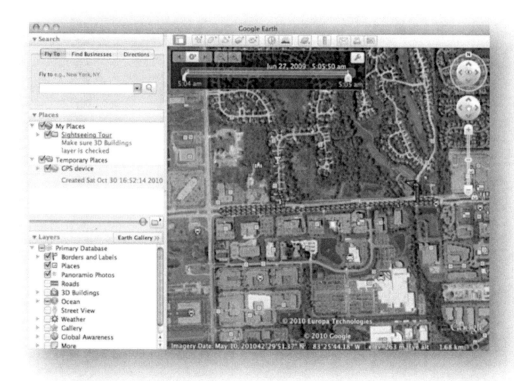

Figure 7–40. *Google output from GPSBabel*

Tom Tom

Another popular application is Tom Tom, which is similar in function to Navigon. The artifacts are located in the `/private/var/com.tomtom.USA2GB` folder. As opposed to Navigon, Tom Tom doesn't save a lot of data in the logical extraction. The most notable piece of data is a screenshot of the last route, as shown in Figure 7–41.

Figure 7–41. *Navigation artifact in Tom Tom*

Tom Tom and Navigon are just a couple of navigation applications that are available for download from the App Store. It's beneficial for an investigator to examine all the third-party apps for navigation aids and look at the data that is contained inside them.

Summary

As you have seen in this chapter, there can be a plethora of geodata on an iDevice. In this chapter, we discussed the history of GPS, the Maps application, and the data that is stored within the application.

Images can also provide a lot of data, which can be very beneficial to an investigation when placing the device at a specific location on a specific date and time. We also discussed the way cell tower data is stored on the phone and also how that can be viewed. This, on top of other artifacts on the device, adds up to giving you a complete picture of the travels of the iDevice and could place the phone in a general area in reference to a crime.

Lastly, we discussed a couple of navigation applications, the data that resides on the device, and how to view the data. GPS is becoming more and more important in our lives, and it is being used more than ever. The iDevice can store a lot of this information and aid an investigator.

Chapter 8

Media Exploitation

In previous chapters, we discussed how to obtain logical data and analyze the acquired data. The iDevice (iPhone, iPod Touch, iPad) was developed by Apple in such a way that the system is *jailed* (or closed), which, in UNIX terms, gives the ability to create a partitioned operating system. On iDevices, the operating system partition is read-only, and this makes the device a jailed system. This, coupled with using the root model found in Unix systems, provides for a secure system. In this situation, the iDevice's mobile user has defined and limited access to certain areas of the iOS. Since the first iPhone came out, some people have taken it upon themselves to develop methods to break that jailed system, which has lead to the development of numerous unsupported versions of iOS and jailbreaks. Law enforcement agencies then demanded that they get access to the physical device, as traditional methods of forensics began to fade away in the wake of the iPhone. Numerous arguments arose in areas from digital rights management, to copyright violations, to poor decisions being handed down by Apple. This chapter will discuss relevant case law, as well as procedures and tools to exploit iDevices.

What Is Digital Rights Management (DRM)?

Digital rights management (DRM) systems are ways to protect copyrighted material. In the very simplest of terms, DRM is nothing more than a set of rules or a lock combination that acts to protect a copyrighted work such as a downloaded song or any other work. If you follow the rules set forth by the holder of the copyright, you are able to open the work and enjoy it.

In today's world, digital rights management is used to regulate and manage the use of digital content. Basically, DRM is a form of encryption that rests on digital media and seeks to prevent the unauthorized use of media by unauthorized persons (Labriola 2004). DRM uses encryption methods to "safeguard against the unauthorized usage and to prevent access by any media player that doesn't enforce its rights-management system" (Labriola 2004). DRM is employed in CD/DVDs, online services, pay-per-view services and can also restrict playing of media in certain countries (Groenenboom and Helberger 2006).

According to Labriola (2004), "DRM is an umbrella term for technologies that let copyright holders control how digital content is used . . . Virtually all DRM systems require a file format that can store licensing information along with audio/video content, which excludes all MP3 and DivX, the two mainstays of unauthorized file-sharing networks." For example, as a result of DRM controls, an owner of a DVD movie is unable to make copies of that movie. Other uses of DRMs would be to "provide limited access to works for paying users only, limit some functions of digital files or even prevent certain uses all together" (Elkin-Koren 2007).

The unique aspect of DRM is that owners of copyrighted works are able to control how their works are used after they are purchased (Elkin-Koren 2007). Digital rights management has been a topic of debate over the past several years as technologies continue to improve and many technologies now involve the exchange of protected content online, such as the exchange of music and other digital copyrighted works (Harwood 2009). Courts are continually battling to define how DRM should operate to protect electronic media that is copyrighted (Rosenblatt 2006).

Legal Elements of Digital Rights Management

To better understand the concept of DRM, it is important to understand the legal roots of digital rights management.

United States Constitution

The legal concept of DRM can be traced back to the United States Constitution. In the U.S. Constitution, Article I, the framers sought to protect the creations of artists and to enable them to have the power to share their works the way they see fit. As explained, Article I of the U. S. Constitution states, in its power to Congress, "to promote the progress of science and useful arts, by securing for limited times to authors and inventors the exclusive right to their respective writings and discoveries" (Harwood 2004). Thus, ever since the birth of this country, a person is granted an exclusive protection right to his or her works.

As time evolved, Congress sought legislation to strengthen and permeate the right given in Article I of the U.S. Constitution (Harwood 2004). In 1790, the Copyright Act was passed, which was the first attempt at legislation to protect creative works, and the original Copyright Act was very limited and offered little protection as compared to the Copyright Act today (Harwood 2004). For instance, identifying that "in the first decade of U.S. copyright law, only five percent of the books published received copyright protection," as opposed to today where "virtually every creative work imaginable is automatically copyrighted." As technology continues to improve, Congress has made and continues to make amendments to the Copyright Act.

The Copyright Act and digital rights management systems are important players in protecting digital media. "According to research from SIMBA Information, a leading U.S. Market research firm, global online information sales are projected to reach US$24 billion," and this figure is from 1998 as consumer Internet use was still in its early stages (Tang 1998).

Digital Millennium Copyright Act (DMCA)

To better understand the concept of digital rights management, it is critical to understand the underlying laws that shape digital protection measures. On the most basic level, the legal authority of digital rights management stems from copyright law (Rosenblatt 2006). Courts look to the concepts of copyright law when deciding cases involving digital rights management. In 1995, Congress passed the Digital Performance Right in Sound Recordings Act (DPRA) to regulate digital recordings on the Internet.

The DPRA enabled holders of copyrights "to perform the copyrighted work publicly by means of a digital audio transmission" (Harwood 2004). As a result, according to, the DPRA required online services to "negotiate royalty payments with copyright owners" (Harwood 2004).

In 1998, in an effort to tighten the regulation of the Internet, the U.S. Congress passed the Digital Millennium Copyright Act (DMCA), which gave more power to copyright holders of sound recordings on the Internet (Harwood 2004). A fundamental change in DMCA as compared to DPRA was the increase in royalty and licensing requirements for internet transmissions. Further, the DMCA contains provisions that make any attempt to circumvent protection measures employed by DRM systems illegal – thus, civil and criminal penalties will apply (Lyon 2007).

First Sale Doctrine

As codified in Section 109 of the Copyright Act, the first sale doctrine "limits a copyright owner's distribution right in that he can only exploit the copyrighted work up to the point of the first sale. . . . The goal of the first sale doctrine was to balance copyrighted work up to the point of the first sale" (Hinkes 2007). Thus, if someone has purchased a copyrighted work, such as a book, he or she is free to dispose or sale that book without permission of the copyright owner.

A critical aspect of the first sale doctrine that Hinkes pointed out in her article, as coded in 17 U.S.C. Section 109(a) (2000), is that it "explains that lawful ownership of an item is not the same as owning the copyright" (2007). Therefore, the owner can do anything with the copyrighted work, including destroying it, as long he or she doesn't make copies of it.

Fair Use Doctrine

The fair use doctrine is also rooted in the Copyright Act (Hinkes 2007), who notes "the Copyright Act grants authors control of the reproduction, public performance, display, and distribution, along with a monopoly on the creation of derivative works." Further explained that with this in mind, the fair use doctrine "functions as a safety valve on this monopoly" mentioned above, thus according to the Copyright Act gives "property rights" to its authors (Hinkes 2007).

Hinkes summarized this concept by stating, "the concept of fair use serves to mediate between these property rights and the constitutional rights of public access and free speech embodied in the First Amendment" (Hinkes 2007). For a consumer, as a result of the concept of fair use, the U.S. Copyright law does not restrict anyone from downloading copyrighted material as long as it is not for commercial purposes (Tang 1998).

Secondary Infringement Liability

The theory of secondary infringement liability is often linked with DRM and copyright law: "If someone infringes copyright, and another party is somehow involved, the latter party could be legally liable; this is called secondary liability" (Rosenblatt 2006).

In 1984, the Sony Betamax case, (*Sony Corp. of America v. Universal City Studios, Inc.* 464 U.S. 417 (1984)), was heard before the Supreme Court. The Betamax case established the principle of "significant noninfringing uses" and further defined this principle as follows, "if a technology can be shown to have significant uses that do not infringe copyright, the maker or distributor of that technology should not be liable for infringement" (Rosenblatt 2006).

Case Study: DMCA

The DMCA also inspired two cases incorporating "consumer discourse within copyright analysis"—the Lexmark and Chamberlain cases (Elkin-Koren 2007). It is important to note that the balance between consumer rights and copyright law is still being fine-tuned through the court system. The main question that these two cases brought up is, what is a legitimate consumer interaction with copyrighted material in the first place? The answer lies in post-purchase control of the material—"copyright law facilitates post-purchase control, allowing copyright owners to restrict the use by purchasers of copies." However, there are no absolute restrictions in copyright law. The law "allows post-purchase restrictions within the limits of the delicate balance between exclusivity and access that defines the scope of copyright" (Elkin-Koren 2007).

This delicate balance tries to "secure incentives to invest in future creation" of new intellectual property while at the same time providing a monopolistic hold over intellectual artifacts (Elkin-Koren 2007). In the Lexmark case, the company tried to prevent an aftermarket for printer cartridges by using an authentication sequence. This attempted control over copyrighted material actually was only ruled to be an unprotected idea, and defendants were free to circumvent the digital management sequence that was intended to prevent copyright infringement (Elkin-Koren 2007).

Case in Point: Jailbreaking the iPhone

The Apple iPhone has quickly become one of the most popular smart phones on the market since its first release in 2007. One the great advantages of having an iPhone is the ability to download custom applications for the device. It has been perceived as a breakthrough technological device for consumers, especially for its built-in features, including a fully functioning web browser, visual voicemail, e-mail, iPod, and more. However, as with its other products, Apple does not officially allow unauthorized applications to be placed on the iPhone that have not been approved through the Apple application process.

One drawback to the iPhone when it was first introduced was its inability to interoperate with third-party applications. Apple limited access to what could be loaded on an iPhone to protect the reliability and security of the operating system on the iPhone and the iPhone overall (Hayes 2009). In March 2008, Apple introduced its iPhone Developer Program (in the SDK) that enabled independent software developers to design applications for the iPhone. The application store was an instant hit, with over 100,000 downloads of the SDK during the first four days of its launch (Apple 2008a). Since its launch, the iPhone application store has been a huge success, with over 10 million application downloads in the first weekend.

Every iPhone has digital rights management (DRM) type technological protection measures built into the device. These measures protect two primary pieces of software that are critical to its functioning, the bootloader and operating system (Hayes 2009). The bootloader's primary function is to load the operating system and the operating system is the core operating software for the iPhone. Apple has implemented protection measures such as cryptographic keys used to validate the bootloader and the operating system and protect their integrity. Further, these protection measures serve to protect Apple's copyright interests, as protected by the Digital Millennium Copyright Act.

Since the onset of third-party application availability, acts of piracy have led to programs being released that defeat, or seek to defeat, the technological, DRM protective measures in place on the iPhone that act as a safeguard to protect its copyrights. These unauthorized, third-party iPhone programs are called jailbreaking programs. When installed, they allow unauthorized programs to be loaded onto the iPhone. A jailbreaking tool is similar to a DVD ripper program that circumvents the protective DRM measures on a DVD, enabling users to make illegal copies, violating the Digital Millennium Copyright Act (DMCA). Apple has taken the stance that jailbreaking an iPhone constitutes copyright infringement and a DMCA violation.

Over the past couple years, there has been much debate, and a movement has arisen to exempt jailbreaking from being considered a DMCA violation. Section 1201(a)(1) of the copyright law requires the Librarian of Congress to determine every three years, whether there are any classes of works that will be subject to exemptions from the DMCA's prohibition against circumvention of technology that controls access to a copyrighted works. In accordance with this rule, the Electronic Frontier Foundation (EFF) formally requested the Copyright Office to recognize a DMCA exemption to permit jail-breaking applications (Elkin-Koren 2007). The EFF takes the stance that Apple's reasoning for the technical locks is to limit iPhone owners to only Apple-approved applications, although Apple does have a viable argument that jail-breaking, on its face, is a form of DRM circumvention under the DMCA (Berka 2009). Apple asserts that jailbreaking an iPhone modifies Apple's bootloader and operating system software, which EFF doesn't deny. However, EFF argues that Apple is doing nothing but attempting to protect its business model, not copyright interests. Further, the EFF firmly advocates that jailbreaking does not violate copyright, so the act of jailbreaking should be granted a three-year exemption under the DMCA.

Apple also argues that the Digital Millennium Copyright Act (DMCA) Section 1201(a)(1)(B) permitted an exemption only where users are adversely affected by virtue of an access control to make "noninfringing uses" of the product (Hayes 2009). However, Apple points out that EFF's proposed exemption results in the act of infringing uses of copyrighted works protected by the protective measures in the iPhone and does not satisfy the fundamental prerequisite of the DMCA statute.

Although Apple takes a firm stance that jailbreaking is illegal, a number of iPhone owners choose to jailbreak their devices. Apple has taken minimal measures to stop users from physically jailbreaking their iPhones (Berka 2009).

In July 2010, the Copyright Office concluded its review of official comments that were submitted to them from iPhone application developers and other members of the general public regarding the proposed DMCA exemption to allow jailbreaking of their iPhones. The Librarian of Congress determined that six classes of works are subject to an exemption to the prohibition against circumvention technology. These classes include DVD movies, computer programs on wireless devices, programs that allow users to unlock their phones to port another carrier, provide good faith testing, investigate or correct flaws in video games, use programs requiring an obsolete dongle, and access literary works in e-book format. For the purposes of this discussion, the Librarian of Congress effectively made an exemption under the DMCA for jailbreaking iPhones by allowing the use of software programs to circumvent a manufacturer's protection measures. For more information on the exemptions granted recently by the Librarian of Congress, see "Statement of the Librarian of Congress Relating to Section 1201 Rulemaking" at www.copyright.gov/1201/2010/Librarian-of-Congress-1201-Statement.html.

Therefore, in plain language, the DMCA considers the act of jailbreaking technically illegal as it is a method of circumventing the DRM measures in place on the iPhone. However, the recent DMCA exemption by the Librarian of Congress grants users the ability to jailbreak their iPhones without infringing upon copyright laws. A cautionary note to remember though is that the law is still unresolved as to whether users are subject to contractual or other obligations specified in a software user license agreements (ULA). Even though users are exempt under the DMCA, they may still be in breach of contractual obligations under Apple's software user license agreement for using the software in a manner that goes against its intended purpose.

Case in Point: *Apple v. Psystar*

Again, in regards to jailbreaking, Apple's firmly held position is that any method used to circumvent its DRM protective measures for its bootloader and operating system is illegal and a direct violation of the DMCA. Further, Apple asserts that its end user license agreement (EULA), which is included with every copy of the Mac OSX software, expressly forbids any installation on a third party computer system on the devide (McDougall 2008). To fight jailbreaking acts against their products, in July 2008, Apple filed a copyright infringement suit in the U.S. District Court, Northern District of California against Psystar, a Miami-based company that sold "open computers," including those with Mac OSX Leopard preinstalled on them (Lawinski 2008).

Psystar was the first company to commercially distribute actual computers not approved by Apple that had Mac OSX Leopard software installed on them. The company also released a product known as Rebel EFI that contained a modified bootloader and other software tools that enabled a typical user to install the Mac OSX operating system onto any PC-based clone or machine.

In their case against Psystar, Apple initially asserted that the Psystar Mac clone computer systems directly violated the Mac OSX EULA, because the agreement does not allow third-party installation of the Mac OSX operating system on unapproved devices or machines (Lawinski 2008; McDougall 2008). Psystar denied any wrongdoing and countersued Apple for anticompetitive practices, monopolistic behavior, and copyright misuse (Evans 2008). In its original complaint, Apple alleged that Psystar violated the DMCA by circumventing the protection measure technologies that Apple uses to protect its operating system, Mac OSX (Elmer-DeWitt 2009). Specifically, Apple asserted in its complaint that Psystar acquired or created code that interfered with a technological protection measure without the express permission of Apple in an effort to access, without authorization, Apple's copyrighted code that supported its bootloader and operating system.

Psystar continued to sell its Mac clone computers pending the ongoing litigation with Apple, and even attempted to file for Chapter 11 bankruptcy protection in an effort to stall Apple's legal efforts to force them to stop selling the Mac clone computers. The company also filed motions claiming that Apple failed to register the Mac OSX operating system with the U.S. Copyright Office (Lawinski 2008; McDougall 2008).

In November 2009, after several hearings and motions, the U.S. District Court, Northern District of California granted Apple's motion for summary judgment, finding that Psystar violated Apple's copyrights and violated the DMCA by installing Apple's Mac OSX operating system onto unauthorized third-party PC systems (Elmer-DeWitt 2009). In December 2009, as a result of the Court's granting of summary judgment in Apple's favor, Psystar agreed to pay Apple $2.7 million for damages including copyright infringement and DMCA violations (Huges 2009).

Although faced with total defeat, a summary judgment and a huge fine, Psystar immediately appealed and continued selling its Rebel EFI product. However, in December 2009, Apple won a permanent injunction against Psystar that barred the company from having any part in a device, technology, or software that circumvented a technological protection measure, which included the Rebel EFI product (Foresman 2009). The legal battle continues, as Psystar is currently appealing this permanent injunction. However, the company is no longer selling any type of product that contains the Mac OSX operating system or technology that enables Mac OSX to be loaded onto PC-type machines.

The Psystar case acted as a precedent for jail-breaking litigation involving the iPhone or any other Apple products as this case solidified Apple's argument that circumventing Apple's technological protection measures to allow Apple's products to function on unapproved third-party devices, or altering Apple's copyrighted works, was a direct violation of the DMCA.

Until recently, by citing the Psystar case, Apple most likely would be able to prevail in future, similar cases against other individuals who employ jailbreaking technology to circumvent Apple's copyrighted works. However, in light of the recent exemption to the copyright law granted by the Librarian of Congress, the law is now unsettled as to whether Apple will be able to continue to prevail with limiting the use of its Mac OSX operating system. Apple most likely still has a legal basis contractually or by implied consent through its EULAs that specify the approved usage and intent of the software. However, that argument is subject to further interpretation by the courts, as laws must continue to keep up with the changing trends of technology.

Case in Point: Online Music Downloading

Online digital music streaming is another issue that has come to the forefront in recent years. "Unlike AM/FM radio stations, who pay a fairly fixed amount for the right to play songs, webcasting fees are assessed based on the number of people who listen to a station" (Harwood 2004). The rates that a Copyright Arbitration Royalty Panel established for these fees were based "on an agreement between the Recording Industry Association of America (RIAA) and Yahoo, Inc. [and] a major webcaster and Internet retransmitter of broadcast signals. . . . Unfortunately, these rates may not have been appropriate for all webcasters because they were negotiated by a webcaster much too large to represent the interests of many in the Internet radio community" (Harwood 2004). Though the library of Congress reduced the rates, they were still too much for many webcasters, who favored revenue-based royalties.

The legislative history behind the DPRA indicates that "Congress did not intend to extend the sound recordings copyright to all forms of streaming media" (Harwood 2004). In fact, Congress explicitly stated that DPRA was "a narrowly crafted response to one of the concerns expressed by representatives of the music community, namely that certain types of subscription and interactive audio services might adversely affect sales of sound recordings and erode copyright owners' ability to control and be paid of use of their work" (Harwood 2004), also citing to S. Rep. No. 104-128, at 15 (1995); H.R. Rep. No. 104-274, at 13 (1995).

Case in Point: The Sony BMG Case

Another case that is closely tied to digital rights management and the Digital Millennium Copyright Act was the Sony BMG case in 2005 (Lyon 2007). This case illustrated the power and controls a DRM system can have on a computer system. During 2003, Sony BMG launched a DRM protection measure known as MediaMax and another measure known as XCP" in 2005[12]. These programs were embedded "on over twenty million discs manufactured by or for Sony BMG" (Lyon 2007).

According to court transcripts and further explained by Lyon, "The software was described as being for the protection of the audio files on the disc" (2007). Consumers were tricked into installing the software onto their computers because it was disguised as "a music player that would allow for protected digital copies of the songs on the disc to be played on the PC" (Lyon 2007).

Further, this software would be installed on users' computers even if they selected the "disagree" option when the software first loaded (Lyon 2007). To remove the software, users had to navigate to the Sony web site and enter their personal information. Even after they did so, the software was not uninstalled. "The software contacted Internet servers operated by Sony BMG, leaving information in the company's records regarding the compact disc usage and listening habits of each user" (Lyon 2007).

Antivirus vendors knew of the presence of the Sony DRM software but hesitated to informing the public or its own customers; they didn't issue a patch or take measures to correct the harm that the software was causing to users (Lyon 2007). In essence, this protection measure acted like a virus that not only protected the Sony copyrighted music on the compact disc but all other copyrighted music on the user's computer and even reported back to Sony with its findings (Lyon 2007).

Legally, antivirus vendors claim that the "anticircumvention provision of the Digital Millennium Copyright Act" gave them no duty to alert users or provide ways to delete the software (Lyon 2007). Lyon identified that numerous class action suits were filed against Sony claiming "violations of the Computer Fraud and Abuse Act, which prohibits accessing a computer without, or in excess of, the authority granted by the owner of the computer; common law trespass to chattels, and unfair or deceptive business practices" (2007). Sony eventually settled the class action claims in 2006, and Lyon explained that as a result of the DRM protection measures that installed themselves on computers, "California and Texas, along with thirty-nine other states, settled their claims with Sony BMG for approximately $4.25 million."

The Future of DRM

From the previously cited cases, the recent Librarian of Congress decision and ongoing discussion by Congress, it is evident that the future of DRM systems and technology remain questionable. Consumers most likely still remember the Sony DMG case today. In her article, Tang noted that "three forces govern the issues surrounding intellectual property and digital information: those of law, business relationships between the producers and owners and users of intellectual property and technology" (1998).

More recently, as the Sony BMG copy protection case demonstrated, consumers have become intolerant of copy protection systems employed on audio compact discs (Lyon 2007). Consumers fear what these copy protection systems do to their computers and other media devices and have chosen not to purchase compact discs that contain DRM systems. However, DRM systems still exist on other forms of media, including DVD movies and online music (Groenenboom and Helberger 2006).

Unfortunately, for the copyright holder, DRM systems on DVDs are easily circumvented by free programs commonly found on the Internet (Lyon 2007). However, new DVD formats, such as Blu-Ray, offer more data capacities and now feature DRM systems that contain technical protection measures to ensure their discs can't be copied. As history has revealed, every new technology brings a creative programmer out there that will eventually crack the code within the DRM protection measure and exploit the key that cracks the code on the Internet.

DRM and similar copy protection systems still exist on some brands of audio compact discs sold today, but they are being phased out due to the consumer outcry and the Sony BMG copy protection case (Lyon 2007). The critical issue facing DRM is that more consumers are now informed that technical protection (DRM) systems exist, and consumers understand that their computer systems could be harmed in a manner similar to that of a virus infecting a computer (Lyon 2007). Consumers faced with buying and using digital media most likely will remember the Sony BMG case when faced with protection measures that affect how they use copyrighted material. As Lyon explained in his article, companies should take proactive steps to inform the customer of DRM systems on their media, be able to "explicitly authorize" the use of the DRM system, and allow the customer to delete the protection measure from their systems.

As this legal review illustrated, technology and the laws that govern it are not always in sync. Courts look to basic laws and even the U.S. Constitution and apply it to technology, such as DRM. In the future, digital rights management systems will most likely continue to evolve, as copyright protection is here to stay in one form or another.

Media Exploitation

Media exploitation is the method used, in either a forensic or nonforensic way, to collect all information from a given media device. Media exploitation is commonly used by intelligence and antiterrorist investigative agencies. In these environments, it may be required to utilize these procedures. Most of the information acquired never sees the light of a courtroom. In the criminal environment, rules of evidence, motion hearings, judges, and juries need to be considered prior to attempting these procedures. As with other investigative procedures that have been either abused or misused in the past, the legality of jailbreaking can be reversed by legislative means or, in any future digital incarnation of the O.J. Simpson case, where a host of defense lawyers and experts utilize the powerful negatives inherent in this practice. One such negative is that there is not any type of write blocking and that jailbreaking gives the operator full access to the device. This creates a window of opportunity for an investigator to be accused of writing to a device in the course of an investigation. Jailbreaking is all its forms must be used judiciously and with the knowledge and approval of the prosecuting legal authority. The National Institute of Standards and Technology (NIST) standards state to utilize the least destructive process to conduct digital investigations. As explained in previous chapters, a vast deal of information and evidence can be garnered from a logical image. Many crimes can be solved by getting call logs and cell tower data from AT&T and records from Internet service providers. The call logs and cell tower records will provide details such as the time of calls and the location where the calls were made, but the call logs of the `call_history.db` from the phone cannot provide that accuracy of the information. Internet service providers can deliver to investigators all e-mails from accounts located on the iPhone. Then too, with the discovery of deleted information found in the logical space, it becomes increasingly less likely that more destructive methods will be needed to forward a case toward prosecution.

Media Exploitation Tools

Some of the early, and cruder, tools to image the iPhone were tools like iLiberty and Pwanage. These third-party software tools were developed by the hacking community and are still used today. These applications entirely overwrote the system partition of the iPhone. As techniques in jailbreaking were developed, a cat and mouse game with Apple began in which jailbreaking techniques are always behind Apple, and investigators are tied at the hip with the hacking community to complete examinations. Recent jailbreaks evolved from splinter hackers such as purplera1n, blackra1n, and Greenp0ison.

Other imaging techniques place files onto the system partition, which still shows that the jailed system partition was broken; therefore, these techniques are still jailbreaking the device. Understanding how these tools and procedures work is vital to see how their use modifies the overall system. Its better know up front than to get blindsided by a defense attorney and not know the answer, which could ruin your integrity in the eyes of unskilled jurors. Also, some examiners have used hacker tools like redsn0w to jailbreak the phone and then create local images over the air. Typically, these are civilian examiners that cannot afford proprietary tools or do not have access to law enforcement. There is one commercially available image tool, iXAM.

iXAM

iXAM (http://www.ixam-forensics.com) runs entirely in RAM and utilizes an engineered RAM disk to image an entire iPhone. Compared to other methods, the iXAM process is terribly slow. However, iXAM can image the system partition, the data partition, and the entire raw disk. The process, at a glance, would resemble other forms of imaging. However, this method has a slight difference; it does hash the images after an acquisition, but both the acquisition and verification hashes are completed one after another when imaging is complete. iXAM doesn't perform any hashing before imaging. iXAM, at the time of this writing, can only image iPhone 2G and 3G, and it is unable to image iPhone 3GS and 4 and iPod Touch 2G and 3G. As compared to Windows-based imaging tools, the cost of iXAM is extremely high, approximately $3,000 (other imaging tools, such as FTK Imager, Guidance Encase in acquisition mode, Linux-based boot disks, and command-line tools, are all free).

The version of iXAM used here is version 1.9.1. iXAM is a Windows-based tool and requires a dongle. The setup for this tool takes some time to complete. Part of the setup is to delete any previous installation of iTunes.

iXAM will install its own drivers, and it has to go out to the Internet to pull down Apple's copyrighted firmware. Therefore, the forensic system must be connected to the Internet. However, specific firmware verified by hash value can be downloaded and installed on the system without exposing the system to the outside world.

The following steps are required to successfully acquire a device image using iXAM:

1. The first step is to power down your iPhone 2G or 3G, or your iPod Touch 1G, as instructed in Figure 8–1.

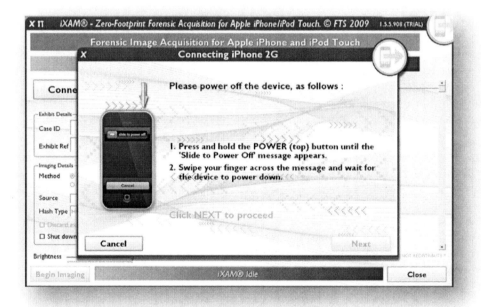

Figure 8–1. *iXAM initial steps in configuring a phone prior to imaging*

2. After the device is powered down, the next step is to connect the device. This is required because iXAM goes through a process that places the iPhone into Device Firmware Update (DFU) mode, which starts up the iPhone without booting into iOS. This was originally devised by Apple as its method for conducting diagnostics on the device. As Figure 8–2 shows, iXAM is ready for the device to connect.

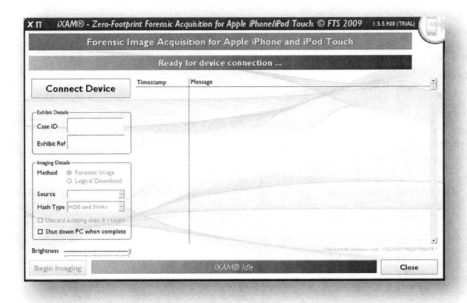

Figure 8–2. *iXAM connecting to the device*

3. After the device is connected. A screen comes up that identifies the model of iPhone or iPod touch. In Figure 8–3, you can see that iXAM cannot image iPod Touch 2G or 3G. iXAM does not support the iPhone 3GS or 4, or the iPad.

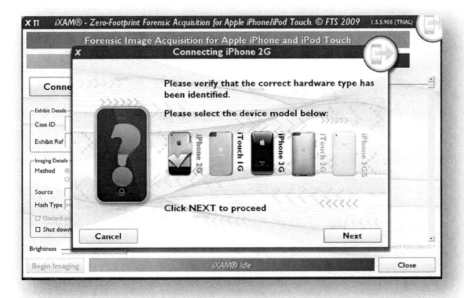

Figure 8–3. *iXAM verifying the model of phone to be imaged*

4. Next, it's time to place the phone into DFU mode. The following steps may look like the same as the steps in tools such as Pwanage.

5. After the device has been place into DFU mode, you'll need to install iXAM's engineered boot loaders, as shown in Figures 8–4 and 8–5.

Figure 8–4. *After iXAM placed the phone into DFU mode, engineered bootloaders are injected.*

Figure 8–5. *The third bootloader is installed.*

6. After the bootloaders have been installed, the device is ready for imaging, as shown in Figure 8–6.

Figure 8–6. *iXAM shows that the device is ready for imaging, and the demonstrated screen is the same as on the device.*

7. The next step is to insert some case information, for example, the case and exhibit numbers (see Figure 8–7).

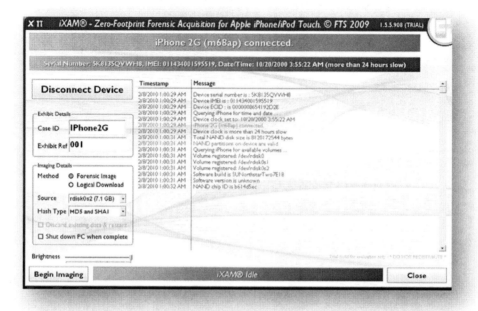

Figure 8–7. *Case information, the type of imaging, and hash value types are provided prior to imaging.*

8. Now, iXAM can create images of `rdisk0`, the full raw disk; `rdisk0s1`, the system partition; and `rdisk0s2`, the data partition. Select the type of acquisition, and iXAM will begin to image the iPhone, as shown in Figure 8–8. For this part, you have to be patient, because it is very slow. An 8–GB iPhone took four hours to image. As with all tools, there are some failures. My first attempt to image an 8–GB iPhone 2G failed at 68%.

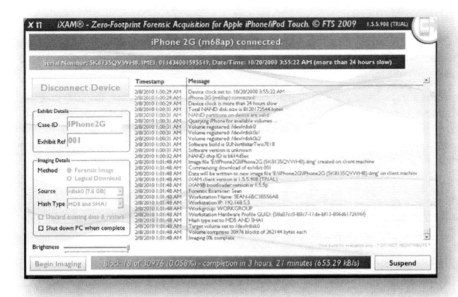

Figure 8–8. *The device is being imaged, and the status bar and log are updated as the process continues.*

iXAM also creates MD5 or SHA1 (or both) hashes of the images that it creates, as shown in Figure 8–9. The hashes are conducted one right after the other; one is labeled "acquisition hash" and the other "verification hash." Again, it must be stated that no hashing was completed prior to imaging for comparison.

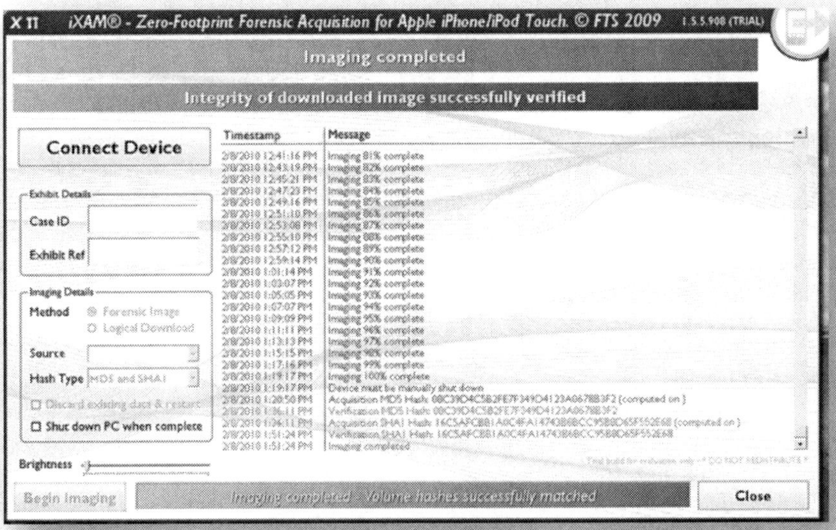

Figure 8–9. *Imaging is complete, and both hashes are then conducted.*

Other Jailbreak Methods

iXAM is a GUI-based tool for imaging a limited set of iDevices. Therefore, examiners and investigators are forced to utilize invalidated tools so that all other devices and versions of iOS can be examined at the physical level.

Some procedures are command-line tools that are derivatives of known hacker tools. Some in the law enforcement community (and the hacker community) do not like the name "hacker," but those who use jailbreaking tools must make their peace with it. The defense is certainly going to be using the term every chance it gets. Due to this fact, and looking toward court, it is imperative that the examiner documents everything that is done.

The first command-line tools developed overwrote the system partition, but they evolved to just breaking the partition and adding two files. These tools morphed from imaging over the air to using high-speed USB. These methods all had some serious drawbacks: they were sometimes complicated and required training and practice prior to implementation. Second, when these procedures were conducted on a piece of media that was corrupted, the tool failed to image the entire data partition.

These command-line procedures also allowed for removal of the passcode on the device. Doing so, however, alters the data partition of the device. Since the examiner has already gained access to the device, it would be wise just to image the disk and maintain the integrity of the data partition. Why allow a window of opportunity for defense attorneys to exploit?

It cannot be stated enough: when using media exploitation methods, document and maintain the integrity of the evidence. This lessens the potential for defense arguments that can threaten the examiner's credibility.

When examiners do not have access to law enforcement tools or can't see the cost versus benefit of iXAM, they have to be more creative in gaining access to the raw data of an iDevice; in other words, these examiners are forced to utilize hacker tools. Some of those tools overwrite the entire OS partition; some jailbreak the phone but place software onto its data partition. One of these hacker tools, called redsn0w, has the ability to prohibit the insertion of additional data to the phone, thereby reducing the intrusion on the device. Once redsn0w was created, simply placing command-line tools such as netcat, ssh, or dd on to the device meant that imaging over the air could be accomplished. This is the least forensic procedure available.

Image Validation

The question is, how can we determine if any partition of an iDevice has been changed when using either command line techniques or vendor programs? As we discussed in Chapter 2, the Catalog ID is given to every file on an HFS system. Therefore, if an iPhone is imaged twice, the Catalog ID number should not increase. We can determine if there are any changes to a volume by imaging the volume twice and using a tool that analyzes volumes to see if the Catalog ID number changes. Since command-line tools, by default, do not image the full raw disk, it is impossible to determine if any changes were made to the device. However, IXAM can image the complete raw disk or the system or data partitions. After an iPhone is imaged, we can use a command-line tool such as hfsdebug to see if the catalog ID changes in anyway. hfsdebug is a command line utility that was developed by Amit Singh, and it can be downloaded at http://www.osxbook.com/software/hfsdebug.

> **NOTE:** hfsdebug is a handy tool for forensic analysis. However, it will probably not be updated any longer, so there is a newer alternative called fileXray, available at http://filexray.com. For the purposes of this task, though, hfsdebug works perfectly well.

After downloading the utility, copy the file into your $PATH directory. The following procedure explains how to analyze an HFSX volume and notate the Catalog ID number:

1. Image an iPhone using your tool of choice.

2. Open a Terminal window.

3. At the command line, type the following command:

```
hfsdebug -V [drag and drop the .dmg] -v
```

4. Press Enter.

5. Review the output to locate the next catalog ID number (see Figure 8–10).

```
# HFS Plus Volume
  Volume size          = 243862672 KB/238147.14 MB/232.57 GB
# HFS Plus Volume Header
  signature            = 0x482b (H+)
  version              = 0x4
  lastMountedVersion   = 0x4846534a (HFSJ)
  attributes           = 1000000000000000010000000000000
                         . kHFSVolumeJournaled (volume has a journal)
  journalInfoBlock     = 0x801
  createDate           = Sat Mar 27 22:21:21 2010
  modifyDate           = Sun Nov  7 09:11:19 2010
  backupDate           = 0
  checkedDate          = Sun Mar 28 01:21:21 2010
  fileCount            = 873308
  folderCount          = 220921 /* not including the root folder */
  blockSize            = 4096
  totalBlocks          = 60965668
  freeBlocks           = 3253108
  nextAllocation       = 6840349
  rsrcClumpSize        = 65536
  dataClumpSize        = 65536
  nextCatalogID        = 2923412  <----
  writeCount           = 182906403
  encodingsBitmap      = 0000000000000000000000000000000
                         0000001000000000000000000010001011
                             . MacRoman
                             . MacJapanese
                             . MacKorean
                             . MacCyrillic
                             . MacChineseSimp
```

Figure 8–10. *hfsdebug output*

If the same device is imaged again, rerun the hfsdebug command. Look at the output, and verify that the nextCatalogID number does not increase. If the number does increase, a change was made to the system. This procedure can also be used on images of the data or system partitions.

The next step is to hash your image. iXAM does complete two sets of hashes after image acquisition. Other command-line methods do not hash at all. If you're using those tools, it will be necessary for you to hash the image after it is acquired. The following steps go through using md5deep, which is a command-line hashing utility. This open source utility can be downloaded from SourceForge at http://sourceforge.net/projects/md5deep/.

1. Follow these instructions to compile md5deep:

   a. Use the cd (change directory) command to move to where the unzipped md5deep folder is located.

   b. Open a Terminal window.

   c. At the command line, type ./configure, and press Enter.

   d. Next, type make, and press Enter.

   e. Type make install, and press Enter.

   f. If you get a permission error, type sudo make install, enter the administrator's password, and press Enter again.

   g. To see if you were successful in compiling md5deep, type which md5deep. The command should return the path where md5deep is installed.

2. After the installation of md5deep, at the command line, type the following, and then press Enter:

```
md5deep -e [drag and drop the .dmg image] | tee ~/Desktop/Imagehash.txt
```

You will see a progress of the hashing, and after completion, a hash value for the image will be shown on the screen, and a text file will be created, as seen in Figure 8–11.

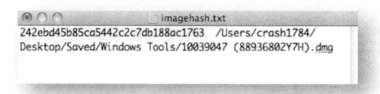

Figure 8–11. *The created hash value*

Summary

One of the biggest debates in the law enforcement community is on the subject of whether or not one should jailbreak. The advocates of jailbreaking also advocate tools that have not been formally validated, even tools that come from potentially questionable sources.

When using these tools, one question constantly crops up: how do they work? It's true that their functionality is not rocket science, but it's incumbent to the members of the digital forensic community to demand answers to some of the most basic questions. For example, how does the tool in question acquire and assure the integrity of a digital image? Also, you, the forensic examiner, will take the stand in court, not the tool developers; therefore, it's your responsibility to know how the tool works, but it's not the responsibility of the author to tell you anything.

Even the ruling from the Library of Congress does not change the rules of forensic practices. To keep the science reputable, examiners must keep the caveats of forensics and see that nothing gets changed in the evidence. However, in the mobile forensics realm, this is extremely difficult to do. In light of that, should mobile forensics receive the title of "forensics"? Or is it more like an offshoot of e-discovery? Because of the limitations and operational parameters of gaining data from the devices, mobile forensics cannot maintain the traditions of forensics. This is the reality that one must live with when advocating jailbreaking.

The opponents of jailbreaking know that to serve forensics in the long term, mitigating the changes in evidence should be central to mobile forensics. Even though jailbreaking appears to be permitted at this time, doing so still changes data, so the jailbreak must be revealed. Opponents of jailbreaking also state that the least intrusive methods should be utilized before more invasive and possibly destructive methods are employed. Another argument in opposition to jailbreaking is that developers may have questionable motives or allegiances. By turning a blind eye to the way the evidence was acquired, examiners forgo normal acceptable practices for the sake of expediency.

The iPhone is a tough nut to crack, but that does not mean that it is impossible to investigate. Have investigators forgotten how to serve court orders on ISP's to retrieve e-mail? Has the art of obtaining provider call records died? As shown in this book, there are other means of recovering evidence quickly. Providers can interrogate their systems faster than any other investigative method when time is a factor in locating suspects or victims. The fact is that cell site records are more accurate than any log found on the iPhone and, in some cases, even more detailed. Is carving for items of unallocated space worth the cost of possible phone destruction, when only fragments of databases are retrieved and most information of a recent crime is in the logical data? Tools like Fernico's ZRT have been used on devices that cannot be retrieved using conventional mobile forensic tools, which have been at the heart of acceptable practice for many years.

The last argument against jailbreaking to obtain evidence is that some of these methods are complex and can potentially damage the very evidence that they are helping acquire if not wielded precisely. In short, there are many schools of thought on jailbreaking, and each case is individual in its own right; what works in one situation may fail in another.

The public isn't always a fan of law enforcement, and if unorthodox media exploitation methods are to be used, the practice of using means from least invasive to most invasive must be part of the examination process. Using traditional methods first and then progressing to jailbreaking only when it's necessary shows jurors that all nondestructive means were exhausted. Because none of the jailbreaking methods have any concrete write protection, image only one partition, and do not hash their images, using a practical approach that is well documented can thwart allegations of tampering with evidence.

References

Apple Inc. Apple iPhone Software License Agreement. Available at
     http://images.apple.com/legal/sla/docs/iphone.pdf.

Apple Inc. 2008. iPhone SDK downloads top 100,000 (press release), March 12,
     http://www.apple.com/pr/library/2008/03/12iphone.html.

Apple Inc. 2008. App Store downloads top 100 million worldwide (press release) September 9,
     http://apple.com/pr/library/2008/09/09appstore.html.

Berka, Justin. 2009. EFF Proposing DMCA exemption for iPhone jailbreaking. *ARS Technica*,
     January 9, http://arstechnica.com/apple/news/2009/01/eff-proposing-dmca-exemption-
     for-iphone-jailbreaking.ars (accessed February 4, 2010).

Electronic Frontier Foundation. 2009 DMCA Rulemaking, http://eff.org/cases/2009-dmca-
     rulemaking (accessed February 4, 2010).

Elkin-Koren, N. 2007. Making room for consumers under the DMCA. *Berkeley Technology Law
     Journal, 22,* 1119-1155.

Elmer-DeWitt, Philip. 2009. Apple Wins Clone Suit. *CNN Money*, November 14,
     http://brainstormtech.blogs.fortune.cnn.com/2009/11/14/apple-wins-clone-suit/
     (accessed February 7, 2010).

Evans, Jonny. 2008. Psystar beats Apple to Blu-ray on OS X computer. *IT World*, October 29,
     http://www.itworld.com/hardware/56947/psystar-beats-apple-blu-ray-os-x-computer
     (accessed February 7, 2010).

Foresman, Chris. 2009. Psystar gets permanent injunction, legal warning form judge. *Ars
     Technica*, December 16, http://arstechnica.com/apple/news/2009/12/psystar-gets-
     permanent-injunction-legal-warning-from-judge.ars (accessed February 7, 2010).

Groenenboom, M. and N. Helberger. 2006. Consumer's guide to digital rights management. *The
     Indicare Project* web site, http://www.indicare.org/consumer-guide (March 8, 2008).

Harwood, E. D. 2004. Staying afloat in the internet stream: Jow to keep web radio from drowning in digital copyright royalties. *Federal Communications Law Journal, 56,* 673–696.

Hayes, David. 2009. Responsive comment of Apple Inc., in opposition to proposed exemption 5A and 11A (Class #1). U.S. Copyright Office, Library of Congress, In the Matter of Exemption to Prohibition on Circumvention of Copyright Protection Systems for Access Control Technologies, Docket No. RM-2008–8.

Hinkes, E. M. 2007. Access controls in the digital era and the fair use/first sale doctrines. *Santa Clara Computer and High – Technology Law Journal, 23,* 685–726.

Hughes, Neil. 2009. Psystar agrees to pay Apple $2.7M in Settlement. *AppleInsider*, December 1, http://www.appleinsider.com/articles/09/12/01/psystar _agrees_to_pay_apple_1_3m_in_settlement.html (accessed February 7, 2010).

Keizer, Gregg. 2009. Apple adds DMCA charge to lawsuit against Psystar: It accuses clone maker of breaking Mac OS copy-protection scheme. *Computer World*, December 30, http://www.computerworld.com/s/article/9121798/Apple_adds_DMCA_charge_ to_lawsuit_against_Psystar (accessed February 7, 2010).

Labriola, D. (2004, May 4). Good-bye, MP3; hello, DRM!: What's on your digital music player? *PC Magazine, 23,* 104.

Lawinski, Jennifer. 2008. Psystar Releases Mac Clone, But Has Apple Shut Them Down? *Channel Web*, April 14, http://www.crn.com/hardware/207200440; jsessionid=QBEDOZSLW2FG5QE1GHRSKHWATMY32JVN (accessed February 7, 2010).

Lyon, M. H. 2007. Technical protection measures for digital audio and video: learning from the failure of audio compact disc protection. *Santa Clara Computer and High – Technology Law Journal, 23,* 643-665.

McDougall, Paul. 2008a. Mac Clone Maker Psystar Vows To Challenge Apple EULA. *InformationWeek Blog*, April 14, http://www.informationweek.com/blog/main/archives/2008/04/mac_clone_maker.html;jsess ionid=1ZR3VLY3RJ3YTQE1GHPSKHWATMY32JVN (accessed February 7, 2010).

McDougall, Paul. 2008b. Apple Failed to Copyright Mac OS X, Psystar Claims. *Information Week*, December 22, http://www.informationweek.com/ news/hardware/mac/showArticle.jhtml?articleID=212501673 (accessed February 7, 2010)

Rosenblatt, B. 2006. DRM, law and technology: an American perspective. *Online Information Review, 31,* 73-84.

Tang, P. 1998. How electronic publishers are protecting against piracy: doubts about technical systems of protection. *The Information Society, 14,* 19-31.

Chapter 9

Media Exploitation Analysis

The Mac is the best platform to conduct any examination of OS X and iOS volumes. Although some Windows tool are getting better, there is no substitute for a Mac, which can view file types that Windows can't discern. Inherently Windows can't read HFS volumes and often requires third-party applications to mount and then view the data.

In this chapter, we will review some of the techniques and tools that can be used to analyze physical images. We will discuss tools on the Mac and delve into Mac and Windows forensic tools such as MacForensicsLab, EnCase, and FTK.

Reviewing Exploited Media Using a Mac

In Chapter 5, we discussed looking at artifacts retrieved from logical analysis tools. In Chapter 8, we covered several means of acquiring the physical disk of the iDevice. Now it's time to look at what is left to investigate from the physical disk. First we'll cover the complete data partition. Figure 9–1 is a representation of the iOS directory structure after a physical acquisition.

Figure 9–1. *iPhone data partition directory structure*

The following are some of the items of interest from the physical image:

- *General log*: Located at `Logs/Applesupport/general.log`, this log file gives the OS version, model, serial number, and created data and time of the operating system (see Figure 9–2).

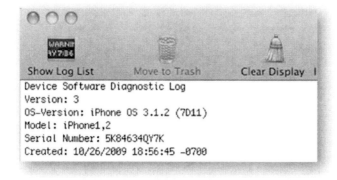

Figure 9–2. *General log*

- *Manifest property list*: The manifest property list is important in the encryption of the backup. This has the same information as in the property list of the backup on any Mac or Windows computer. This file is located at `tmp/manifest.plist`. This holds the keys to the encryption and the password for the backup encryption.

- `Mobile/Librarycom.apple.mobile.installation.plist`: This holds the following:

  - System information, shown under the Metadata key, and the installed applications, as shown in Figure 9–3.

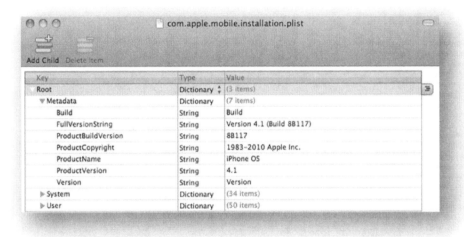

Figure 9–3. *Mobile installation plist*

  - The System list consists of Apple-installed applications, which includes extensive application information.

  - The User list consists of user-installed applications, which also contains application information, as shown in Figure 9–4.

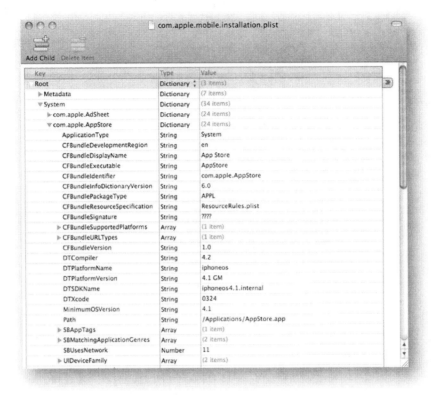

Figure 9–4. *Application information from* `mobile.installation.plist`

- ▨ `Mobile/Library/Caches/Safari/Thumbnails`: This contains screenshots of web pages.

- ▨ `Mobile/Library/Caches/snapshots`: This contains screenshots from the following applications:

    - ▨ AppStore

    - ▨ Calculator

    - ▨ Compass

    - ▨ Maps

    - ▨ AddressBook

    - ▨ Mobilecal—Calendar

    - ▨ Mobilemail—Mail

    - ▨ Mobilephone

    - ▨ Mobiletimer

    - ▨ Preferences

- /library/configurationProfiles/Passwordhistory.plist: This property list tracks passcodes that were entered by a user. This list continues as different passcodes are used. The passcodes themselves are encoded and not the actual passcodes that were on the device.

- Maptiles: This can be a treasure trove of data. As part of the Maps application, the app saves screenshots of the map tiles that it receives from Google Maps and stores them in an SQLite database. There are two locations of this database: /Library/Cache/Maps/MapTiles and /Library/Cache/MapTiles. The former file seems to be more current and larger than the latter. To effectively utilize the data in these files, it is necessary to extract the images from the database. This can be accomplished by using SQLite commands from Terminal. Once the images have been extracted, they can be reconstructed to view complete maps.

Mail

One of the biggest things that doesn't get brought over by a logical extraction is e-mail. On the iPhone there are numerous types of e-mails that can be configured, including those from any IMAP or POP account or Microsoft Exchange account. But as you saw with the logical data, all the e-mail settings can be located in the logical space, which is useful for investigators to put preservation letters and search warrants to gather even more historical data.

The iDevice can automatically set up Gmail, AOL, Yahoo, MobileMe, and Exchange mail accounts (see Figure 9–5). The user needs to input required information from the Mail application. Also, any other IMAP or POP account can also be added to the Mail application. First you need to understand the difference between the major configurations of IMAP, POP, and Exchange.

Figure 9–5. *Mail application setup interface*

IMAP

Internet Message Access Protocol (IMAP) is one of two more prevalent types of e-mail accounts that are used. The IMAP e-mail lets the user access only those e-mails requested from the server and is stored on the iDevice. On the iDevice, the same method is used; however, the contents of the mail are not stored on the device. For example, let's look at a Gmail account that was set up from an iPhone. The system automatically sets up the account as an IMAP account. As the users access their e-mail, the interface will show snippets and address information from that particular e-mail. To read the e-mail, the user clicks that mail, and then it is brought down from the server and shown on the device; however, nothing is stored on the device. Figure 9–6 shows the directory structure of a Gmail account.

Figure 9–6. *Gmail IMAP directory structure*

As shown in Figure 9–6, there aren't any e-mails, but there are a handful of .emlxpart files. These files are e-mail attachments that are base64 encoded. The same is seen in Yahoo. Nothing is seen within the mailbox. In MobileMe accounts, there are a few e-mails, but the rest are attachments.

POP Mail

Post Office Protocol is the most widely used e-mail protocol. There have been three versions of this protocol, with POP3 being the latest and the one generally used. The biggest difference from IMAP is that this form mostly downloads all the e-mails from the server vs. leaving them on the server, even though there is an option to do so. Therefore, there will be more artifacts to find in these types of e-mail accounts. As shown in Figure 9.7, you can see more .emlx files, which are the e-mails themselves and attachments. The .emlx files can be opened with TextEdit, which can show all the e-mail headers and content. Figure 9–7 shows an example of a POP e-mail account inbox.

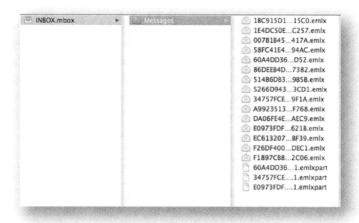

Figure 9–7. *POP e-mail inbox files*

Figure 9–8 shows an e-mail that has been opened with TextEdit, and you can see the data within an `.emlx` file.

Figure 9–8. *Contents of an* `.emlx` *file*

Exchange

The most widely used form of enterprise e-mail is Exchange. This is a Windows e-mail messaging system that is a server- and client-based system that is mainly used by larger organizations. Since the iPhone 3GS and iOS 3.0+, Apple iDevices have been capable of supporting Microsoft Exchange technology. The artifacts on an iDevice from Exchange are the largest on any iDevice, because this type of e-mail protocol keeps more e-mail in `.emlx` format than any other account type on the device. This can become an e-discovery gold mine. Hundreds of e-mail can be mined, even including attachments.

The location of all the mail on the iPhone is `Mobile/Library/Mail`. Each mail account will have its own folder, which keeps incoming e-mails, sent e-mails, and deleted e-mails. Conventional wisdom would dictate that using normal Mac tools, and even Mail, to open these `.emlx` files would be a simple task. However, this is not the case.

One of FTK's strengths is its ability to parse e-mail artifacts. This is no different on the iPhone. FTK can parse all e-mails from the iPhone and attachments. The e-mails on the iPhone are in the `.emlx` and `.emlxpart` formats. FTK can present this data in the manner that it has in the past, which gives the sender's and recipient's e-mail addresses, the date and time of the e-mail, and the body of the text. FTK can parse the `.emlx` file extremely well and can present the data in an excellent visual manner. FTK 3.2 automatically mines these e-mails and can even parse them by month and year. This is by far the best tool to view e-mail from an iDevice. Figure 9–9 shows an example of an e-mail viewed in FTK.

Figure 9–9. *FTK and its e-mail view*

NOTE: Viewing mail in FTK+ is accomplished by either extracting e-mail artifacts from a jailbroken iPhone or iPod touch or using the methods that were discussed in Chapter 9. Make sure that your legal authority is aware of the method of extraction and why normal investigative methods of subpoenas and search warrants can't be utilized to gather these types of artifacts.

Carving

At one point, we thought that we could not locate deleted data in the logical space. But we now know that there are deleted items within the logical image. You can use common tools to locate deleted data. One such application, TextEdit, can find deleted records within any SQLite database. One database, for example, is SMS. There are deleted SMS messages within the logical database. One way to search for deleted SMS messages is to use your Windows tool from your virtual machine. Export the SMS.db file from the image, and import it into EnCase as a logical evidence file; then you can locate the deleted SMSs. Keyword searching by a known phone number will reveal numerous deleted text messages. There are also tools in development that will assist in locating deleted data from SQLite databases. For normal carving, there are Mac and Windows tools that can be used in any physical image examination.

MacForensicsLab

One Mac-based forensic application from SubRosaSoft is MacForensicsLab, which can mount and examine all HFS volumes including the iPhone's HFSX. Since this is a native Mac tool, mounting HFSX is seamless and easy. MacForensicsLab (which can be purchased at www.macforensicslab.com) has a built-in carver called Salvage. This carves mainly for Mac-based files types and has the ability to carve from specific file types that are contained in its vast file listing. This tool can traverse the file system of Mac volumes, bookmark data, and generate reports. The one thing that this tool does very well is carving from free space. The following are the steps to carve data from unallocated space on the iDevice using MacForensicsLab:

1. Open MacForensicsLab.

2. Make sure the Devices tab is selected, as shown in Figure 9–10.

3. Highlight the data volume.

4. Select Salvage.

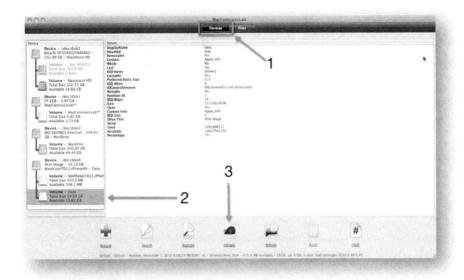

Figure 9–10. *MacForensicsLab interface*

5. In the next dialog box that appears, select Free Space Only (Deleted Files).

6. There are also selections for block-by-block or byte-by-byte scans, which you can set if necessary.

7. Then click "Start a new scan" (see Figure 9–11).

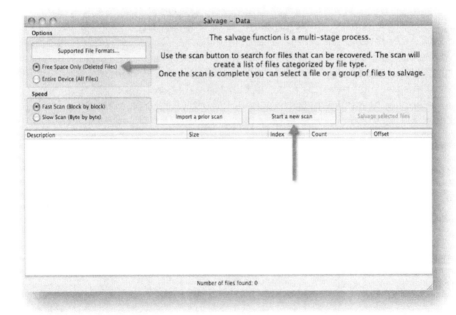

Figure 9–11. *Salvage interface*

8. MacForensicsLab's Salvage tool will then perform a scan of artifacts it can carve from unallocated space (see Figure 9–12).

Figure 9–12. *MacForensicsLab scanning for deleted data*

9. When the scan is done, the user can select the file types that will be cared by using the command+trackpad/mouse, or the user can highlight all the files to be carved (see Figure 9–13).

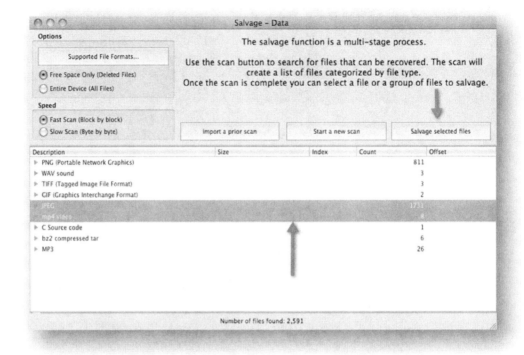

Figure 9–13. *Salvage after scan*

10. Once all the file types of interest are selected, then select "Salvage Selected files."

11. Then enter a location for the carved items to be placed, enter a filename, and navigate to the location that you would like the items saved.

12. After the carve is completed, MacForensicsLab attempts to rebuild the filenames of the carved items.

13. Navigate to the folder that you determined as your saved folder, and examine the artifacts. There can be just about anything, including JPEGs of contacts, e-mails, call logs, instant messages from other programs, or videos. Anything that can possibly happen on an iDevice can be gathered and saved as screenshots when one screen transitions to another. These images get placed into unallocated space and with carving tools can be brought back. Figure 9–14 shows examples.

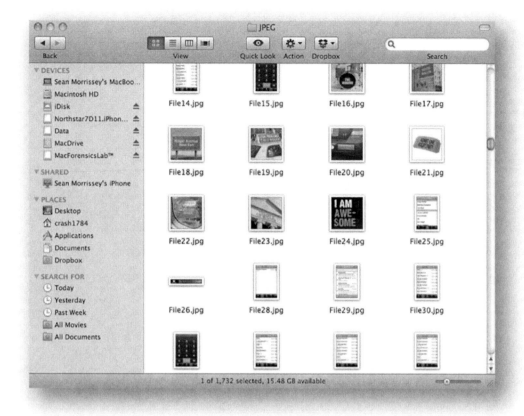

Figure 9–14. *Recovered deleted images from MacForensicsLab*

Access Data Forensic Toolkit

Access Data's FTK has made great strides in support of Mac-based images. FTK 3.2 has support for HFS, HFS+ and HFSX, which is of great importance to the iPhone. FTK is the only Windows-based forensic tool that can identify and bring in the whole disk image and produce a complete file system in its interface. Once the image file is brought into FTK, the file system of the iPhone will eventually populate. Once this is completed, you can start an analysis of the iPhone. FTK has some strengths and some deficiencies, which is inherent in Windows-based tools. Therefore, it will necessary to bring the DMG into a Mac platform and complete the examination. FTK can do very well with images but fails to parse out GPS data from 3G iPhones. It can see all databases, but the data has to be exported and opened with a SQLite application. Property lists are parsing quite well within FTK. With the prebuilt set of file types to carve, numerous items can be gathered from the free space of the iDevice. Since this is the case, FTK 3.2 can now carve for specific file types. But all in all, FTK is a good tool for examining iOS images.

When the whole raw image that was created with iXAM is brought into FTK and began its processing, you'll see the file structure of the iPhone, as in Figure 9–15.

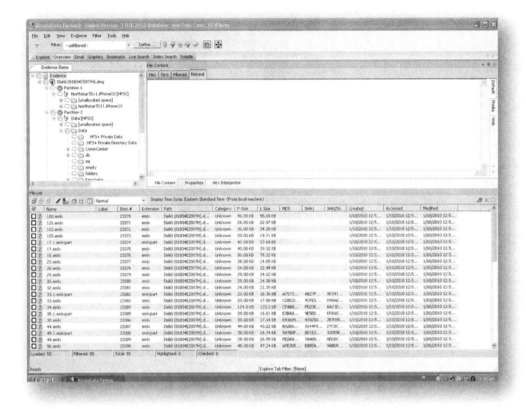

Figure 9–15. *iXAM image brought into FTK and visible file structure*

Figures 9–16, 9–17, and 9–18 are some examples of carved images and HTML files. Some of the JPEGs that could be carved could be screenshots of movies, images, e-mails, contacts, maps, and just about anything. Because of the foil transition of the iPhone from one screen to the other, the OS places the previous screen saved as JPEGs in unallocated space.

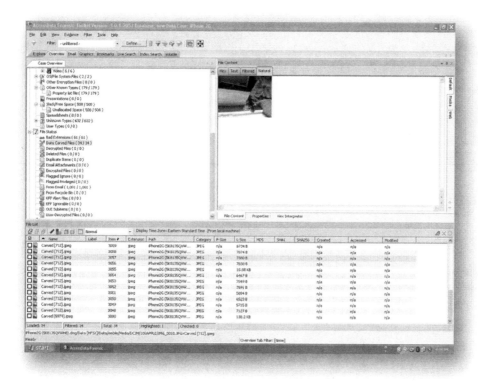

Figure 9–16. *Carved image using FTK*

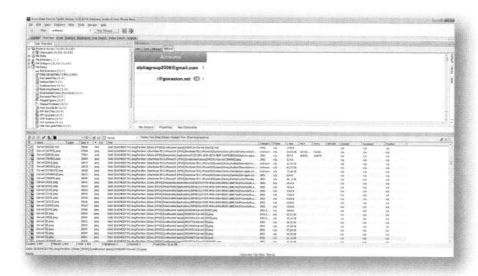

Figure 9–17. *Deleted screenshot recovered from carving using FTK*

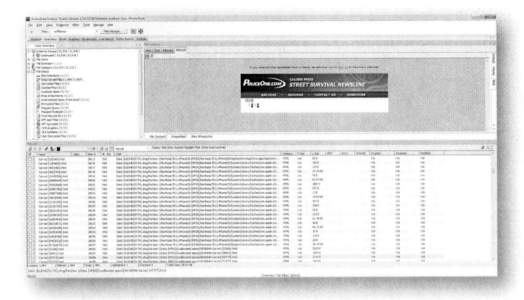

Figure 9–18. *HTML page seen in FTK*

FTK and Images

The process of examining EXIF data and GPS tags has gotten much better with FTK. FTK 3.2 can parse EXIF data on images that were taken from the iPhone, but it sometimes fails to parse GPS tags. Figure 9–19 is an example of how FTK parses EXIF data and GPS tags.

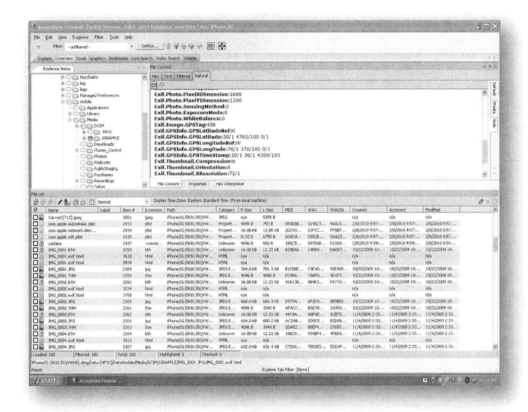

Figure 9–19. *Image EXIF and geodata*

When FTK fails to produce GPS data, you can use Irfanview, a free utility, to gather that data. This free utility can be downloaded from www.irfanview.com. It is also important to download the plug-ins so that the geodata can utilize Google Maps. To export images from FTK to Irfanview, follow these steps:

1. From a selected image, right-click, and select **Open With...** ➤ **External Program**, as in Figure 9–20.

Figure 9–20. *Exporting image for viewing with third-party viewer such as Irfanview*

2.   From the dialog box shown in Figure 9–21, select Irfanview.

Figure 9–21. *Selecting Irfanview for viewing images*

3. Irfanview will automatically open; from the top menu bar, click the Blue circled *i*, as shown in Figure 9–22. After you click the *i*, an "Image properties" window will appear. To see the EXIF data, click the EXIF info* button, as in Figure 9–22.

Figure 9–22. *Viewing images and EXIF data selection in Irfanview*

4. The EXIF Info window will show all EXIF and geodata from the image. Also, there is an option to open the image with Google Earth and see the location of where the image was taken. (Note that Google Earth needs to be installed on the computer.) Figure 9–23 shows the EXIF data.

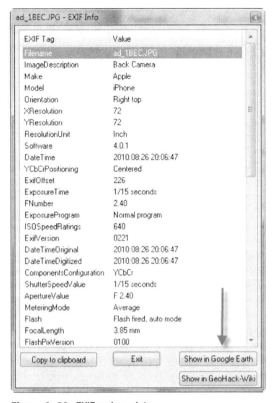

Figure 9–23. *EXIF and geodata*

As we've previously mentioned, the synced images from iTunes and iPhoto are placed into proprietary `.ithmb` files. Prior to 3.2, the images on an iPhone as synced with iTunes were placed into these Apple-proprietary file types. FTK attempts to carve out these images without much success, as shown in Figure 9–24.

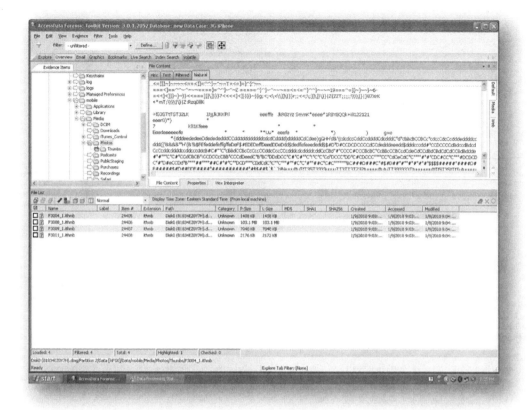

Figure 9–24. .ithmb *image files as seen in FTK*

The only way to see these images are with Mac-based tools such as File Juicer on the Mac platform. There are command-line tools, but the previously mentioned tool, File Juicer, is a quick and efficient way to view these images. Since these are synced images, they will not have any EXIF data. File Juicer is downloaded from http://echoone.com/filejuicer/ and has a cost of $18. The location of these file is at /mobile/Media/Photos/Thumbs. Here you can find multiple files with the .ithmb extension. The filenames start with the letter *F* and four numbers. Here are the steps in order to view .ithmb files:

1. Open the File Juicer application.

2. From a Finder window, navigate to the /mobile/Media/Photos/Thumbs, and drag and drop an .ithmb file into the File Juicer window, as shown in Figure 9–25.

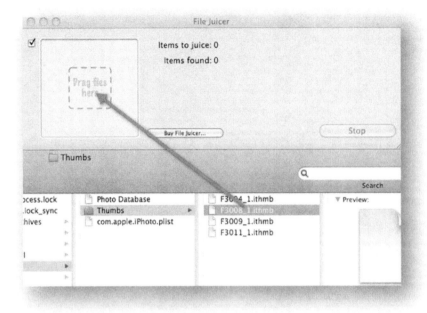

Figure 9–25. *Drag-and-drop technique used with File Juicer*

3. File Juicer will extract the images and will create a folder name with the same name of the `.ithmb` filename. From here you can examine the images from these files (see Figure 9–26).

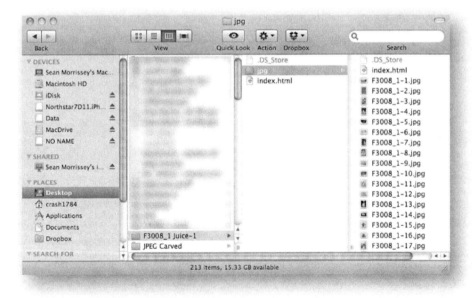

Figure 9–26. *File Juicer export*

SQLite Databases

FTK can in some instances parse out some of the databases that are located on the iPhone. SMS and Notes databases are some of the databases that FTK can parse out quite well in FTK, while others like CallHistory and AddressBook aren't, so exporting to a third-party viewer would be necessary. Figure 9–27 shows an example of the SMS database parsed by FTK.

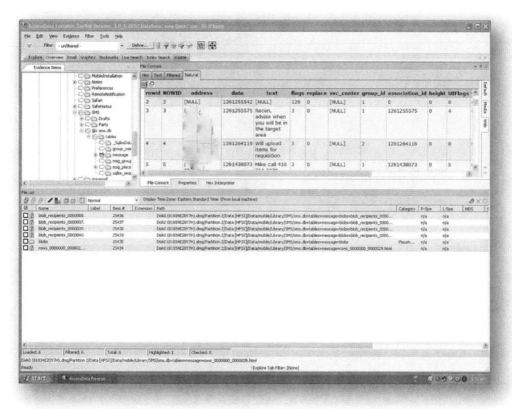

Figure 9–27. *SMS database viewed in FTK*

Database can be exported and opened with SQLite. The same procedure that was discussed in the .ithmb files can be replicated here except that tools like SQLite Database Browsers would be replaced as the associated program. SQLite Database Browser is used exactly the same as on the Mac. The view and options are the same as well.

After the exporting is done, the data such as the date, time, and flags have to be translated manually. To translate the date and time, a good Windows tool is Timelord, a free tool that can be downloaded at http://computerforensics.parsonage.co.uk/timelord/timelord.htm.

EnCase

A raw DMG (disk image) of the complete iDevice disk can be brought in, even when giving EnCase the correct starting offsets from disk view. EnCase can see that there are two partitions, but no file structure is seen. Figure 9–28 shows how an iPhone image looks in EnCase.

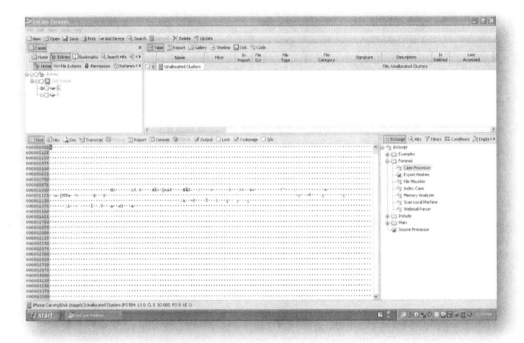

Figure 9–28. *EnCase and iPhone image*

So, since we can't see any file system, what can we do with EnCase? One, you can change the volume header from HFS+ to HFSX, which would change the hash value of the image or just use EnCase to Carve. EnCase does a pretty good job of carving the iPhone image. EnCase also has the ability to create a custom file signature for the enscripted File Finder to locate iPhone-specific file types such as binary plists, AMR, M4A, M4V, MVP, and other Mac-specific file types. The best way to run EnCase on a Mac is in Boot Camp. Using EnCase in a VM is very resource intensive and sometimes very slow. Installing EnCase on the superior Mac hardware makes for a good match to carve for data on the iPhone. The following steps can assist in carving for items from an iPhone image file:

1. From the Enscript pane, select Case Processor.

2. Next give the process a name such as Data Carve (see Figure 9–29).

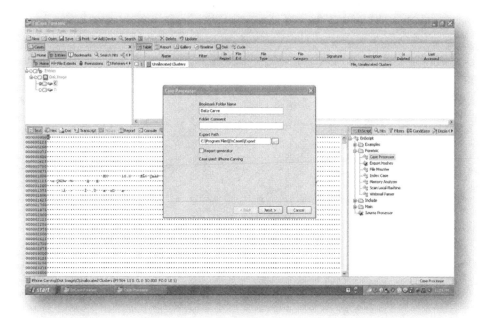

Figure 9–29. *Carving using EnCase*

3. Click Next.

4. In the Case Processor dialog box, click File Finder (see Figure 9–30).

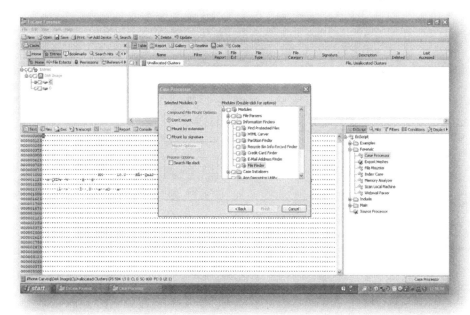

Figure 9–30. *File Finder enscript*

5. From the File Finder dialog box, you can select the file types to carve for.

6. If you want to select other file types not listed, there are two ways; one is to import from a table within EnCase, and the other is to create your own from the create custom signature button. Figures 9–31 and 9–32 show samples of those windows.

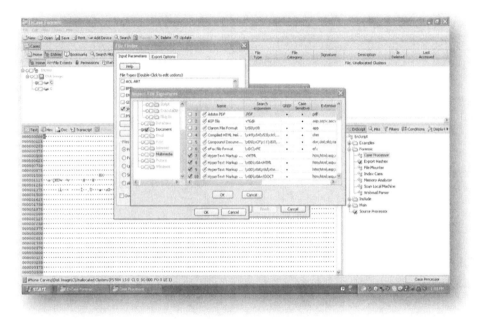

Figure 9–31. *Adding additional file types within the File Finder enscript*

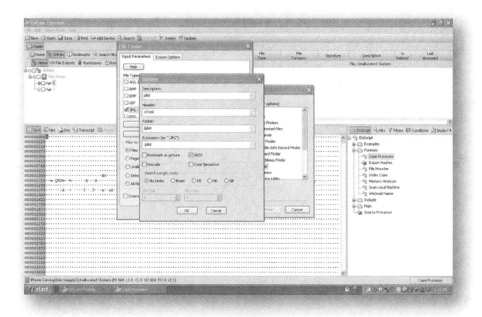

Figure 9–32. *User-created file types within the File Finder enscript*

7.   After you either created your own or selected from the import table, return to the File Finder window, and check all the ones that you just added.

8.   Once that is complete, return to the Case Processor window, and click Finish.

9.   When the data carve is complete, the results will be populated in the Bookmarks tab.

10. Review and bookmark the relevant artifacts.

EnCase can carve more items than its counterpart FTK, because of its flexibility to add custom file types. This illustrates that using more than one tool is wise. In cell phone forensics, it is well known that not one tool will solve a case; sometimes it takes a multitude of tools.

Spyware

Two of the most common spyware applications are Mobile Spy and File Spy. A lot has been made about these applications, but not much has been seen in labs. Either the examiners don't know what to look for or the applications are just hype. These applications can work only on jailbroken phones. Each needs to utilize the Cydia application in order to inject the apps onto the iPhone. The intended target has to give up physical access to their iPhone in order for these programs to be installed. The applications are made to be stealthy. The reason is that all the interfaces are hidden and all other icons that are associated with the jailbreak are removed from the Home screens. Since the phones are meant to be jailbroken, then it also allows an examiner to traverse the directory structure and locate these applications.

Mobile Spy

This software package can be purchased at www.mobile-spy.com. These are paid-for applications. Mobile Spy costs $49 every quarter. This application can monitor the following:

- Call logs
- SMS
- GPS
- Contacts
- Tasks
- Memos
- Cell ID locations
- E-mail log
- Calendar
- Web history
- Photos and video

The application Mobilephone.app resides in the /private/var/stash/Applications directory.

There are several files of relevance to Mobile Spy:

- Library/Preferences/com.rxs.smartphoneplist
  - Gives the access code to be placed into Phone.app
  - GPS interval time
  - User name and password
  - All data that is mined
- /System/Library/LaunchDaemons/com.rxs.ms.plist
- /Preferences/ com.rxs.msdaemon.plist
  - Access code
  - Last photo date and time
  - Web history

- /Msdeamon directory, `Contactlogs.dat`: Tracks the data and time that a contact is used from `Addressbook.db`. Figure 9–33 shows an example of this file opened with the TextEdit application.

```
ContactLogs.dat
2010:10:24    10:33:51    (410) 224-5877    Annapolis Apple Store
2010:10:24    10:33:51    14106904577       Residence
2010:10:24    10:33:51
2010:10:24    10:33:52
2010:10:24    10:33:52
2010:10:24    10:33:52
2010:10:24    10:33:52
2010:10:24    10:33:52
2010:10:24    10:33:52
2010:10:24    10:33:53
2010:10:24    10:33:53
2010:10:24    10:33:54
2010:10:24    10:33:54
2010:10:24    10:33:54
2010:10:24    10:33:54
2010:10:24    10:33:55
```

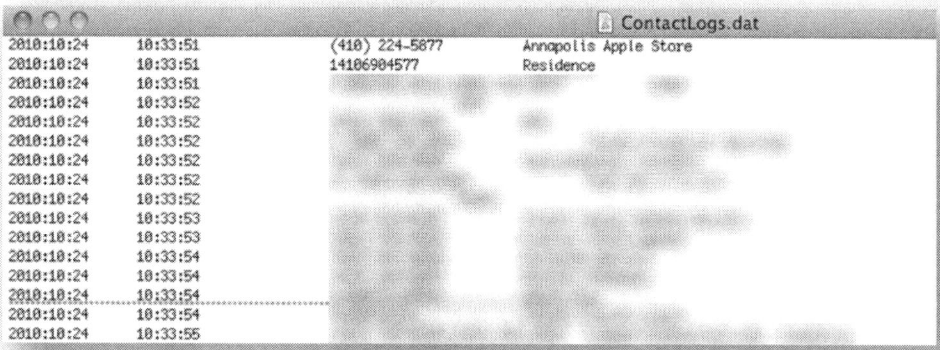

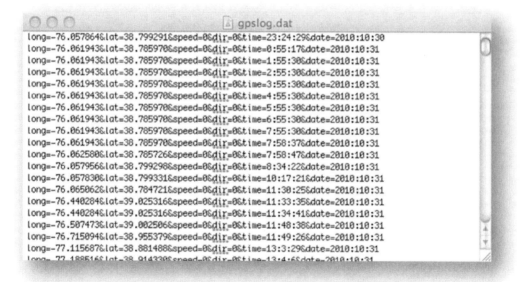

Figure 9–33. *`Contactlogs.dat`*

- `Gpslog.dat`: Latitude, longitude, date, and time of values from the GPS system (see Figure 9–34).

```
gpslog.dat
long=-76.057864&lat=38.799291&speed=0&dir=0&time=23:24:29&date=2010:10:30
long=-76.061943&lat=38.785970&speed=0&dir=0&time=0:55:17&date=2010:10:31
long=-76.061943&lat=38.785970&speed=0&dir=0&time=1:55:30&date=2010:10:31
long=-76.061943&lat=38.785970&speed=0&dir=0&time=2:55:30&date=2010:10:31
long=-76.061943&lat=38.785970&speed=0&dir=0&time=3:55:30&date=2010:10:31
long=-76.061943&lat=38.785970&speed=0&dir=0&time=4:55:30&date=2010:10:31
long=-76.061943&lat=38.785970&speed=0&dir=0&time=5:55:30&date=2010:10:31
long=-76.061943&lat=38.785970&speed=0&dir=0&time=6:55:30&date=2010:10:31
long=-76.061943&lat=38.785970&speed=0&dir=0&time=7:55:30&date=2010:10:31
long=-76.061943&lat=38.785970&speed=0&dir=0&time=7:58:37&date=2010:10:31
long=-76.062580&lat=38.785726&speed=0&dir=0&time=7:58:47&date=2010:10:31
long=-76.057956&lat=38.799298&speed=0&dir=0&time=8:34:22&date=2010:10:31
long=-76.057830&lat=38.799331&speed=0&dir=0&time=10:17:21&date=2010:10:31
long=-76.065062&lat=38.784721&speed=0&dir=0&time=11:30:25&date=2010:10:31
long=-76.440284&lat=39.025316&speed=0&dir=0&time=11:33:35&date=2010:10:31
long=-76.440284&lat=39.025316&speed=0&dir=0&time=11:34:41&date=2010:10:31
long=-76.507473&lat=39.002506&speed=0&dir=0&time=11:48:38&date=2010:10:31
long=-76.715094&lat=38.955379&speed=0&dir=0&time=11:49:26&date=2010:10:31
long=-77.115687&lat=38.881488&speed=0&dir=0&time=13:3:29&date=2010:10:31
```

Figure 9–34. *`GPSLog.day` file*

- `Sms.dat`: Contains several SMS messages to conclude the number, date and time, and content from the message (see Figure 9–35).

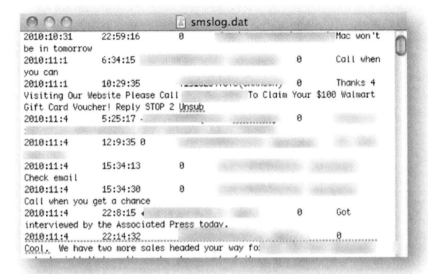

Figure 9–35. *The* `smslog.dat` *file*

- `Email.db`: Stores a lot of data in reference to all e-mail accounts on the iDevice. Figure 9–36 shows the series of tables in this database.

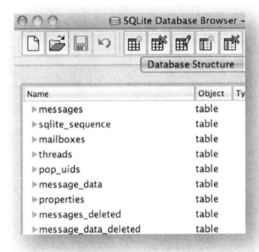

Figure 9–36. `Email.db` *structure*

From the interface in Figure 9–37, if the smartphone application is seen, then Mobile Spy has been installed onto the device.

Figure 9–37. *Mobile Spy icon*

FlexiSpy

This is another application that acts the same as Mobile Spy. This one is hidden better and is more costly. Flexispy can be purchased at www.flexispy.com. The costs range from $349 per year to $145 per year. The application is stored in the same location as Mobile Spy and is called `Mobiefonex.app`. Everything is contained within the app, even the log file, which is called `logevents.db`. An SQLite database, this database records all the data that is logged such as SMS, GPS, and e-mail.

There are also property lists that can be examined, in particular, `com.mobiefonex` `.Mobiefonex.launch.plist`. This can be found in `/System/Library/LaunchDaemons`, and it points to a library that the program uses.

In the iPhone interface, the app is named MBackup, and the icon is shown in Figure 9–38.

Figure 9–38. *FlexiSpy icon*

Summary

In this chapter, we covered many topics, including how to carve from unallocated space using both Windows and Mac tools. Now that e-mails are easily viewed with FTK, even those from jailbroken phones, you can look for spyware and understand where those apps store their data and where the application lives.

Remember, Mac-based tools have a greater success rate of gathering all the data from the iPhone. Using Windows-based tools has been ingrained in the psyche of the examiner for so long that going out of the comfort zone of Windows to the Mac seems to some daunting. When the subject comes up on using Macs to conduct examinations, many investigators say, "It is too cost prohibitive." However, all the processes, tools, and procedures in this book were done a $600 Mac Mini. There is always a solution to a problem, such as virtual machines and Boot Camp, which is a simple platform that can do both Windows and Mac processes for less than $1,000.

Chapter 10

Network Analysis

Looking at how the fabric of human communication is changing, one of the most significant factors is mobile communication. Whether for personal or commercial application, the ability for someone to stay connected has never been easier. As humans continue to become more reliant on mobile devices, the amount of information that can be gathered about the user continues to grow. Therefore, the ability of forensic analysts to extract and make sense of the data on mobile devices becomes immensely important. This is compounded by the ability of modern computing to house larger and larger amounts of data as time passes.

The key aspect of iOS devices has been their portability. In an always-on, always-connected world, the various functions of these mobile devices pave the way for rich forensic data to be harvested. From chat conversations to geo-locational databases, the data that is being generated and stored on Apple mobile devices is creating a new area of forensics.

Whereas pictures and text messages are the data of choice for today's forensic analyst, one key area that can produce substantive forensic data points is networking. With iOS devices using Wi-Fi connections and Internet-based applications, a new world of forensic data is being discovered atop the network stack.

Custody Considerations

With these new devices, you must consider new techniques for evidence acquisition and chain-of-custody procedures. Because these devices reside in a state of persistent connections, various forensic issues could invalidate any evidence the device might yield. For example, over-the-air remote wipe is a feature that Apple includes in its MobileMe service, which allows a user, through a web portal, to erase a device that has a current Internet connection (3G or Wi-Fi) without being near it. Thus, once you obtain a device, you must take steps to remediate any remote tampering to prevent data loss.

In addition, if the device settings are accessible at the time, make sure to put the device in Airplane Mode. Be sure to note the time (and time zone) at which this was performed in order to clearly indicate on the forensic timeline when this step took place and what data might have been generated on the phone after the seizure. If this configuration is not accessible at the time, a Faraday cage for both Wi-Fi and GSM/3G must be utilized until the device can be moved to a shielded, EMI/RFI-sanitized room.

Further, a network analysis should be performed of the surrounding area, especially in the event the area is the suspected crime scene. Any locations the suspect has been known to frequent should also have a site survey performed in order to understand the various network environments the suspect might have had a connection to. This will be valuable later to correlate data found on the device to other physical locations. Of course, obtain a warrant before performing such surveys.

Networking 101: The Basics

Within the Apple mobile device family (iPod touch, iPhone, and iPad), there are a few different ways network connections can be made. Internally, the devices contain one or more radios. Although some have GSM cellular radios or 3G data network radios, all contain a 802.11 variant radio for wireless Internet connectivity. Older models, such as the original 2G iPhone and iPod touch devices, have 802.11b/g, while newer models such as the iPad or iPhone 4 have 802.11/b/g/n. Each of the three letters—b, g, and n—denotes a revised standard of the original 802.11 wireless communication protocol.

The standard is governed by the Institute of Electrical and Electronics Engineers (IEEE), and revisions are released every few years to keep emerging technologies compatible. The base standard, IEEE 802, is heavily known within the networking community, because many of the groups within the 802 family are critical components of network functionality, 802.11 being one of them.

Within the 802.11 standard, there are five variants: the original 802.11, 802.11a, 802.11b, 802.11g, and 802.11n (see Table 10–1). Each has their own implementation, with unique traits such as frequency, bandwidth, and modulation type. There has been good emphasis on backward compatibility, so usually devices that adhere to newer standards are capable of connecting to devices of an older standard, using the older standard as the connection protocol. All of this is invisible to the user, however.

Table 10–1. *802.11 Variants*

Version	Release	Frequency (GHz)	Indoor (Ft)	Outdoor (Ft)	Max Data Rate
802.11	1997	2.4	60	300	2Mbps
802.11a	1999	5	100	350	54Mbps
802.11b	1999	2.4	120	450	11Mbps
802.11g	2003	2.4	120	450	54Mbps
802.11n	2009	2.4 / 5	230	800	150Mbps

The 802.11 family is one of many communication standards that an iOS device uses to make network communication with the world around it. To better understand how this communication takes place from a logical perspective, a brief history and overview of RFC 1122 (Internet Protocol suite) will prove a valuable concept in performing network analysis.

Since the birth of networking from the Defense Advanced Research Projects Agency's research, there have been ideas about how to logically construct a network model. This began to take shape in the 1970s and now provides a clear view into how Internet communication takes place. The best way to do this was with the concept of layers. By taking like functionality protocols and layering them on top one another, a wide range of systems were able to communicate at high layers on the stack, even if the bottom layers were different as the data traversed the Internet.

Inside RFC 1122, there are four layers, each performing a specific, but critical, function in network communication. From the bottom up, the layers are Link, Internet, Transport, and Application (see Figure 10–1). A good way to think of this is encapsulation. As an application on one computer prepares to send data to another application on a different computer across the Internet, it takes the data it wants to send and gives it to the operating system it's installed on. That operating system then divides the data into chunks for transport, uses Internet addressing to determine how to get across the Internet to the destination machine, and then sends it onto the network using its physical link. Because the destination receives it through its own link, it knows the data is for its system since the Internet address matches, so it reassembles it at the Transport layer and pushes the data up to the application for processing by the recipient application.

Encapsulation

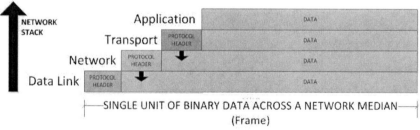

Figure 10–1. *Encapsulation transmitted across networks*

This is a difficult concept to comprehend, but its implementation is what allows all devices to communicate across networks. The world of networking is full of system compatibility—many different systems working together. By implementing standards defined inside the Internet Protocol suite, an iPhone can send an e-mail to another mobile device halfway across the world.

Within the Link layer, protocols are designed to allow connectivity from a host to the immediate network around it. This includes the physical connection (wired or wireless) and the basic protocols for sending and receiving bits. Carrier Sense Multiple Access with Collision Avoidance (CSMA/CA) is a protocol used by wireless devices to share common airwaves with one another. CSMA/CA is a standard implemented inside the 802.11 family. Consider the Link layer as a gateway to physical bits flowing across the network connection medium. The Link layer has its own way of addressing, commonly known as *MAC addressing*, that defines the physical hardware address of a device. MAC addresses are used in the Ethernet 2 protocol, which is also used in the 802.11 family (notice the commonality—lots of protocols!). CSMA/CA and Ethernet 2 will not get information from New York to California, but it will get information from an iPhone to the immediate access point nearest to it.

Figure 10–2 outlines how bytes are broken up into parts to create frames. From the iPhone to the router, the destination (DST) MAC address is of the router, and the source MAC address is of the iPhone (see Figure 10–3 for the MAC addresses, both Wi-Fi and Bluetooth, of the iPhone). Once this reaches the router, the Link layer is stripped off, the IPv4 IP header (see Figure 10–4) is interpreted, the router determines where to send it next, and then the router reencapsulates the IPv4 packet inside a new Link layer for the next device-to-device transmission it makes.

Ethernet II Frame Header & Payload

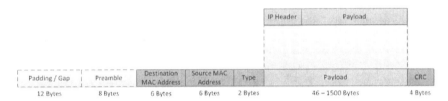

Figure 10–2. *A breakdown of the data contained inside an Ethernet 2 (Link layer) header*

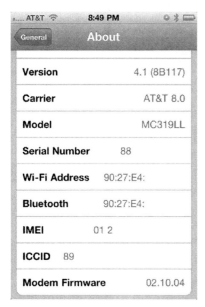

Figure 10–3. *Important hardware network addresses on an Apple mobile device, specifically, Wi-Fi and Bluetooth. Note that various digits have been hidden for privacy purposes.*

That is where the Internet layer comes in. The bits are transmitted from the iPhone to the wireless access point, and now they are transferred over a wire to another device. Once at the access point, the frame (a piece of Link layer data) is forwarded to the router. A router is a device used to link networks together. Commonly using the Internet Protocol (IP) addressing scheme, they send packets from one router to the next until they reach their destination. There are algorithms and standards that govern where a router actually sends its data, but that's outside the scope of this book. Realize that the Internet, at its core, is a multitude of networks both big and small, connected through lots and lots of routers.

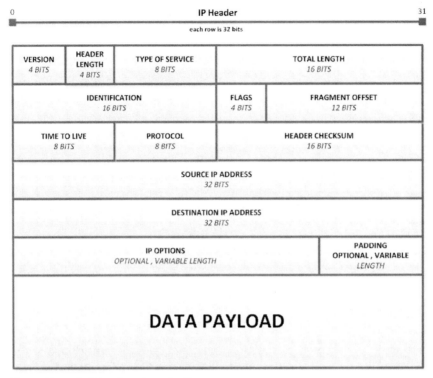

Figure 10–4. *An IP header schematic diagram*

An IP address consists of four numbers between 0 and 254 in what is referred to as dotted-quad notation. 8.8.8.8 is the IP address of a Google domain name server on the Internet, for example. IP addresses are the means by which information is sent from one node on the Internet to another. Whether it's a Mac, PC, iPhone, or other Internet-enabled device, it will use IP to send and receive information on the Internet.

The next layer in the stack is the Transport layer. (See Figure 10–5 for a complete view of the network stack, and see Figure 10–6 for the network flow between access points.) Although this layer is still transparent to the user, it is a critical link in application traffic between two hosts on the Internet. The Transport layer is largely made up of two protocols: Transport Control Protocol (TCP) and User Datagram Protocol (UDP). Although fundamentally different, almost every host on the Internet uses these protocols continuously while connected. For example, when a user navigates to a web site (for example, Google.com), their web browser will seemingly connect to Google's web server. Behind that, two critical things are happening, both with UDP and TCP. Using IP as the network layer protocol, an IP address must be specified. The Domain Name Service (DNS) is a global system that uses the UDP protocol to pair host names (for example, Google.com) with a given IP address (for example, 72.14.204.103). A host machine will query known DNS servers with a host name. The server will respond with the corresponding IP address. The host application and operating system can effectively construct data and conform to the RFC 1122 standard.

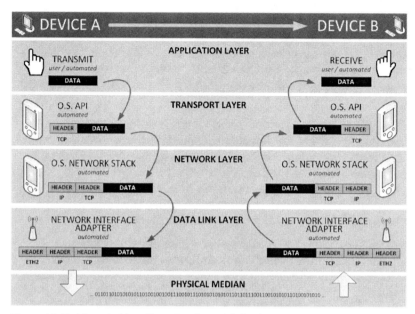

Figure 10–5. *A layout of how the network stack is implemented on a device*

NETWORK FLOW

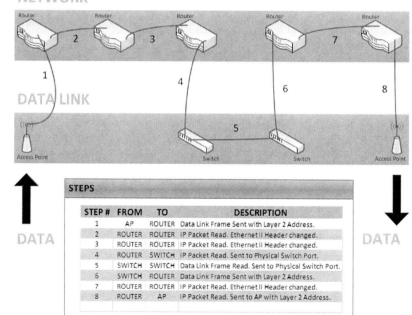

Figure 10–6. *How traffic flows through networks between layers 2 and 3*

Once the DNS service has resolved the IP address, the host browser, using the Hypertext Transfer Protocol (HTTP), requests a web page. This request is at the Application layer, and HTTP will be covered in more depth later. This request is made through a logical connection between the web server and the host machine. This connection's persistence is maintained with the use of the TCP protocol at the Transport layer.

TCP is a very complex protocol, but its creation helped change the way computer systems communicated. It is known as a connection-oriented protocol and uses many algorithms and functions to maintain data from one host to another. Consider that the data "ABCDEFG" is sent from Host A to Host B. The two hosts, using TCP, will communicate to ensure that not only is it sent and received but that it's ordered correctly and is the same data that was intended to be sent. This functionality is why TCP is considered to be a reliable communication transport protocol.

Using a mesh of protocols (see Figure 10–7), you can see how effective global communication is possible. This is how everything from mobile devices to servers communicate on the Internet. Every application that a user interacts with on a device will communicate in this manner.

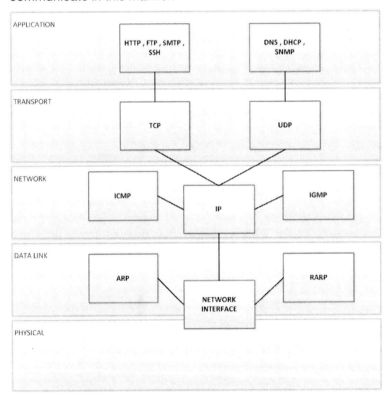

Figure 10–7. *Network protocols by layer and how they interoperate with the network stack*

Networking 201: Advanced Topics

Now that you better understand networking, it's time to look at some of the more advanced areas inside networking. There are networking artifacts scattered around mobile devices that hold significant relevance, but to apply them forensically, it's important to understand what they are from a networking standpoint.

DHCP

Looking back to the Internet Protocol, the pinnacle functionality becomes addressing. When two nodes on the Internet communicate, they must have effectively addressed one another. This is where Dynamic Host Control Protocol (DHCP) comes in. Although most servers and other static devices on the Internet get their addresses from organizations such as IANA, small mobile devices are assigned their IP addresses through the DHCP service operating on the local network. When a device is connected to a local Wi-Fi network, the device will broadcast at the Link layer, with a message saying, "I'm new, and I'd like to communicate using IP; is there a DHCP server that can give me an address?" The DHCP server on the local network (typically the router on most home and SMB equipment) will answer them, and the two will negotiate an address for them to use on the local network. This is usually a private address. Private addresses are specific ranges of IP addresses that have been designated for use on private networks and are not publicly accessible on the Internet. On networks that use private addressing, the router performs Network Address Translation (NAT). In NAT, the router will have a public IP address (usually assigned by the ISP) on one connection and then will perform DHCP services for all other connections. When a host on the private address space wants to access the Internet, they are routed through the public connection. The router manages what hosts have made what connections and can pass information back and forth from the public Internet to the hosts on the private network. Figure 10–8 shows how NAT works on a home network. Table 10–2 shows the ranges of private IP addresses (you'll usually only see Class C private addresses on a home network).

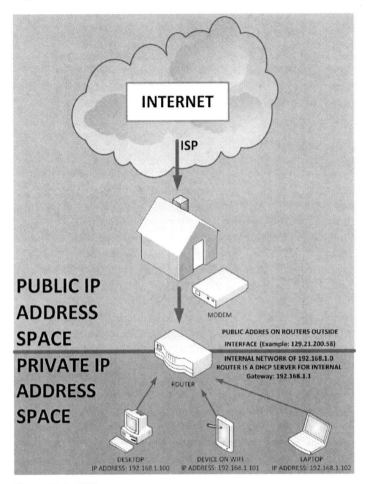

Figure 10–8. *NAT*

Table 10–2. *Private IP Address Ranges*

Beginning Address	End Address	Class	# of Hosts Possible
10.0.0.0	10.255.255.255	A	16,777,216
172.16.0.0	172.31.255.255	B	1,048,576
192.168.0.0	192.168.255.255	C	65,536

Aside from assigning an IP address to the device, DHCP can and will frequently pass along additional information about the local network. The most important of this information is the IP address of a DNS server. The host from that point on will query that DNS for all address resolutions. Figure 10–9 shows the address information your iPhone will pick up from a DHCP server.

Figure 10–9. *iPhone network settings screen*

Wireless Encryption and Authentication

When talking about mobile networking, it's almost certainly through 802.11 Wi-Fi. As time has progressed, several Wi-Fi encryption and authentication standards have emerged. Although compatible with all Apple devices, some networks today still do not utilize these technologies. The major types are WEP and WPA.

Wired Equivalent Privacy (WEP) is the oldest and least secure. Its creation was to thwart the ability to eavesdrop on 802.11 networks. Within the last several years, many cryptographic weaknesses have been identified in its design, and it has been depreciated, although many networks have not transitioned off of it. WEP has a few variants, which are dependent on the length of the key. The key is in essence the password to the network and part of the encryption cipher. It can be either 40, 106, or 232 bits in length and is usually entered as hexadecimal when a connection is attempted.

The standard chosen to replace WEP is called Wi-Fi Protected Access (WPA). It has a newer version of it called WPA2. WPA/WPA2 has much stronger security in its implementation than WEP. Even still, it is possible from a security standpoint to break WPA/WPA2 encryption in some cases. This is dependent on the implementation. Using algorithms such as Advanced Encryption Standard (AES) and strong passphrases will usually thwart most attacks. A passphrase is a password that can be long and complex, such as an entire sentence. WPA can also be used in conjunction with enterprise services such as RADIUS and EAP to authenticate users against enterprise directories.

Forensic Analysis

Where most forensic analysis relies on the discovery of user activity on the phone, network artifacts are quite opposite. Most are invisible to the user and cannot always be viewed from within the phone. Although this might not incriminate a user based on input, network artifacts are one of the best sources to corroborate location. By analyzing the network data stored on the phone cross-referenced with the network heuristics of networks surrounding a suspected location, a forensic analyst can prove the location of a device, even if all the user did was come near the access point in question. There are multiple files on an iOS device that can lead to this discovery.

com.apple.wifi.plist

This plist configuration file located at `/Library/Preferences/SystemPreferences/com.apple.wifi.plist` is used to cache Link layer and physical network information for 802.11 and its subprotocols, such as WPA, WEP, and so on. Data pertains to what Wi-Fi networks the user has connected to and when it is stored here. Information such as the access point's MAC address and the type of encryption used are present within this plist. All artifacts are stored in this document as Apple plist <key>/<data> pairs. Table 10–3 shows the significant artifact keys to identify and document when investigating the contents of this file.

Table 10–3. *Artifact Keys in* `com.apple.wifi.plist`

Artifact Keys	Explanation
BSSID	Link layer MAC address of the access point associated
SSID_STR	The name of the network the user connected to
Strength	An indicator of the signal strength at the time of connection
lastJoined	The date and time (local to the phone) of when the user joined to the network
lastAutoJoined	The date and time (local to the phone) of when the phone automatically joined to the network

If the network was a WPA2 enterprise network, an XML subtree named `EnterpriseProfile` will also exist and contain `EAPClientConfiguration`. An enterprise-level user name is typically found in here and could be useful in an investigation to note, for example, in the case of a stolen account.

com.apple.network.identification.plist

Like `wifi.plist` preserved data relating to 802.11 and its Link layer configurations, `network.identification.plist` (located at `/Library/Preferences/com.apple.network.identification.plist`) contains the mirroring information for

Internet Protocol network configurations. Inside the XML tree, there is a branch for every network the device has connected to. Inside each network <dictionary>, there is data pointing to the network's gateway and DNS servers, among other data. Table 10–4 shows artifacts that should be documented for an investigation.

Table 10–4. *Artifact Keys in* com.apple.network.identification.plist

Artifact	Explanation
Identifier	Default gateway (router's network address) as well as the MAC address for that interface.
DNS/server addresses	The DNS servers that were pointed to while on the network
IPv4/addresses	The IP address of the device at the time of connection
IPv4/router	The IP address of the router at the time of connection
IPv4/subnet masks	The subnet mask (used in routing network layer traffic)
Time stamp	A time stamp of when this information was generated

Using the information in both of these plists combined with an analysis of the site surveys performed, a forensic analyst could prove that the suspect device was accessing resources on or through this network at a specific time. This could be used to put a suspect at the location of a crime or to correlate an IP address to a suspect's device through Internet routing logs.

consolidated.db (iOS 4+)

consolidated.db (located at /Library/Caches/locationd/consolidated.db) is potentially one of the most forensically rich files an analyst can use. To view the data, open a Terminal window and navigate to the directory that contains consolidated.db using the cd (change directory) command. For more information on the syntax, type man cd at the Terminal prompt. Once there, open the database using the command sqlite3 consolidated.db. A prompt for sqlite will appear. If you type .tables, you'll see the following output:

```
iOSForensics # ls
consolidated.db
iOSForensics # sqlite3 consolidated.db
SQLite version 3.6.12
Enter ".help" for instructions
Enter SQL statements terminated with a ";"
sqlite> .tables
Cell                          CellLocationLocalBoxes_rowid
CellLocation                  CellLocationLocalCounts
CellLocationBoxes             CompassCalibration
CellLocationBoxes_node        Fences
CellLocationBoxes_parent      Location
CellLocationBoxes_rowid       LocationHarvest
CellLocationCounts            LocationHarvestCounts
CellLocationHarvest           TableInfo
CellLocationHarvestCounts     Wifi
CellLocationLocal             WifiLocation
CellLocationLocalBoxes        WifiLocationCounts
CellLocationLocalBoxes_node   WifiLocationHarvest
CellLocationLocalBoxes_parent WifiLocationHarvestCounts
sqlite>
```

The two important tables relating to networking are WifiLocation and WifiLocationHarvest. Although similar in structure, they represent two data sets. WifiLocation is a database of MAC addresses of access points the phone has "heard." In a wireless network, an access point broadcasts a beacon frame—a Link layer piece of data to alert possible devices of the network's existence. This allows the phone to discover the available Wi-Fi networks within its range. WifiLocation records the MAC address, time stamp, latitude, longitude, altitude, and other geo-locational references when it hears one of these beacons. If a phone moves across a given area, you could theoretically track the phone by interpreting the beacons the phone has seen against a map of known Wi-Fi networks. The data set inside WifiLocation is quite large—regularly in the hundreds of thousands of rows. WifiLocationHarvest is similar but only lists the access points that the phone has actually made a connection to.

To view the data contained within these tables, simple SQL queries can be made. For example, to print all the data within the WifiLocation table, the command SELECT * FROM WifiLocation; can be issued at the prompt. There is a lot of information about SQL queries—specifically SQLite syntax—on the Internet. Finally, to quit, execute the command .exit at the sqlite prompt. This will bring you back to the working directory the consolidated.db file is in. If you want to generate a more detailed view of the information contained, simple scripts written in Perl or Bash can be a quick solution, or third-party applications can convert entire tables into HTML or CSV files. Finding any SQLite export utility should be sufficient here.

Network Traffic Analysis

In extreme cases, network traffic analysis may need to be performed. This could be used to identify malware operating on the device or to identify certain information sent over plain-text protocols on a device. For this to occur, there are special requirements that need to be met.

Inside the forensics lab, a forensic analyst will need the following hardware:

- A wireless access point (not a router!)
- A wired router
- Multiple CAT5/6 cables
- A hub
- A computer
- An Internet connection (optional but sometimes helpful)

Besides this hardware, the analyst will need to be able to configure these devices specifically to fulfill their purpose. The hub is a crucial part of the topology. Without it, an analyst will not be able to effectively sniff the traffic from the phone. Figure 10–10 shows the topology to set up and use.

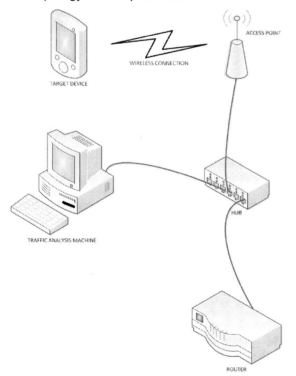

Figure 10–10. *Topology of a forensic traffic analysis network*

After building and configuring the hardware and the network (assigning IP addresses of the traffic analysis machine, creating the wireless network and connecting the device, and configuring the router), next we will cover the analysis tool Wireshark. Wireshark is a network protocol analysis utility that is platform independent and shows the user all network traffic seen by the device it's installed on in a nice GUI. To download the latest version of Wireshark, visit www.wireshark.org.

Once you've installed and configured Wireshark to sniff the traffic on the network interface tied into the forensic network, you will be able to see the network traffic in the GUI. There are three main views within Wireshark's GUI: Packet List, Packet Details, and Packet Bytes (see Figure 10–11).

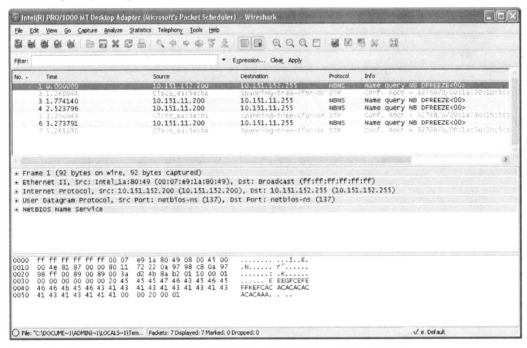

Figure 10–11. *In order from top to bottom: Packet List, Packet Details, and Packet Bytes*

Notice the similarities between the Packet Details view and the network layers of RFC 1122. From Wireshark, you can effectively view *all* encapsulated data at every layer simply by expanding the plus sign next to the corresponding layer's protocol name.

From a forensic standpoint, when searching for possible connection attempts from malware on a device, the best indicator is DNS traffic. A piece of malware or a spy agent might attempt to make a remote connection to a endpoint on the Internet by first making a DNS query against a host name. This would give the malware an IP address to connect to. If that IP address goes down, the malware operator simply points the host name at a different IP address and continues. This is a common way malware operators maintain persistence.

Although these packets are viewable from the default view inside Wireshark, using a filter will help narrow down the list of packets inside the Packet List view. Using a filter to find DNS traffic is just one of the many applications a forensic analyst might use when analyzing traffic sent and received by a device. To filter for DNS, type **dns** into the Filter field, and click Apply. This will give a list view of only DNS traffic, as shown in Figure 10–12.

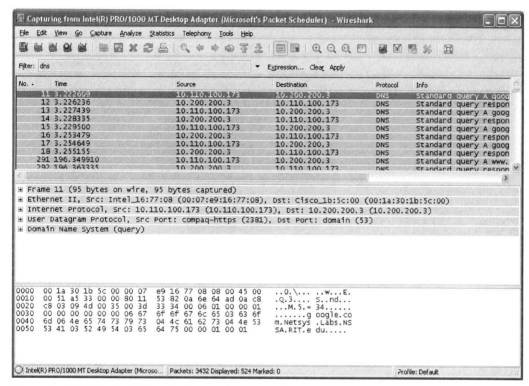

Figure 10–12. *A Wireshark filter showing only DNS traffic*

Many other filters might prove valuable. For example, to filter based upon IP address, use the `filter` command `ip.addr == 10.200.200.17` to view any traffic relating to the 10.200.200.17 IP address; see Figure 10–13.

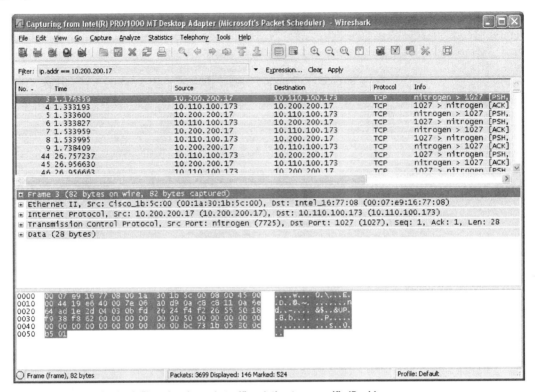

Figure 10–13. *A Wireshark filter showing only traffic relating to a specific IP address*

To view only HTTP traffic, use the filter `tcp.port == 80` in the Filter field. Afterward, expand the HTTP protocol information inside the Packet Details view to find data relating to the specific HTTP packet selected in the list (see Figure 10–14).

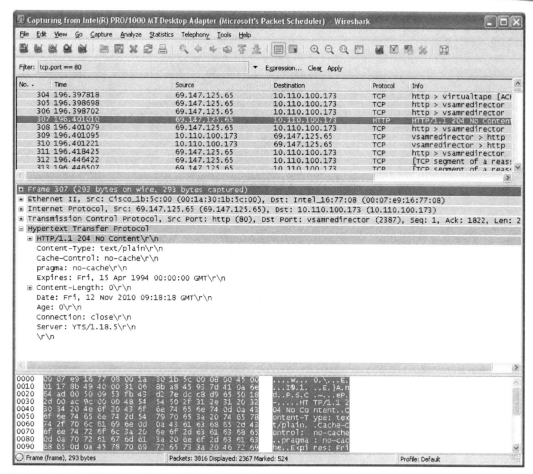

Figure 10–14. *A Wireshark filter showing HTTP traffic with the HTTP protocol details expanded*

Using Wireshark, the analysis of the data being sent and received from a device is not only possible but easy for a forensic analyst. Many applications use plain-text HTTP traffic to send and receive data on mobile devices. Using the network forensic techniques described earlier will allow a forensic analyst to uncover and document this data on the device. Once finished with the analysis, an analyst will want to save a PCAP file of the capture. A PCAP file is a binary file that contains all the data recorded and can be reopened using Wireshark and many third-party utilities as well. To do this, stop the capture by selecting Capture ➤ Stop Capture and selecting File ➤ Save As. The capture can also be saved through that Save As dialog box in many different formats for various reporting purposes.

Summary

While conventional forensics analyzes typical phone data, network analysis can yield data that can go beyond hearsay and into technical truth. By uncovering connection logs and other empirical evidence, investigators are given not just insight into users' actions, but data by which they can continue to correlate and build a forensically rich timeline.

Consider the difference in an investigation it would make for an investigator to take connection data to a judge and get a warrant for the network the phone was connected to. Had network analysis not been conducted, the warrant would more than likely have not been granted, and the investigation could not use another vector to mine data. Using live traffic analysis, a forensic analyst might discover malware installed on the device or sensitive information transmitted in an insecure or plain-text fashion. Both of these examples can make a difference in the course of an investigation.

As the world becomes more integrated, the systems that run servers will continue to power more and more of the devices, giving birth to new areas of forensic data that were previously nonexistent. Being versed in the concepts of networking, a forensic analyst can begin to decode this data and build a case off evidence rooted in various standards and protocols invisible to the suspect for viewing or change—something that cannot be negotiated in a court of law.

Index

■Numbers

2G iPhone, 4
3 Minutes setting, 79
3G network, 72

■A

ABGroup table, 49, 139, 142
ABGroupChanges table, 49
ABGroupMembers table, 49, 139, 142
ABMultiValue table, 49, 139, 142
ABMultiValueEntry table, 49, 139, 142
ABMultiValueEntryKey table, 49
ABMultiValueLabel table, 49
ABPerson table, 49, 139, 142
ABPersonChanges table, 49
ABPersonMultiValueDeletes table, 49
ABPersonSearchKey table, 49
ABPhoneLastFour table, 49
ABRecent table, 49
ABStore table, 49
ABThumbnailImage table, 144
Accelerometer iPad hardware, 18
Access Data FTK (Forensic Toolkit) tool
    and images, 306–313
    overview, 303–306
    SQLite databases, 313
Accountsettings.plist, 113
Acquire icon, Lantern app, 94
Add button, 64
Add Files, CocoaSlideShow menu bar, 242
Address_bcc message ID, 165
AddressBook database, 1, 49, 142–144
AddressBook.sqlitedb, 138
Address_cc message ID, 165
Address_replyTo message ID, 165
Address_to message ID, 165
AES (Advanced Encryption Standard), 333
Airplane Mode, 75–76, 323

All Applications, 64
Allocation file, 34
Alternate volume header, 35
Always Open With box, 64
analysis window, 220
analytics, 191
antiforensic applications, 197–206
    image vaults, 198
    incognito web browser, 200–201
    invisible browser, 201
    Picture Safe, 198–199
    Picture Vault, 199–200
    tigertext, 202–206
AOL AIM, 184
AOL Instant Messenger artifacts, 184
API (application programming interface), 29
App Store, history of, 19–22
Apple Message Pad, 1
Apple TV, 36–37
Apple v. Psystar, 273–274
AppleTV 2G iOS device, 18
Application directory, 42
Application processor 2G hardware, 11
Application processor 3G hardware, 13
Application processor 3GS hardware, 15
application programming interface (API), 29
applications
    antiforensic, 197–206
        image vaults, 198
        incognito web browser, 200–201
        invisible browser, 201
        Picture Safe, 198–199
        Picture Vault, 199–200
        tigertext, 202–206
    MacForensicsLab app, 299–303
    Maps, 227–237
    navigation, 260–265
        Navigon, 260–264
        Tom Tom, 265
    spyware, 317–322
        FlexiSpy, 321

Mobile Spy, 318–321
third-party, 178–196
analytics, 191
AOL AIM, 184
Bing, 194
Craigslist, 189–190
documents and document recovery,
194–196
Facebook, 182–183
Google Mobile, 192–193
Google Voice, 186–189
iDisk, 192
LinkedIn, 184–185
MySpace, 185–186
Opera, 193
Skype, 180–182
social networking analysis, 180–196
Twitter, 185
artifacts
from Mac, 209–212
changes to backup files, 211–212
lockdown certificates, 212
MobileSync database, 210
property list, 209–210
from Windows, 212–214
iPodDevices.xml, 212–213
lockdown certificates, 214
MobileSync backups, 213–214
Attributes file, 35
Audio 2G hardware, 11
Audio 3G hardware, 13
Audio 3GS hardware, 15
Audio iPad hardware, 16
Audio Processor iPad hardware, 18
authentication, wireless, 333
Auto-Lock setting, 78–79
Autowake.plist, 168

B

Back Up option, iTunes app, 91
backed-up data, 211
Backup Extraction Wizard interface, 220
Backup Extractor tool, iPhone, 214–216
backup files, 220–225
changes to, 211–212
FTK 1.8 tool, 222–223
FTK Imager tool, 221
tips, 223
Baseband iPhone 4 hardware, 16
Baseband processor 2G hardware, 11

Baseband processor 3G hardware, 13
Baseband processor 3GS hardware, 15
Berka, J., 272
Bin directory, 42
Bing, 194
Blacklist applications, 250
Bluetooth iPad hardware, 18
Body message ID, 165
Bookmark.plist, 154–155, 230, 232–234
Browse Data tab, 54–55
Browse tab, 57
BSSID artifact key, 334
B*trees, 33
buyer bewares, 130

C

Cache.plist, 253
Caches directory, 140–141, 144–146
Calendar app, 100–101
Calendar directory, 140–141
Call History database, 49–52, 97, 147–148
Call History directory, 140–141
Call history log, 112
Call Log database, 51
Call logs, 97, 123
Call table, 51
CallHistory database, 147–148
Camera 2G hardware, 11
Camera 3G hardware, 13
Camera 3GS hardware, 15
Camera application, 27, 174
Camera iPhone 4 hardware, 16
Carrier Sense Multiple Access with Collision
Avoidance (CSMA/CA), 326
carving, 299–317
Access Data FTK tool
and images, 306–313
SQLite databases, 313
EnCase tool, 314–317
MacForensicsLab app, 299–303
case directory, Lantern app, 93
case number, Lantern app, 93
Catalog file, 35
catalog ID numbers, 34
cell phone, tracking individual by, 69
Cell table, 259
cell tower data
GeoHunter technology, 255–259
overview, 248–255

Cellebrite UFED (Universal Forensic
  Extraction Device), 125–130
  results, 132
  setting up, 126–130
  supported devices, 126
CellLocation table, 259
CellLocationCounts table, 259
CellLocationHarvestCounts table, 259
CellLocationLocaBoxes_parent table, 259
CellLocationLocal table, 259
CellLocationLocalBoxes table, 259
CellLocationLocalBoxes_node table, 259
CellLocationLocalBoxes_rowid table, 259
CellLocationLocalCounts table, 259
Cells.plist, 249
CFAbsoluteTimeConverter, 146
Class C private addresses, 331
Clients-b.plist, 249
clients.plist, 259
Clients.plist database, 145
Clients.plistproperty list, 145
Cocoa component, 30
CocoaSlideShow, 241, 244
com.apple.accountsettings.plist property
  list, 156
com.apple.AppStore.plist property list, 156
com.apple.AppSupport.plist property list,
  156
com.apple.commventer.plst property list,
  156
com.apple.compass.plist property list, 156
com.apple.locationd.plist property list, 156
com.apple.Maps.plist property list, 157
com.apple.MobileBluetooth.devices.plist
  property list, 157
com.apple.mobilephone.settings.plist
  property list, 157
com.apple.mobilephone.speeddial.plist
  property list, 157
com.apple.mobilesafari.plist property list,
  157
com.apple.mobiletimer.plist property list,
  157
com.apple.network.identification.plist, 157,
  334–335
com.apple.preferences.datetime.plist
  property list, 157
com.apple.prefernces.network.plist property
  list, 157
com.apple.springboard.plist property list,
  157
com.apple.stocks.plist property list, 157
com.apple.weather.plist property list, 157
com.apple.wifi.plist, 157, 334
com.apple.youtube.plist property list, 157
comma-separated value (CSV) format,
  55–56
command-line tools, 87
CommCenter directory, 47
Compass application interface, 240
CompassCalibration table, 259
configuration profiles, 149
ConfigurationProfiles directory, 140–141
connection wizard, Oxygen Forensic Suite
  2010 program, 118–119
Connectivity 2G hardware, 11
Connectivity 3G hardware, 13
Connectivity 3GS hardware, 15
Connectivity/80211 and GPS iPhone 4
  hardware, 16
Connectivity iPhone 4 hardware, 16
consolidated.db CellLocation table, 145
consolidated.db file, 145
consolidated.db (iOS 4+), 335–336
Contact data, 123
Contactlogs.dat, 319
Contacts pane, 98–99
Content_type, 162
Conversation ID message ID, 165
cookies, 149–150
Cookies directory, 140–141
cookies.plist file, 150, 201
Core Services component, 31
Cores directory, 42
Craig Phone app, 190
Craigslist, 189–190
CS folder, 196
CSDatabase.sqlite folder, 196
CSMA/CA (Carrier Sense Multiple Access
  with Collision Avoidance), 326
CSV (comma-separated value) format,
  55–56
custody, 323–324
Cydia application, 317

 D

Damaged files directory, 42
dat file, 105
data acquisition, 87–133
  buyer bewares, 130
  Cellebrite UFED, 125–130

results, 132
setting up, 126–130
supported devices, 126
from iPhone, iPod touch, and iPad, 87–92
Lantern application, 92–107
Calendar app, 101
call logs, 97
Contacts pane, 98–99
directory structure, 107
Dynamic Text data, 105–106
Internet history, 102
iPod and media, 103
Maps pane, 106
messages, 99
notes, 100
phone information pane, 96
photos, 103–105
results, 132
Voicemail pane, 98
Oxygen Forensic Suite 2010 program, 118–125
connection wizard, 118–119
data extraction wizard, 120
results, 131
supported devices, 118
viewing backup data, 121–125
Paraben Device Seizure tool
overview, 115–117
results, 131
support, 133
Susteen Secure View 2 tool, 107–114
acquiring data, 110–111
reporting data, 111–114
results, 132
setting up and navigating interface, 107–110
data extraction wizard, Oxygen Forensic Suite 2010 program, 120
data partition, for iOS, 46–49
Data table, 51
Database Browser, 53–55, 138, 140, 143, 221, 313
database format, 49
Database Viewer, SQLite, 221
date and time, photo evidence, 82
Date voicemail.db, 163
dateMS conversation ID, 166
Db directory, 47, 61
DC Regulator iPad hardware, 18

Defense Advanced Research Projects Agency, 325
DES algorithm, 43
Desktop Accounts folder, 196
Developer directory, 42
Developer Program, iPhone, 31–32
Device Firmware Update (DFU), 278
Device information, 124
Device Seizure, 115–117, 131
DFU (Device Firmware Update), 278
DHCP (Dynamic Host Control Protocol), 331–332
Dhcpclient directory, 47
Dictionary pane, Lantern app, 106
Digital Millennium Copyright Act (DMCA), 269–270, 272
Digital Performance Right in Sound Recordings Act (DPRA), 269
Directions To Here, 229
Directions.plist, 234–237
Directory data, 125
directory structure, 107
Display 2G hardware, 11
Display 3G hardware, 13
Display 3GS hardware, 15
Display iPad hardware, 18
Display iPhone 4 hardware, 16
DMCA (Digital Millennium Copyright Act), 269–270, 272
.dmg files, 223, 225
DNS (Domain Name Service), 328, 332, 338–339
DNS/server addresses artifact, 335
Documents folder, 196
documents, recovery of, 194–196
Documents to Go app, 196
Domain Name Service (DNS), 328, 332, 338–339
downloading music online, 274
DPRA (Digital Performance Right in Sound Recordings Act), 269
DRAM memory iPhone 4 hardware, 16
DRM (Digital rights management), 267–276
Apple v. Psystar, 273–274
DMCA, 269–270
fair use doctrine, 269–270
first sale doctrine, 269
future of, 275–276
jailbreaking iPhone, 271–272
online music downloading, 274
secondary infringement liability, 270

Sony BMG case, 275
United States Constitution, 268–269
Duration voicemail.db, 163
Dynamic Host Control Protocol (DHCP),
    331–332
Dynamic Text data, 105–106
dynamic-text.dat file, 150

E

e-mail, 295–298
    Exchange, 298
    IMAP, 296
    POP, 296–297
Ea directory, 47
Earthpoint output, 257
Earthpoint web interface, 256
Elkin-Koren, N., 268, 270–271
Elmer-DeWitt, P., 273
Email.db structure, 320
EMI/RFI-sanitized room, 324
.emlx file, 297
encapsulation, transmitted across networks,
    325
EnCase tool, 194, 213, 216, 221, 299,
    314–317
encryption, wireless, 333
Enter Passcode screen, 77–78
Etc directory, 42
Ethernet 2, 326
Evans, J., 273
Exchange e-mails, 298
EXIF (Exchangeable Image File Format),
    103, 114, 138, 171, 237, 310
Expiration Date voicemail.db, 163
export data from Froq application, 59
Export KML File, 245
Export resultset screen, 60
Extents overflow file, 35
extraction wizard, 120

F

Facebook, 182–183
Faces tool, 174
fair use doctrine, 269–270
Farley, T., 67
Fences table, 259
File Finder enscript, 315–317
File Juicer app, 177, 312

File Spy application, 317
file system, for iOS, 33–36
    HFS+, 33–35
    HFSX, 35–36
Files report, 114
Find My iPad feature, 73
Find My iPhone service, 72–73
first sale doctrine, 269
FirstSortSectionCount table, 49
Flag, CocoaSlideShow menu bar, 242
Flags voicemail.db, 163
Fletcher, F., 69
FlexiSpy app, 321
Folders directory, 47
forensic analysis, 334–336
    com.apple.network.identification.plist,
        334–335
    com.apple.wifi.plist, 334
    consolidated.db (iOS 4+), 335–336
forensic tools, 220–225
    FTK 1.8 tool, 222–223
    FTK Imager tool, 221
    tips, 223
forensic workstations, setting up, 135–140
Foresman, C., 274
Fourth Amendment of U.S. Constitution, and
        search and seizure, 68–69
Froq application, 56, 58–59, 140, 153
fstab file, 41
FTK 1.8 tool, 222–223
FTK (Forensic Toolkit) tool
    and images, 306–313
    SQLite databases, 313
FTK Imager tool, 221

G

General log, 292
Geo-location data, 227
Geodata, entered into Google Maps, 231
GeoHunter technology, 255–259
geospatial metadata, 237
geotagged EXIF data, 239
geotagging images, and videos, 237–248
Gershowitz, A., 69–72
Get Info dialog box, 63
Get Info option, 222
Gmail account contact information, 189
Google Map button, CocoaSlideShow, 243
Google Maps, 6, 103, 130, 172, 236,
        241–243

Google Mobile, 192–193
Google Voice, 186–189
GoogleDocDatabase.sqlite folder, 196
GPGGA data, 261
GPRMC values, 261
GPS 3G hardware, 13
GPS 3GS hardware, 15
GPS coordinates, 172–173
GPS data, 114, 171–172, 303
GPS (Global Positioning System), 227–265
    cell tower data
        GeoHunter technology, 255–259
        overview, 248–255
    geotagging images and videos, 237–248
    Maps application, 227–237
    navigation applications, 260–265
        Navigon app, 260–264
        Tom Tom app, 265
GPS Visualizer, 257–258
GPSBabel app, 262–264
Gpslog.dat, 319
GPSLog.day file, 319
graphical user interface (GUI), 1, 51, 87, 103,
    139
Graphics 2G hardware, 11
Graphics 3G hardware, 13
Graphics 3GS hardware, 15
Groenenboom, M., 267, 276
GUI (graphical user interface), 1, 51, 87, 103,
    139
GUI tools, Mac, 177
Gyroscope iPhone 4 hardware, 16

H

H-cells.plist, 250–251
H-Wifi.plist, 252–253
hackers, of iPhone, 22
Hafner, K., 70
hardware, internal
    for iPad, 16–17
    for iPhone 2G, 9–11
    for iPhone 3G, 12–13
    for iPhone 3G[S], 14–15
    for iPhone 4, 15–16
Harwood, E.D., 268–269, 274
hasAttachment conversation ID, 166
hasAttachment message ID, 165
Hayes, D., 271–272
Hdiutil program, 37
Helberger, N., 267, 276

Henderson, S., 68–69
HFS+ (Hierarchical File System), 33–36
HFS volume, 33, 40
HFSX, file system for iOS, 35–36
Hierarchical File System (HFS+), 33–36
Hinkes, E.M., 269–270
history of Apple mobile devices, 1–23
    and App Store, 19–22
    iPad, 8
    iPhone 2G, 3–5
        competitive advantages, 5
        web apps for, 4
    iPhone 3G, 5–6
    iPhone 3G[S], 6–7
    iPhone 4, 7
    iPhone hackers, 22
    iPod, 2
    ROCKR, 2–3
history.plist, 158, 230
home screen, iPhone, 26
HTC, 5
HTML report, 128
HTTP (Hypertext Transfer Protocol), 330,
    340
https_www.google.com_0 directory, 167
Huges, N., 273
Hypertext Transfer Protocol (HTTP), 330,
    340

I

Identifier artifact, 335
iDevice backups, 214–220
    iPhone Backup Extractor tool, 214–216
    JuicePhone app, 216–217
    mdhelper app, 218–219
    Oxygen Forensics Suite 2010 program,
        219–220
iDisk, 192
IEEE (Institute of Electrical and Electronics
    Engineers), 324
iErase app, 197
Image direction reference, 241
Image EXIF, 307
image validation, 284
image vaults, 198
images
    Access Data FTK tool, 306–313
    geotagging, 237–248
IMAP (Internet Message Access Protocol),
    296

incognito web browser, 200–201
info.plist, 138
Inspector GPS data, 240
Institute of Electrical and Electronics
        Engineers (IEEE), 324
internal hardware
    for iPad, 16–17
    for iPhone 2G, 9–11
    for iPhone 3G, 12–13
    for iPhone 3G[S], 14–15
    for iPhone 4, 15–16
Internet bookmarks, 102
Internet history, 102
Internet Message Access Protocol (IMAP),
        296
Internet Protocol (IP), 327
invisible browser, 201
iOS, 25–66
    development of applications for, 31–33
    feature comparisons for, 25–31
        iOS 1, 25–27
        iOS 2, 27–28
        iOS 3, 28–29
        iOS 4, 29–31
    file system, 33–36
        HFS+, 33–35
        HFSX, 35–36
    partition and volume information, 36–49
        data partition, 46–49
        OS partition, 41
        system partition, 41–45
    property lists in, 61–66
    SQLite databases in, 49–66
        Address Book database, 49
        Call History database, 50
        retrieving data from, 53–60
        SMS database, 50
IP address, 328, 339
IP header, 328
IP (Internet Protocol), 327
iPad
    data acquisition, 87–92
    history of, 8
    internal hardware for, 16–17
iPad 3G+ WiFi iOS device, 18
iPad WiFi iOS device, 18
iPhone
    data acquisition, 87–92
    jailbreaking, 271–272
iPhone 2G
    history of, 3–5

competitive advantages, 5
    web apps for, 4
    internal hardware for, 9–11
iPhone 3G
    history of, 5–6
    internal hardware for, 12–13
iPhone 3G[S]
    history of, 6–7
    internal hardware for, 14–15
iPhone 4
    history of, 7
    internal hardware for, 15–16
iPhone Backup Extractor tool, 214–216
iPhone Developer Program, 31–32
iPhone home screen, 26
iPhone Twitter application, 179
iPhoto photos, 176–177
iPod, history of, 2
iPod Touch 1G iOS device, 18
iPod Touch 2G iOS device, 18
iPod Touch 3G iOS device, 18
IPod Touch 4G iOS device, 18
iPod Touch, data acquisition, 87–92
iPodDevices.xml, 212–213
IPv4/addresses artifact, 335
IPv4/router artifact, 335
IPv4/subnet masks artifact, 335
Irfanview, 308–309
isinbox conversation ID, 166
isinbox message ID, 165
isolating device, from networks, 75–77
isStarred conversation ID, 166
isStarred message ID, 165
isUread conversation ID, 166
isUread message ID, 165
.ithmb files, 138, 311
iTunes, 3, 121, 177–178
iXAM tool, 277–283

J

jailbreak methods, 284
jailbreaking
    iPhone, 271–272
    overview, 207
jailbroken iPhones, identifying, 79–80
John the Ripper tool, 43
JPEGs, 302, 304
JuicePhone app, 216–217

K

Kerr, O., 71
Key column, 64–65
key logger, 150
keyboard, 150–152
Keyboard directory, 140–141
Keychain directory, 47, 61
keyword search, in TextEdit, 151
Keyword search option, 100
KML export, 245–247
KML file, 244

L

Labriola, D., 267–268
Lantern application, 92–107
    Calendar app, 101
    call logs, 97
    Contacts pane, 98–99
    directory structure, 107
    Dynamic Text data, 105–106
    Internet history, 102
    iPod and media, 103
    Maps pane, 106
    messages, 99
    notes, 100
    phone information pane, 96
    photos, 103–105
    results, 132
    Voicemail pane, 98
Last visited date value, 158
lastAutoJoined artifact key, 334
lastJoined artifact key, 334
Latitude
    history.plist, 230
    North Pole settings, 241
Lawinski, J., 273
LED Driver iPad hardware, 18
LED flash, 7
Library/AddressBook directory, 48
Library/Caches/Com.apple.itunesstored
        directory, 48
Library/Caches directory, 48
Library/Calendar directory, 48
Library/CallHistory directory, 48
Library/Carrier Bundles directory, 48
Library/ConfigurationProfiles directory, 48
/library/configurationProfiles/Passwordhistor
        y.plist, 295
Library/Cookies directory, 48

Library/DataAccess directory, 48
Library directory, 43
Library domain, 140–167
    AddressBook database, 142–144
    Caches directory, 144–146
    call history database, 147–148
    configuration profiles, 149
    cookies, 149–150
    keyboard, 150–152
    Logs directory, 152–154
    Map history, 155
    Maps app, 154–155
    Notes database, 156
    Preferences folder, 156–157
    Safari browser, 157–158
    SMS and MMS databases, 160–162
    Suspended State property, 159–160
    voicemails, 162–163
    WebClips folder, 163–164
    WebKits folder, 164–167
Library/Keyboard directory, 48
Library/Logs directory, 48
Library/Mail directory, 48
Library/Maps directory, 48
Library/Mobileinstallation directory, 48
Library/Notes directory, 48
Library/Preferences/com.rxs.smartphoneplist,
        318
Library/Preferences directory, 48
library property list, 210
Library/RemoteNotification directory, 48
Library/Safari directory, 48, 61
Library/SafeHarbor directory, 48
Library/SMS directory, 48
Library/Voicemail directory, 48
Library/Webclips directory, 48
Library/WebKit directory, 48
LinkedIn, 184–185
Locate button, GPS data box, 172
Location Harvest table, 259
Location table, 259
lock passcode, remote, 75
LockBackground.jpg directory, 140–141
lockdown certificates
    copying from computer, 84
    overview, 212–214
Lockdown folder, 84
Log directory, 47
logical data analysis, 135–207
    antiforensic applications and processes,
        197–206

image vaults, 198
incognito web browser, 200–201
invisible browser, 201
Picture Safe, 198–199
Picture Vault, 199–200
tigertext, 202–206
jailbreaking, 207
Library domain, 140–167
AddressBook database, 142–144
Caches directory, 144–146
call history database, 147–148
configuration profiles, 149
cookies, 149–150
keyboard, 150–152
Logs directory, 152–154
Map history, 155
Maps app, 154–155
Notes database, 156
Preferences folder, 156–157
Safari browser, 157–158
SMS and MMS databases, 160–162
Suspended State property, 159–160
voicemails, 162–163
WebClips folder, 163–164
WebKits folder, 164–167
Media Domain, 170–178
iPhoto photos, 176–177
Media directory, 170–175
multimedia, 177–178
PhotosAux.sqlite database, 175
Photos.sqlite database, 175
recordings, 176
setting up forensic workstations,
135–140
System Configuration data, 168–170
third-party applications, 178–196
analytics, 191
AOL AIM, 184
Bing, 194
Craigslist, 189–190
documents and document recovery,
194–196
Facebook, 182–183
Google Mobile, 192–193
Google Voice, 186–189
iDisk, 192
LinkedIn, 184–185
MySpace, 185–186
Opera, 193
Skype, 180–182
social networking analysis, 180–196

Twitter, 185
Logs directory, 152–154
Longitude
history.plist, 230
North Pole settings, 241
Lyon, M.H., 269, 274–276

■ M

Mac
artifacts from, 209–212
changes to backup files, 211–212
lockdown certificates, 212
MobileSync database, 210
property list, 209–210
reviewing exploited media, 291–295
MAC addresses, 326
Mac GUI tools, 177
MacForensicsLab app, 299–303
MacFUSE, 40
Mail application, 295
Managed Preferences directory, 47, 61
Manifest property list, 293
Map history, 155
Maps application, 154–155, 227–237
Maps bookmarks, 155
Maps data, 106
Maps directory, 140–141
Maps pane, 106
Maptiles, 295
MCDataMigration.plist, 149
McDougall, P., 273
.mdbackup files, 211
mdhelper app, 88–92, 218–219
Media/Books directory, 49
Media component, 30
Media/DCIM directory, 48
Media directory, 170–175
Media Domain, 170–178
iPhoto photos, 176–177
Media directory, 170–175
multimedia, 177–178
PhotosAux.sqlite database, 175
Photos.sqlite database, 175
recordings, 176
media exploitation, 267–289, 291–322
carving, 299–317
Access Data tool, 303–313
EnCase tool, 314–317
MacForensicsLab app, 299–303
DRM, 267–276

Apple v. Psystar, 273–274
DMCA, 269–270
fair use doctrine, 269–270
first sale doctrine, 269
future of, 275–276
jailbreaking iPhone, 271–272
online music downloading, 274
secondary infringement liability, 270
Sony BMG case, 275
United States Constitution, 268–269
e-mail, 295–298
Exchange, 298
IMAP, 296
POP, 296–297
image validation, 284
reviewing exploited media using Macs,
291–295
spyware applications, 317–322
FlexiSpy, 321
Mobile Spy, 318–321
tools, 277–284
iXAM, 277–283
other jailbreak methods, 284
Media /iTunes_Control directory, 48
Media/PhotoData directory, 48
Memory 2G hardware, 11
Memory 3G hardware, 13
Memory 3GS hardware, 15
Memory iPad hardware, 18
Memory iPhone 4 hardware, 16
Message Pad, Apple, 1
Message_id, 162
messages, 99
mini-SIM card, 77, 79
MMS data, 99
MMS database, 160–162
Mobile/Application directory, 48
Mobile directory, 47
Mobile installation plist, 293
Mobile/Library/Caches/Safari/Thumbnails,
294
Mobile/Library/Caches/snapshots, 294
Mobile/library/Cookies directory, 61
Mobile/Library/Mail directory, 61
Mobile/Library/Preferences directory, 61
Mobile/Librarycom.apple.mobile.installation.
plist, 293
Mobile/Library.Maps directory, 61
Mobile Safari browser, 149
Mobile Spy application, 318–321
MobileDevice directory, 47

MobileInstallation directory, 140
mobile.installation.plist, 294
MobileMe account, 72, 192
MobileSync backups, 213–214
MobileSync database, 176, 209–210
ModifyDateMs conversation ID, 166
Motorola Droid, 5
MOV files, 247–248
Move to trash, CocoaSlideShow menu bar,
242
Mow, L., 69
/Msdeamon directory, Contactlogs.dat, 319
Msg_group, 50
Msg_Pieces, 50
msg_pieces table, 162
multimedia, 177–178
music, downloading online, 274
MySpace, 185–186

N

NAT (Network Address Translation),
331–332
National Institute of Standards and
Technology (NIST), 277
navigation applications, 260–265
Navigon, 260–264
Tom Tom, 265
Navigon app, 260–264
Network Address Translation (NAT),
331–332
network analysis, 323–342
custody, 323–324
DHCP, 331–332
forensic analysis, 334–336
com.apple.network.identification.plist,
334–335
com.apple.wifi.plist, 334
consolidated.db (iOS 4+), 335–336
network traffic analysis, 337–342
wireless encryption and authentication,
333
Network protocols, 330
network traffic analysis, 337–342
Network.identification.plist, 168–169
networks, isolating device from, 75–77
Never setting, 79
Newton, 1–2
NIST (National Institute of Standards and
Technology), 277

North Pole settings, Compass application, 241
notes, 100
Notes database, 156
Notes directory, 140–141
Notes pane, 100
Notes table, 156
Numbers directory, 195
numMessages conversation ID, 166

O

OmniOutliner application, 62, 64–65
online music, downloading, 274
Open icon, 53
Opera, 193
OS X kernel component, 31
Oxygen connection wizard, 118, 121–122, 125
Oxygen Forensic Suite 2010 program, 118–125
    connection wizard, 118–119
    data extraction wizard, 120
    results, 131
    supported devices, 118
    viewing backup data, 121–125
Oxygen Forensics Suite 2010 program, 219–220

P

Pages files, analyzing, 194
Paraben Device Seizure tool
    overview, 115–117
    results, 131
partitions, for iOS, 36–49
    data partition, 46–49
    OS partition, 41
    system partition, 41–45
Parts subdirectory, 162
passcode lock, turning off, 77–79
PCAP file, 341
phone information pane, 96
Phone Setup Wizard, 108
photos, 103–105
Photos pane, 104
PhotosAux.sqlite database, 175
Photos.sqlite database, 175
Picture Safe application, 198–199
Picture Vault app, 199–200

Pinch Media, 191
PList Editor, 221
plists (property lists), 87
pmap option, 37
POI (points of interest), 227
POP (Post Office Protocol), 296–297
Power amp iPhone 4 hardware, 16
/Preferences/ com.rxs.msdaemon.plist, 318
Preferences folder, 47, 140–141, 156–157
Preferences menu, iTunes app, 89
Preferences.plist, 169–170
Prevent iPods and iPhones from syncing automatically option, iTunes app, 90
Preview application, 103, 238
Preview_id, 162
Primary key, 175
private directory, 43
Processor iPad hardware, 18
Processor iPhone 4 hardware, 15
property list, 209–210
Property List Editor application, 62, 64, 138, 146, 149, 155, 232–234
property lists, in iOS, 61–66
Pwnage, 80

 # Q

QuickTime geodata, 248
Qwkpwn, 80

R

Radio/amplifier iPhone 4 hardware, 16
Radio/transmit and receiver iPhone 4 hardware, 16
RAM iPad hardware, 18
RAW disk, 41
Read Backups button, 215
ReceiveddateMS message ID, 165
Recommended Applications, 64
Recording Industry Association of America (RIAA), 274
recordings, 176
RecordModDate, 175
Recovered iPhone Files, 91, 140
Remote Notification directory, 140
remote user, 74
remote wipe, 72

remotely locking device, 72–75
remotely wiping device, 72–75
Remove, CocoaSlideShow menu bar, 242
report mode, selecting, 116
Research in Motion (RIM), 5
RFC 1122, 325, 328
RIAA (Recording Industry Association of
        America), 274
RIM (Research in Motion), 5
Roberts, M., 71
ROCKR, history of, 2–3
Root directory, 47
Rosenblatt, B., 268–270
Rotate Left, CocoaSlideShow menu bar, 242
Rotate Right, CocoaSlideShow menu bar,
        242
ROWID (row identification), 50, 160, 162
Run directory, 47

▮ S

Safari app, 102
Safari browser, 102, 157–158
Safari directory, 141–142
Safari History property list, 158
Salvage interface, 300, 302
Save As dialog box, 341
sbin directory, 43
SDK (Software Development Kit), 6, 27
search and seizure, 67–86
        collecting information from iPhone,
                80–83
        copying lockdown certificates from
                computer, 84
        and Fourth Amendment of U.S.
                Constitution, 68–69
        identifying jailbroken iPhones, 79–80
        incident to arrest, 69–71
        iPhone is considered cell phone, 71–72
        isolating device from networks, 75–77
        and remotely locking device, 72–75
        and remotely wiping device, 72–75
        tracking individual by cell phone, 69
        turning off passcode lock, 77–79
Search.db folder, 196
secondary infringement liability, 270
Secure View 2 home screen, 108
Sender and Callback_num voicemail.db, 163
senderListHTML conversation ID, 166
Sensors 2G hardware, 11
Sensors 3G hardware, 13

Sensors 3GS hardware, 15
Set Directory,CocoaSlideShow menu bar,
        242
Settings icon, 78
Shredit HD app, 198
SIM card, 77, 79
Skype Analyzer, 182
Skype application, 180–182
SkypeLogView, 181
Slideshow, CocoaSlideShow menu bar, 242
SMS data, 99, 124
SMS database, 50, 160–162
SMS directory, 141–142
SMS messages, 111, 161, 299
SMS.db file, 161, 299
smslog.dat file, 320
SnippetHMTL conversation ID, 166
SnippetHMTL message ID, 165
social networking analysis, 180–196
Software Development Kit (SDK), 6, 27
Sony BMG case, 275
spyware applications, 317–322
        FlexiSpy, 321
        Mobile Spy, 318–321
SQlite commands, 139
SQLite Database Browser, 53–55, 138, 140,
        143, 313
SQLite Database Viewer, 221
SQLite databases, 49–66, 313
        Address Book database, 49
        Call History database, 50
        retrieving data from, 53–60
        SMS database, 50
_SqliteDataBaseProperties, 50
SqliteDatabaseProperties table, 51
Sqlite_sequence table, 49–51
SSID_STR artifact key, 334
Startup file, 35
Stillwagon, B., 68–69
Storage 2G hardware, 11
Storage 3G hardware, 13
Storage 3GS hardware, 15
Strength artifact key, 334
String value, 158
Subject conversation ID, 166
Subject message ID, 165
Suspended State property, 159–160
Susteen Secure View 2 tool, 107–114
        acquiring data, 110–111
        reporting data, 111–114
        results, 132

setting up and navigating interface,
    107–110
System Configuration data, 168–170
System Configuration directory, 141
System directory, 43
system information, photo evidence, 83
/System/Library/LaunchDaemons/com.rxs.
    ms.plist, 318
system partition, for iOS, 41–45
SystemProfiles directory, 149

T

Table drop-down list, 54
TableInfo table, 259
Tang, P., 269–270
TCP (Transport Control Protocol), 328, 330
TextEdit application, 41, 211–212, 233
third-party applications, 178–196
    analytics, 191
    AOL AIM, 184
    Bing, 194
    Craigslist, 189–190
    documents and document recovery,
        194–196
    Facebook, 182–183
    Google Mobile, 192–193
    Google Voice, 186–189
    iDisk, 192
    LinkedIn, 184–185
    MySpace, 185–186
    Opera, 193
    Skype, 180–182
    social networking analysis, 180–196
    Twitter, 185
tigertext app, 202–206
tigertext database, 204–206
Time stamp artifact, 335
Time stamp, North Pole settings, 241
Tmp directory, 42, 47
Tom Tom app, 265
Touchscreen iPad hardware, 16
tracking individual, by cell phone, 69
Transport Control Protocol (TCP), 328, 330
Trashed date voicemail.db, 163
TV, Apple, 36–37
Twitter, 185

U

UDP (User Datagram Protocol), 328
UFED (Universal Forensic Extraction
        Device), 125–130
    setting up, 126–130
    supported devices, 126
UI (user interface), 26
Uniform Resource Locator (URL), 113, 158
United States Constitution, 268–269
UNIX jail, 41
UNIX time, 33, 50
URL (Uniform Resource Locator), 113, 158
USB 2G hardware, 11
USB 3G hardware, 13
USB 3GS hardware, 15
User Datagram Protocol (UDP), 328
User directory, 42
user interface (UI), 26
userLabelIds conversation ID, 166
Usr directory, 43

V

Value column, 64–65
Var directory, 42
Video geotag data, 247
videos, geotagging, 237–248
Vm directory, 47
Voice memos, 176
Voicemail data, 163
Voicemail directory, 141–142
Voicemail pane, 98
voicemail.db, 163
voicemails, 162–163
Volume header, 34

W

Web apps, and history of iPhone 2G, 4
web-based MobileMe account, 74
web interface, Earthpoint, 256
Webclip directory, 141–142
WebClips folder, 163–164
WebClips info.plist data, 164
WebKit directory, 141–142, 164–167,
        187–188
WEP (Wired Equivalent Privacy), 333
Wi-Fi Protected Access (WPA), 333
WiFi Location Harvest table, 259
WiFi table, 259

WifiLocation table, 259
WiFiLocationHarvestCounts table, 259
Wifi.plist, 169
Windows
    artifacts from, 212–214
        iPodDevices.xml, 212–213
        lockdown certificates, 214
        MobileSync backups, 213–214
    forensic tools and backup files, 220–225
        FTK 1.8 tool, 222–223
        FTK Imager tool, 221
        tips, 223
Windows 7, 88, 214
Windows command-line tools, 177

Windows Vista, 88, 214
Windows XP, 88, 214
Wired Equivalent Privacy (WEP), 333
wireless encryption and authentication, 333
Wireshark filter, 340–341
WPA (Wi-Fi Protected Access), 333

X, Y, Z

XML files, 61–62
XML plist format, 149